D1301610

# Citizens of Rome

# Citizens of Rome

Simon Goodenough

Consultant: Dr Richard Reece

CROWN PUBLISHERS INC.
NEW YORK

**Devised and created by**
**Berkeley Publishers Ltd,**
**9 Warwick Court, London WC1R 5DJ**

Copyright © The Hamlyn Publishing Group
Limited 1979

All rights reserved. No part of this publication may
be reproduced, stored in a retrieval system, or
transmitted, in any form or by any means,
electronic, mechanical, photocopying, recording or
otherwise, without the permission of the Hamlyn
Publishing Group Limited.

First published 1979 in the United States of
America
By Crown Publishers Inc., New York.

Phototypeset by Filmtype Services Ltd.,
Scarborough, Yorkshire.

Colour separations by Metric Reproductions Ltd.,
Chelmsford, Essex.

Printed in Spain by Graficromo

Library of Congress Cataloging in Publication Data

Main entry under title:

Citizens of Rome

1. Rome – Civilization. I. Reece, Richard.
DG77.C57 1979          937.6          78–24210
ISBN 0–517–53750–8

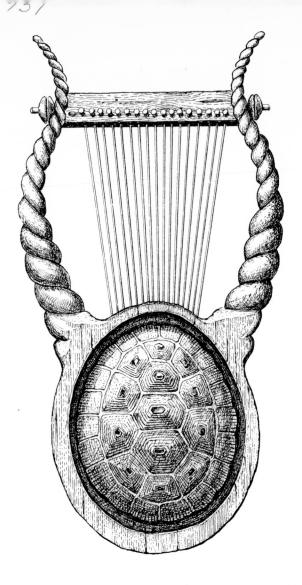

# CONTENTS

*'An empty pageant; a stage play; flocks of sheep, herds of cattle; a tussle of spearmen; a bone flung among a pack of curs; a crumb tossed into a pond of fish; ants, loaded and labouring; mice, scared and scampering; puppets, jerking on their strings — that is life. In the midst of it all you must take your stand, good-temperedly and without disdain, yet always aware that a man's worth is no greater than the worth of his ambitions.'*

# I

# Introducing the Romans

The marble statue stands proud and severe. The face is dignified, the folds of the toga are perfectly draped, the authority of the figure commands respect. Who is this Roman? What lies behind the calm face of empire? The furrows on his brow signify great events but his daily problems are not unlike our own. He complains of urban stress and toothache, high-rise apartments and tourism; he lines up for the dole and suffers from inflation; he is an energetic social climber, ambitious for his children, unfaithful to his wife.

The likeness goes deeper for he believes himself to be very modern and so he is, a civilised man in a barbaric world. But his busy, practical confidence conceals an underlying sense of insecurity. He may look self-sufficient but behind the mask he wants very much to be admired and to belong within the universal scheme of things. His mania for building says that he does not wish

He is one of the two highest magistrates in Rome. His face expresses all those virtues the Romans most admired – firmness, fairness, sober judgement. He is a Consul, an apotheosis of the Roman ideal.

to be forgotten. At heart he is conscientious, responsible and traditional but he has a reputation for extravagance and cruelty. Once you unwrap the toga that protects him like the cloak of Victorian respectability, you will find that he is full of such paradoxes and enigmas.

He faces many of the same tricky social issues that perplex and divide us today but they do not seem to trouble his conscience. His attitudes to human rights, the rights of women, religious tolerance and social responsibility are often contradictory to our way of thinking and yet he takes the contradictions in his stride. He shows no inclination either to resolve or to explain them. Has human nature changed or can we understand such a man? His character is complex and intriguing.

He loves his home without sentimentality, a sensitive parent who believes devoutly in family tradition and continuity, who keeps an ever-watchful eye on the generations past and the generations still to come. He represents the stability of the State, humanely authoritarian, wholly responsible for all those under his roof. And yet he will expose weakling children or unwanted girl-babies to die on the rocks, at the mercy of the weather and the wolves.

He is a devoted and affectionate husband, as many tombstones testify. The Roman wife is reputedly the rockbed of the home; the Roman mother is praised by famous sons who acknowledge a profound debt to their upbringing. The influence of Greece adds an irresponsible frivolity to Roman independence and women seem freer than they will be for the next two thousand years. And yet they have virtually no political rights. A Roman husband can put his wife to death.

His attitude to Greece is itself a paradox. The wonders of ancient Greek cities are destroyed by Roman armies in punishment for revolt; Greek slaves and philosophers are blamed for spreading immorality; Greek merchants are mistrusted. And yet the Roman looks to Greek buildings and culture as a vital part of his inheritance; he relies heavily on the skills of Greeks in teaching, administration and trade; he embraces the Greek philosophy of Stoicism; he seeks to emulate the empire of Alexander the Great.

His 'polite' literature has been a model for successive civilisations. Pliny's letters shine with reasonableness and honesty; Horace and Juvenal are repulsed by excesses; Seneca's level-headed commonsense stands as a measure of civilisation for all time. And yet their contemporaries are capable of diabolical cruelties which compare with the worst tortures of the Inquisition and the horrors of Hitler's extermination camps. Human candles blaze in the arena and are half-choked, half-grilled to death; they are dragged away with hooks, leaving a broad, black trail behind them in the sand.

This same Roman deeply loves the country for he is a farmer by tradition. He seeks success in life by co-operation with the 'natural' forces that surround him, not by flying independently in the face of the gods and the common good. He believes in something greater than himself, the underlying forces of continuity, the spirit or 'genius' of the Roman people which has given him his sense of destiny and purpose. And yet his appreciation of great themes and his love of nature does not extend, like ours, to admiration for the harsh and wild. He likes a gentle, fertile nature: fresh springs, running water, meadows, groves of trees and the peaceful lapping of the sea. The sense of awe instilled by mountains, rocks and deserts is nothing more positive than fear of the unknown. He sees them as arid, unfruitful and godless.

He is a brilliant engineer. His practical ability is evident in the skilful construction of massive buildings, beautiful domes and arches, one hundred thousand kilometres of major roads. And yet he scorns creative ingenuity as

*'Mislead yourself no longer; you will never read those notebooks again now, nor the annals of bygone Romans and Greeks, nor that choice selection of writings you have put by for your old age. Press on, then, to the finish; cast away vain hopes; and if you have any regard at all for self, see to your own security while still you may.'*

*'How strange are the ways of men! They will spare no word of praise for their contemporaries, who live in their very midst, and yet they covet greatly for themselves the praise of future generations, whom they have never seen and never will see. They might as well grumble at not having praise from their ancestors!'*

unworthy of a Roman citizen. He has developed little or nothing that is genuinely new. Perversely he seems to avoid mechanical or scientific progress in favour of primitive manpower.

Here lies the answer to some of the paradoxes. Roman society is an elitist society. Roman citizens live on top of a precarious edifice of potentially explosive material which they must control with an absolutely firm grip. Roman civilisation is not a veneer; it runs deep enough to influence the twentieth century. But to preserve the delicate balance on which it is based, it has to be tough and rigidly disciplined. The elitist structure relies on an abundant supply of slaves, whose numbers are such that they must be kept permanently busy and ruthlessly suppressed in case they turn against the State. It is not in the Roman interest to replace them with mechanical power. And yet these slaves often live in Roman homes as part of the family; sometimes they run their own businesses and hold down important government jobs; even slaves have slaves of their own. In one moment they can be killed at the whim of their master; in the next they may be freed for their children to become Roman citizens and join the elite. This fluid system actually supports the structure as newcomers grasp at their privileges and guard them carefully.

*'Never let the future disturb you. You will meet it, if you have to, with the same weapons of reason which today arm you against the present.'*

The worthiest quality of the Roman is his sense of civic and imperial responsibility for the people in his care. Despite savage action against insurrection, he is concerned for the people he has conquered; despite powers of life and death over slaves, they are still members of his household; despite great wealth, there is also great poverty and the rich adopt responsibility for the poor. There are responsibilities to the State and the municipality, as well. The Roman may demonstrate these by substantial public benefactions, for buildings, schools, baths, temples and statues, although altruism is strongly tinged with self-satisfaction. In many cases, his responsibility to his fellows is demonstrated in an equally harmless way, with gifts, patronage and influence. And yet fear determines these actions, too. Free hand-outs of grain and the thoughtlessly cruel entertainments of the amphitheatre – bread and circuses – are the one sure way to keep the less fortunate satisfied and silent.

*'When a loaf of bread is in the oven, cracks appear in it here and there; and these flaws, though not intended in the baking, have a rightness of their own, and sharpen the appetite. Figs, again, at their ripest will also crack open. When olives are on the verge of falling, the very imminence of decay adds its peculiar beauty to the fruit.'*

These attitudes and paradoxes varied in intensity during the thousand years of Roman pre-eminence, just as attitudes have changed enormously in the last thousand years. To imagine a modern equivalent to the timespan of Roman history, we have to go back to the Norman conquest of Britain, in 1066, and think of the changes since then. Even so, many Roman paradoxes are recognisable in subsequent civilisations: the polite society of Jane Austen's eighteenth-century novels made no mention of the barbarities of public executions, which continue today in certain countries; children were cruelly set to work even in the supposedly serene domesticity of the nineteenth century; women who were admired and respected at the beginning of the twentieth century had no political rights; scientific and mechanical advances are still resisted by those who fear the perils of unemployment; few societies have avoided a structure wherein there is one rule for the rich and another for the poor. The elitist paradoxes of the Romans were no more extraordinary than those of many other empires. What enabled the Roman structure to last so long was its fluidity.

Possibly the greatest Roman paradox lies in the relationship of the State with Christianity. In general the Romans were tolerant of other religions, so long as Roman authority was recognised. But the Christians would not bow to the emperor or to the Roman gods and the Romans were forced to persecute them or accept the challenge to their authority. And yet the Roman State provided a remarkable framework for the growth of Christianity. Those Roman virtues of self-denial and 'gravitas' seemed tailor-made for the stern ethics of puritan Christianity. Stoicism and Mithraism spread the concept of a universal power infused by one spirit. The vast slave population welcomed the compassion of Christianity and its belief in the sanctity of human life. It is this that we miss in Roman attitudes, despite their tolerance and despite their sense of responsibility. The paradox was carried to its ultimate extent when Christianity became the religion of the State. The elite structure could not live side-by-side with Christian compassion, although Christianity cannot be blamed for the fall of Rome. In fact, many of the traditions of the western empire survived through the Church, which assumed the fabric of the fallen State and did not lose its grip until the re-emergence of temporal nationalism at the time of the Reformation. It was only in the Byzantine Empire that a purely Roman society did live side-by-side with the Church and where it was the Church that compromised and lost many of its ideals and values.

We have much to learn from Roman attitudes, despite – or because of – the paradoxes. What the Romans can teach us, they tell us themselves in letters packed with the sharp detail of daily life, in lyrical or cryptic poems, in essays that are full of wisdom, in biting epigrams or world-weary satires that let us know just what they find moving, comic, ridiculous or important about the fashions and morals of their day. They have left thousands of inscriptions on tombs and memorials to provide insights into their private lives and they have scratched graffiti quite as liberally as we do to demonstrate their prejudices. Roman writers are at their best when they speak for themselves and so they have been quoted often in the following pages. They are almost always biased in one way or another but that adds to the fun and the flavour of their comment. Although most of them belong to the elite, we can hear the occasional voice of the common people. If we keep a sharp ear well tuned, we will catch the contrasts that are the essence of the story.

It would be hard to reflect all the changes in life and attitudes that occur during the thousand years of Roman dominance. Most of the best contemporary commentators write during the two or three hundred years roughly in the middle of that period, from the last century BC to the first two centuries AD. Those years are the main theme of this book. Likewise, there has not been space to range throughout the empire, giving examples of lifestyles in every province. The empire is too extensive. Roman armies push north into the unwelcome fogs of Britain; they gaze in awe at the tides of the Atlantic; they build their monuments among the ruins of ancient eastern empires; they stare across the sands of the Sahara. But Rome itself links every corner, giving the lead in laws, customs, buildings, language and dress. And so this book concentrates on life in Rome, drawing examples from elsewhere that contrast with or confirm Roman attitudes.

These Roman attitudes and virtues often make Roman citizens seem unduly serious and sober. At first glance you would not guess they thoroughly enjoy the lewd antics of the latest comic farce on the stage and that it would be hard to match the flow of enthusiasm, criticism and earthy innuendo in their conversation. It may be a surprise to discover how much they love colour and gaudy decoration. That classically pure, marble statue with which we began was once brightly painted. We are going to restore the faded colours and reveal the secrets within the folds of the thick woollen toga. But before we begin there is time to spend a few moments looking back, as the Romans themselves do, on the events that lead up to their greatness, for these events are always in their minds.

*'The whole universe is change and life itself is only what you think it is.'*

*'Everything that happens is as normal and expected as the spring rose or the summer fruit; this is true of sickness, death, slander, intrigue, and all the other things that delight or trouble foolish men.'*

10

# II

# Events and deeds

Trajan's column is one of the most celebrated of all Roman remains. The reliefs on the column show episodes from the Dacian wars of 101–102 AD and 105–106 AD. One of the bonuses reaped by Trajan as the result of the Dacian campaigns was the acquisition of the Dacian gold mines.

L ike all good stories, the origins of Rome soon became legend. There may be little truth in the tale of Romulus and Remus but their story was reverently passed down and given substance just as the twins themselves were cherished by the wolf. The tale began in another, older story, when the Greeks sacked Homer's Troy. Fleeing from his stricken city, the mighty Aeneas reached Italy, where his son Ascanius, also known as Julius, founded the town of Alba Longa, nineteen miles south-east of the future site of Rome.

One of his descendants was called Numitor. This king had a daughter who was a Vestal Virgin but she lost her virginity to Mars, the god of war, so it was said, and gave birth to twins. Numitor also had a younger brother, who deposed him and ordered the twins to be thrown into the River Tiber in case they laid claim later to the throne he had seized. Someone had pity on the boys and they were placed in a wooden trough which floated downstream with the current. The trough caught on a shoal or in the bushes along the bank and a passing she-wolf found the brothers and suckled them. Brought up subsequently by a local herdsman, Romulus and Remus gathered together a group of young men, killed their wicked great uncle and restored their grandfather to his throne.

The brothers then founded the city of Rome at the point where their wooden trough had come to land, in recognition of their miraculous escape. But they quarrelled. Romulus built a wall around the city and Remus contemptuously leapt over it. Furious at being flouted, Romulus killed his brother. Surprisingly the gods did not take revenge for this impious act. Romulus ruled supreme and Rome flourished. He increased the male population by granting asylum to fugitives from neighbouring tribes and he provided his soldiers with wives by inviting the nearby Sabines to a feast and seizing their women. His death occurred mysteriously in a storm. It was believed that he had been carried away and transformed into the god Quirinus, whose warlike responsibilities were similar to those of Mars, the father of the twins.

We owe the grandest expression of the legend of Aeneas to the poet Virgil, whose *Aeneid* was written with the encouragement of the emperor Augustus. The poet's main desire was to please his patron, so he chose a flattering theme. Augustus was the adopted heir of Julius Caesar, whose family claimed descent from Aeneas himself and from Aeneas' son who bore the family name of Julius. Virgil's epic established a direct link with that magnificent past and forged a legend that reflected gloriously upon Augustus by associating him with the heroic qualities and fundamental Roman virtues exemplified by Aeneas.

The historical story is, at first, less dramatic but, in the end, no less triumphant. Indo-European migrants from the north had settled in the fertile plain south of the Tiber by about 1000 BC. One of these tribes recognised the geographical and strategical advantages of the crossing point on the river, which became the site of Rome. At first the people lived in primitive compounds on two or three of Rome's famous seven hilltops. In time the tribal settlements grew down the slopes of the hills and the tribesmen met and exchanged simple goods in the marshy plain between. They established a larger, common compound that embraced their original settlements. The traditional date of the founding of Rome was in 753 BC.

For several centuries Rome was ruled by kings. Several of these kings were called Tarquin. They were Etruscans, a people neighbouring Rome whose origins are still uncertain, but at an early stage in their development they were strongly influenced from the East. By the time the Roman settlements had established themselves the Etruscans had already achieved an advanced state of civilisation and they had a considerable influence over the young kingdom. They were skilful merchants, clever at warfare and fond of music and dancing. It was from them, too, that the Romans acquired their knowledge of architecture and engineering as well as many elements in their religion. Since there is still much to be learnt about the Etruscans, we may well find that the Romans were even more indebted to them than we think.

By tradition a defensive wall was built around the main hills by King Servius Tullius in the sixth century BC. In fact his name has been attached to a wall built much later and now known as the Servian Wall. By that time a forum had been established between the Capitoline and Palatine Hills, which formed the active centre of the city.

*'If thou wouldst know contentment, let thy deeds be few.'*

*'This mortal life is a little thing, lived in a little corner of the earth; and little, too, is the longest fame to come.'*

The last king was Tarquin the Proud. He was expelled from Rome in about 510 BC because of a scandal in which his son raped a kinsman's wife who subsequently committed suicide. The inhabitants of the city decided that henceforth they would govern themselves. They did so for 500 years. The new Republic was headed by two consuls, elected for one year at a time, who were advised and assisted by the heads of the patrician families, the Senate, and two assemblies of the people.

Rome's first concern was to defend itself against the attacks of rival tribes and, through alliances and force if necessary, to carve for itself a secure position among the other Latin cities. Despite a serious setback in 390 BC, when barbarians from Gaul invaded Italy, sacked Rome and left only after exacting a large ransom in gold, the Romans recovered and within about fifty years had succeeded in dominating central Italy. Their intermittent wars with the Samnites and Greek colonies of southern Italy brought them up against the colonial interests of King Pyrrhus of Epirus, a powerful state across the Adriatic. This was their first major overseas adversary.

Pyrrhus landed an army in Italy and immediately won two resounding victories against the Romans. But he suffered heavy losses himself in the process. A third such victory, he said, would be the end of him. It was. The cost of his first two 'Pyrrhic' victories had exceeded their strategic value. His weakened army was defeated decisively and the Republic had passed its first international test: Rome was a power to be reckoned with in the eastern Mediterranean. Pyrrhus was finally crushed at Beneventum in 275 BC. Two years later the Romans had established diplomatic relations with Egypt.

There was no hope that the existing powers in the Mediterranean would allow Rome to grow peacefully, as she wished. One after another she came up against jealous rivals with whom she had to fight more out of self-protection than in a spirit of open imperialism. Rome acquired her empire almost apologetically but, once challenged, she fought with determination and steadfast competence.

The longest and most bitter struggle was with Carthage, the original home of the Phoenicians, a powerful seafaring and trading people who had founded

*'Live not as though there were a thousand years ahead of you. Fate is at your elbow; make yourself good while life and power are still yours.'*

It is something of a paradox that the reign of perhaps the most enlightened and civilized of all the Roman Emperors – Marcus Aurelius Antoninus, who reigned from AD 161 to AD 180 – should have been commemorated in one of the most savagely realistic of all the triumphal Roman victory columns. The column of Marcus Aurelius, which stands in Rome's Piazza Colonna, has a special frieze noted for its unusually high reliefs and also for the savagery and drama of their representations of scenes from the Danubian Wars.

Romulus and Remus with the wolf which, according to Roman legend, suckled them in their infancy. The twins were revered as the founders of Rome.

The story is, of course, a myth and probably originated some three hundred years before the birth of Christ. Greek literature is full of stories of abandoned babies and the practice of finding a hero figure to link with a city name – and Romulus is a derivation from Rome rather than the other way round – was a Greek habit.

This bronze sculpture from the Capitol dates from about 500 BC but the figures of Romulus and Remus were added during the Renaissance.

*'We seek consolation in sorrow in the busts of our dead we set up in our homes; still more then should we find it in the statues standing in public places, for these can recall men's fame and distinction as well as their forms and faces.'*

the city on the north coast of Africa between 800 and 750 BC. It was the Roman word for the Phoenicians, or Poeni, that provided the word 'Punic' for the succession of conflicts between the two nations. The first clash occurred over territory in Sicily in 264 BC. Against their natural instincts the Romans were compelled to fight at sea, for the Carthaginians had inherited the Phoenician skill in seamanship. But the Romans found a stranded Carthaginian warship and within two months constructed enough copies of it to produce a fleet of their own. Since they still lacked the necessary technique and experience to outmanoeuvre the Carthaginians they developed boarding tactics that enabled them to transform a sea-fight into some kind of land battle, in which they were much better practised. They were able to throw the Carthaginians out of Sicily by 241 BC.

One of the generals in that first Punic War was Hamilcar and it was not long before his brilliant son, Hannibal, was determined to make amends for their defeat. He moved into Spain. A Roman ally appealed for help and war began again. Hannibal took the initiative, left Spain, crossed the Alps with his elephants, took the Romans by surprise and defeated them in a series of battles. A Roman army of 50,000 soldiers was destroyed at Cannae. Hannibal marched down Italy but failed to march directly on Rome. He spent fifteen years harassing the Romans in their own homeland, waiting for his brother to come with reinforcements. But his brother was defeated at Metaurus and Hannibal himself had to withdraw to Carthage to defend his capital against a Roman counter-offensive led by Scipio Africanus. Hannibal was defeated at the battle of Zama in 202 BC, not far from Carthage itself, and the Carthaginians were forced to give up Spain.

An everyday rural scene. The goatherd is milking his goat. It has clearly been a fruitful summer for the sheaf of corn has a look of abundance. The Romans liked 'reliefs' of everyday scenes and Rome depended on a prosperous agriculture.

*'Never allow yourself to be swept off your feet: when an impulse stirs, see first that it will meet the claims of justice; when an impression forms, assure yourself first of its certainty.'*

The Roman armies almost immediately had to turn east to stop the expanding policy of King Philip V of Macedon, inheritor of one part of the empire of Alexander the Great. Alexander had died in 323 BC, at a time when the Romans were still struggling to dominate Italy. On his death, his empire was divided into three main parts: Macedon, Syria and Egypt. Rome annexed each in turn. Philip was defeated at Cynoscephalae, in 197 BC, and his son, Perseus, was routed at Pydna, almost thirty years later, when the Romans finally broke through the long spears of the Macedonian phalanx. Macedon and Greece fell to Rome. Syria had already fallen when King Antiochus, trying to take advantage of Roman preoccupation with the Macedonian armies, had landed in Greece and been defeated at Magnesia.

Finding herself with extensive power, Rome tried to rule tolerantly, forming alliances, creating buffer states to protect her frontiers, allowing self-government on condition of non-aggression wherever possible, experimenting with the balance of power to consolidate her rule. But whenever there was trouble, her armies acted ruthlessly. Corinth was completely destroyed in 146 BC for refusing to co-operate with a Roman order and for attempting to form an alliance of Greek states in opposition to Rome. In the same year Carthage was obliterated. M. Porcius Cato had persistently demanded that 'Carthage must be destroyed' or it would remain a continual threat to Roman power. His demands were justified when Carthage attacked Numidia. A Roman army sacked the city. The buildings were pulled down. The male survivors, the women and children were sold into slavery. The site of the city was ploughed up and the land was sown with salt so that no crops would grow. It remained one of Rome's most ferocious examples of revenge.

The Carthaginian wars and the wars with Macedon and Syria left Rome temporarily exhausted. She had her own problems at home and the wars only emphasised them. Her manpower was sadly diminished. Between 250 and 200 BC, the male population over the age of seventeen was reduced from about 300,000 to about 200,000. It is not hard to imagine what effect this had on the young state. The wealthy became richer, the poor became poorer. The steps that had been taken to overcome the conflict between patrician and plebeian were largely nullified by the years of conflict. Plebeian, non-property-owning interests, had won the protection of their own tribunes, elected by them specifically to guard against the dominance of the patrician, property-owning families who held the main religious and magisterial posts and who supplied all members of the Senate. Gradually the plebeians had won the equal rights they demanded: the right to marry into patrician families, the right to enter into the sacred college of priests, the right to be elected consul and the right to pass laws in their own assembly without reference to the state. Rome was on the verge of being ruled by the people in fact as well as intention.

But land and property still meant power and the effect of war was to allow landowners to become even bigger landowners. The smallholdings of the average man were swallowed up by the estates of the rich, who still controlled all the main public offices and were in a position to increase their wealth by receiving bribes and by profits they made from becoming provincial governors in the newly conquered territories. There was plenty of corruption long before the time of the empire. As Rome grew in power and wealth, it became an arena for ambitious individuals to compete for control of the remarkable machine of State.

The brothers Tiberius and Gaius Gracchus attempted some reforms to improve matters. They saw the division of land as the hub of the problem. As

15

'Hour by hour resolve firmly, like a Roman and a man, to do what comes to hand with correct and natural dignity, and with humanity, independence and justice.'

'Time is a river, the resistless flow of all created things. One thing no sooner comes in sight than it is hurried past and another is born along, only to be swept away in its turn.'

tribune of the people, and therefore protector of their interests, Tiberius tried to persuade the Senate to allow some of the large areas of public land to be allocated for use by the plebeians; the land was currently monopolised by the wealthy landowners. When Tiberius pressed his reforms against the inevitable opposition of the Senators, who were still predominantly patrician, he was murdered. His brother Gaius, who became tribune in 123 BC, pressed for similar reforms and suggested that Roman citizenship should be extended to other Italian cities. Gaius avoided his brother's fate only by ordering his own servant to kill him before his enemies captured him.

Gaius Marius was the next figure to dominate the Roman scene. He, too, was a champion of the common people. He was also a highly successful soldier. First, he put an end to the triumphant campaigns of Jugurtha, King of Numidia; then he defeated the Cimbri and Teutones in the north, whose slaughter of a Roman army had so frightened the Romans that they had granted Marius the consulship for five years in succession. He managed to keep social unrest in check for a while and provided some release for the frustrations of the common people by extending military service even to the poorest and by supplying them with pay and equipment at the expense of the State. Instead of an army drawn primarily from the property-owning classes and called up for specific campaigns, he organised a permanent, professional structure.

Marius withdrew from power and matters got worse again. This time it was the thorny question of citizenship that Gaius Gracchus had tried to anticipate earlier. Marcus Livius Drusus took up the theme and once again proposed that Roman citizenship should be granted to all cities throughout the peninsula. Romans of all parties united in their objections to this: they considered themselves infinitely superior to other cities and feared that their own influence in the State would diminish if the franchise was extended. Drusus should have learnt the lesson of the Gracchi: he was murdered the same year that he took office as tribune, in 91 BC. But at least that brought matters to a head. The other cities promptly set up a rival capital, 'Italia'. There was a bloody war for two or three years and eventually the Senate capitulated and citizenship was conferred on Rome's Italian allies. This was known as the Social war – the war of the 'socii', or allies.

Social War sounds more like 'armchair warfare' but the Romans found it far from being a comfortable experience. The authority of the Senate, already threatened by the attempted reforms of Marius, was undermined even further by the result of the struggle. This gave Lucius Cornelius Sulla his opportunity to step into the breach. Despite the continued efforts of Marius to advance the cause of the plebeians, Sulla restored power to the Senate, filled it with his friends, disposed of Marius and his supporters and became virtual dictator of Rome. He also found time to defeat King Mithridates of Pontus, who had dared to massacre Roman colonials and was marching against Rome in the east. Then he turned against the Greek allies of Mithridates and sacked Athens. Since the Romans were greatly in awe of ancient Greek culture and increasingly paid homage to Greek customs and Greek civilisation during the empire, the sacking of Athens was possibly one of Sulla's most unfortunate deeds.

Among Sulla's successful young lieutenants was Gnaeus Pompeius, who became Pompey the Great. The Romans by now were getting used to the idea of popular heroes and Pompey became one of the youngest and best. He cleared the Mediterranean of pirates, he turned back a threat in the east, he survived a conspiracy to replace him in his absence. He returned to Rome,

## The Calendar

The year itself was reckoned by the number of years since the mythical foundation of Rome, in 753 BC. Therefore 1 BC was the 753rd year in the Roman calculation and AD 1 was the 754th year. They called it the 754th year AUC, or 'ab urbe condita' (from the foundation of the city). The Christian system of dating years from the Birth of Christ (AD = Anno Domini = In the Year of the Lord) did not begin until the sixth century. The use of BC (Before Christ) was introduced much later still.

For more recent years, the Romans referred to the names of the consuls for that particular year. Since one consul might easily serve two or three times with a different partner each time, you had to have quite a good memory to get the year right. One of Julius Caesar's partners was a nonentity called Bibulus, so people sometimes referred to the consulship of Julius and Caesar.

Being closely tied to agriculture, the Romans first divided their year into ten months, beginning on March 1 and ignoring the worst winter period. (September to December mean the 'seventh' to the 'tenth' month.) Later, January and February were included to make twelve months but the year still began on March 1. In 153 BC, January 1 became the beginning of the year and magistrates took up their office on that date.

The total number of days in those twelve months was 355, which gradually pushed them out of phase with the true reckoning of the solar pattern, so an extra month of twenty-two or twenty-three days was slipped in every few years to restore the average of 365 days per year. In 46 BC Julius Caesar reorganised the calendar. He made that year 446 days to set things to rights and then established the present-day length of a year with an extra day introduced every fourth year in February. In honour of his decisive move, the sixth month was changed from Quintilis to Julius and, later, the seventh month was changed from Sextilis to Augustus in honour of the emperor. The remaining months stayed the same.

The month itself was divided into phases. Romans did not count from the first to the thirty-first. The Kalends were the first day of the month; the Nones were on the fifth day (except in March, May, July and October, when they were on the seventh day – these had previously been the longest months); the Ides were on the thirteenth day (except in the same longer months when they were on the fifteenth day). All days were reckoned before one or other of these three phases, and the number of days that were counted included the day of the phase. In theory this sounds complex; in practice it is quite easy to get the hang of. If January 5 was the Nones, then January 4 would be the day before the Nones (pridie Nones) and January 3 would be three days before the Nones. The Romans wrote it like this:

| | |
|---|---|
| January 3 | AD III Non Ian |
| January 4 | pridie Non Ian |
| January 5 | Non Ian |

(a.d. = 'ante diem' or 'before the day': the whole phrase literally means 'The third day before the Nones of January')

The days of the week were named after Saturn, the Sun, the Moon, Mars, Mercury, Jupiter and Venus. Every eighth day was usually a market day. There was no weekend. Interest on loans had to be paid back on one of the three main days of the month: Kalends, Nones or Ides. Officially, the College of Pontiffs was in charge of regulating the calendar.

As Rome extended her empire, she left solid symbols of her presence wherever she went. In newly conquered or colonised territories, the temple was one of the first buildings to be erected, a focus for attention.

*'It is the fate of princes to be ill spoken of for well-doing.'*

loaded with honours and could have seized complete control. Instead he formed an alliance with two other powerful men: Crassus was the leading financier of his day; Caesar was the popular politician. These three formed what was known as the First Triumvirate. They used their considerable influence to control the government of Rome.

Matters did not stand still for long. Caesar immediately decided to gain military experience and concentrated on his brilliant conquest of Gaul and two visits to Britain, which he described in his famous *Conquest of Gaul*. Crassus died in 53 BC and Caesar and Pompey collided headlong in a bid for supreme power. Pompey gained the support of the traditionalists; Caesar, an aristocrat himself, gained the goodwill of the popular party. The crunch came when Caesar was not allowed to stand for Consul while still fighting in Gaul and Germany. He refused to disband his army on the orders of Pompey and the Senate and he marched his army across the River Rubicon, toward Rome. Pompey was finally defeated at Pharsalia, in Greece, in 48 BC. He fled to Egypt and was murdered as he stepped ashore. Caesar followed him to Egypt, seized control of the country, took Ptolemy's sister, Cleopatra, as his mistress and then returned to Rome to become sole dictator. He imposed a strong central government and reorganised much of the administration. In his few years of absolute power he laid the basis for a strong Rome but he also aroused the jealousy of rivals. He was murdered in 44 BC.

Once again there was a struggle for power. A Second Triumvirate was formed as a compromise between Caesar's adopted son and great-nephew Octavian, his military second-in-command Marcus Antonius and the influential Senator Lepidus. The Triumvirate defeated the party of Caesar's murderers at Philippi in 42 BC. They then indulged in an orgy of recriminations against their previous enemies. Among the victims was Cicero, the great orator and statesman, the very man who, as co-consul with Pompey, had defeated the Catiline conspiracy against Pompey. But Cicero had spoken out fiercely against Marc Antony and Marc Antony was keen on revenge.

Inevitably the Triumvirate quarrelled. Lepidus was quickly pushed aside and Octavian and Antony took up the struggle. Antony made the mistake of setting aside his wife Octavia in favour of Cleopatra. It was a mistake because Octavia was the sister of Octavian. When Octavian produced a document before the Senate that he claimed was Antony's will and that seemed to offer Cleopatra all Rome's eastern conquests on Antony's death, the Senate did not hesitate to back Octavian against Antony. Octavian triumphed at the battle of Actium in 31 BC. It was a turning point in Roman history. It was the end of the Republic.

Octavian did not see it quite like that. It was certainly a turning point. After the years of struggle he meant to establish peace. But three years after Actium he stated that the Republic had now been restored and he offered to lay down his power. According to plan, you might think, the Senate at once made him 'princeps', or first citizen, and granted him the title of Augustus. He knew full well they could do little else. The Republic was mismanaged and corrupt. He alone could control the empire that had been created. But he took care never to call himself emperor. He ruled with the titles of the old Republican offices: consul, tribune and 'father of his country'. It was many years before Republican sympathisers under succeeding emperors gave up all hope of a return to the Republic. But in fact Rome continued to be ruled by an emperor for the next 500 years.

The Romans welcomed Augustus as the salvation of the State; in the eastern provinces, accustomed to absolute rulers, he was worshipped as a god.

*'Long, I pray, may foreign nations persist, if not in loving us, at least in hating one another. Fortune can bestow on us no better gift than discord among our foes.'*

An ox being sacrificed to Jupiter on the Capitol. This scene comes from a relief on a silver cup found at Boscoreale in Italy.

A fortified gateway. The building is of brick and the towers of such gateways housed a formidable range of defensive weapons. The towers could be as high as thirty metres. In a sense, the Aurelian Walls of Rome signified the beginning of the end, for the barbarians were reaching into Italy. Aurelian began to build his walls in 272 AD. They had a perimeter of nineteen kilometres and enclosed the main city. The walls themselves finally reached a height of about ten metres. There were fourteen main gates.

By treading carefully between his human and divine welcome and recognising the sensitivity of his Roman 'colleagues' in the Senate, he gained a free hand to establish the majesty – and the efficiency – of the empire. The 'Age of Augustus' brought the Roman State to maturity.

With the help of his forceful and often dominant wife, Livia, he established a highly organised and competent civil service. He was particularly successful in choosing his administrators, who were often drawn from the lower levels of Roman society, including freedmen and slaves. The upper classes disdained bureaucratic work; they learnt to revise their opinion when the posts created by Augustus in his household were seen to become increasingly influential. At the same time Augustus set about rebuilding Rome, putting up scores of new temples and repairing and enriching important public buildings. He tried to reform public morals and to encourage childbirth among citizens. He became an enthusiastic patron of poetry. He nurtured overseas colonies of ex-soldiers and he began the conquest of Germany. But his military policy changed after the disastrous loss of three legions under Varus in the Teutoburger Forest. From then on he consolidated his position in the hopes of further advances later. His legions in fact became settled in their frontier posts.

Augustus gave Rome an uninterrupted breathing space of forty years. He also managed to establish the tradition of succession. It was not always family succession. Some of the emperors that followed were carefully trained and chosen by their predecessor; some were put into power by their legions; once, the Senate appointed its own choice. Some were competent, some were wholly inadequate; some were extravagant, others were frugal; some were tolerant, some were cruel.

After the death of his nephew and grandsons, it was his stepson Tiberius whom Augustus recommended as his successor, ensuring that he held all the necessary public offices to find acceptance by Republican sympathisers.

963726

Augustus died in AD 14 and Tiberius was already fifty-five when he became 'princeps'. He did his best to maintain the extent of the empire, for he had been an efficient and successful general under Augustus. But his constant fear of being deposed led to a reign of terror in which informers were encouraged to denounce even their own relations and whole families were put to death on the slightest pretext. Finally Tiberius retired to Capri for the last eleven years of his rule and left control of the empire to the equally ruthless Sejanus, who was hated by all and plotted to become emperor himself. But Sejanus fell, too, and much later the satirist Juvenal celebrated his downfall, typical of many:

> 'Some men are overthrown by the envy their great power arouses; it's that long and illustrious list of honours that sinks them. The ropes are heaved, down come the statues, axes demolish their chariot wheels, the unoffending legs of their horses are broken. And now the fire roars up in the furnace, now flames hiss under the bellows: the head of the people's darling glows red-hot, great Sejanus crackles and melts. That face only yesterday ranked second in all the world. Now it's so much scrap metal, to be turned into jugs and basins, frying pans and chamber pots.'

Tiberius himself died soon after. His popular young grand-nephew, Gaius, soon proved that he was not only a great deal more cruel that Tiberius but mad as well. Gaius is better known as Caligula. The name means 'Little Boot'. He won it as a child when he became the heroic mascot of the legions on the German front. Caligula proclaimed himself a god and put his horse Incitatus up for election as a consul. He was murdered by his own guard when he was still thirty.

There was immediate talk of returning to a Republic and the Senate began to deliberate on whom they should choose. But they were beaten to the choice by the Praetorian Guard who found Caligula's uncle Claudius hiding fearfully in the Palace after the assassination. They hauled him out and proclaimed him emperor on the spot. He was fifty and had a reputation as an idiot; his body was ungainly, he stuttered and slobbered. His only activity to date had been writing history and avoiding elimination by Tiberius or Caligula. In his imaginative reconstruction of the life of Claudius, the novelist, poet and scholar Robert Graves implies that Claudius was clever enough to emphasise his ungainly characteristics to offset the fears of those who would otherwise have killed him as a rival.

Claudius proved himself a reasonably competent administrator, although the elder Pliny, who wrote a scientific encyclopedia, disapproved of the expense of some of his public works. He enlarged Rome's harbour at Ostia, he built bridges, he cut roads through the mountains. He gave greater powers to provincial governors and he was freer than Augustus had been in granting citizenship to foreigners: by this means he helped to 'Latinise' the empire. He also went briefly with an expedition to complete the conquest of Britain, to secure that frontier of the empire. But he fell victim to treachery in the end. He was poisoned by his fourth wife, Agrippina, after she had persuaded him to nominate her son Nero as his successor in preference to his own son Britannicus.

Nero began by killing Britannicus and then, after several failures, he killed his mother Agrippina. He became emperor when he was sixteen. His early portraits on coins make him out to have been quite good looking but he quickly became bull-necked and jowled. He gained himself a bad reputation with equal speed. His reign is notorious for his involvement with the Great Fire of AD 64 and his persecution of the Christians who, he claimed, were almost certainly responsible. He used them as human torches to light up the

*'Germany – with its forbidding landscapes and unpleasant climate – a country that is thankless to till and dismal to behold for anyone who was not born and bred there.'*

*'It seems likely that Gauls settled in the island (of Britain) . . . There is the same hardihood in challenging danger, the same cowardice in shirking it when it comes close. But the Britons show more spirit.'*

20

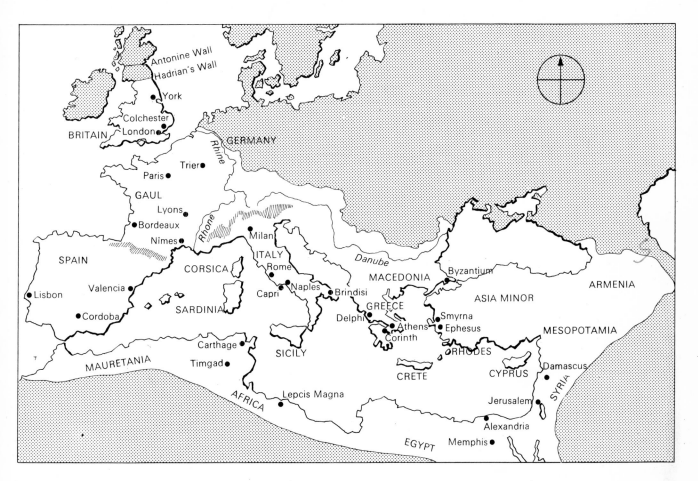

This map shows the Roman Empire at its period of maximum extent around the end of the first century AD. Most of Western Europe is included – Britain is firmly divided by Hadrian's Wall which represents the northern limit of the Empire. Ireland was not included and great tracts of 'Germania' were also blank. The Roman grip on the Mediterranean coast of North Africa can be seen and the limits of the Eastern advance into Asia Minor.

show in the amphitheatre. The public welcomed his magnificent gladiatorial displays but there were others less amused by his lustful tastes and his musical impositions. Nero fancied himself as a poet, singer and player and forced his audiences to listen to his performances whether they liked them or not. Suetonius, who wrote in detail about the lives and vices of *The Twelve Caesars*, described the ordeal:

> 'No one was allowed to leave the theatre during his recitals, however pressing the reason, and the gates were kept barred. We read of women in the audience giving birth, and of men being so bored with the music and the applause that they furtively dropped down from the wall at the rear, or shammed dead and were carried away for burial.'

Resistance to his rule eventually forced Nero to flee from the city. The Senate, no doubt emboldened by his absence, condemned him to death but he anticipated the sentence by committing suicide. Civil war followed as first Galba, then Otho, then Vitellius used Rome's armies to seize the imperial power, all within the space of one year, AD 68–69. It was Vespasian who eventually took control and restored the authority of the emperor and the Senate.

Vespasian established a new dynasty. His own family, the Flavians, came from Spain and, for the first time, a non-patrician ruled Rome. Vespasian was the son of a Spanish tax collector. He was already a highly successful general, conscientious, abstemious and hard-working and he re-established order in the empire. He extended the citizenship once again, strengthened the frontiers with new roads and forts, raised money to give substance to the State economy and established thriving colonies in the more distant parts of the provinces. More important still for the peace of the empire, he restored the confidence of the Senate in the good-intentions of the emperor and the stability of Roman rule.

Vespasian's son Titus reigned for only two years and had little chance to further his father's aims. He was followed by Vespasian's second son Domitian, who was quite an able administrator but emulated Tiberius and Caligula in the use of informers to terrorise his opponents for fear of being deposed. His tactics were evidently successful: he survived fifteen years as emperor. When he was murdered, in AD 96, the Senate for the first time took matters into their own hands and appointed their own choice. Their man was Nerva, a respectable lawyer who succeeded in training an excellent successor during his brief rule.

His trainee was Trajan, whom we know best from his sensible correspondence with the younger Pliny about provincial government and from his famous column which he erected in Rome to celebrate his triumph in the Dacian Wars. The empire prospered under Trajan and the philanthropic social conscience of the averagely wealthy Roman citizen reached new heights in innumerable private endowments of public buildings. Trajan himself instituted a system of cheap loans for the support of orphans and the children of the poor. This was continued under his successor, Hadrian, who travelled widely around the empire and set firm limits to any further expansion. He carried the policy of welcoming provincials as citizens even further than his predecessors and played down the special status of Italy within the empire.

Hadrian's Wall across northern Britain is one of his most famous achievements. It was intended as a demarcation line to keep out the barbarian Picts. Possibly, Rome would have done much better to conquer all of Scotland and Ireland and thus secure a frontier on the sea itself. But Domitian had already put an end to that idea when he recalled the brilliant Roman governor of Britain, Agricola, before he had a chance to complete his subjugation of the island.

A second wall was built across Britain by Hadrian's successor, Antoninus Pius. It was called the Antonine Wall. Antoninus also carried on Hadrian's work of integrating the empire into a single community of countries and colonies bound by a common law. The last of the 'five good emperors' was Marcus Aurelius, the philosopher-emperor. Rome achieved its greatest security and splendour under these men, although it lacked the freshness of the Augustan age. But the pressure of barbarians from the north was already making itself felt and Marcus Aurelius was forced to spend much of his time on his frontiers securing his position. On top of that, plague swept through the empire and Marcus Aurelius himself fell victim in AD 180.

This is the appropriate moment to break off the description of Roman 'deeds' and go back to the affairs of the Roman people. Most of the contemporary Roman 'guides' who we shall be using as evidence of the Roman way of life lived at the end of the Republic and in the first century or two of the empire. The younger Pliny, the letter-writer, and the historian Tacitus lived into the reign of Trajan and Hadrian respectively. Suetonius and Juvenal both survived into the reign of Antoninus Pius. The novelist Apuleius only just outlived Marcus Aurelius.

The city of the seven hills has become a vast empire. What kind of society did its people enjoy? How were they organised and what opportunities were there for them?

*'Names that were formerly household words are virtually archaisms today . . . Scipio and Cato; Augustus, too, and even Hadrian and Antoninus. All things fade into the storied past, and in a little while are shrouded in oblivion.'*

*'Treat with respect the power you have to form an opinion.'*

# The social structure

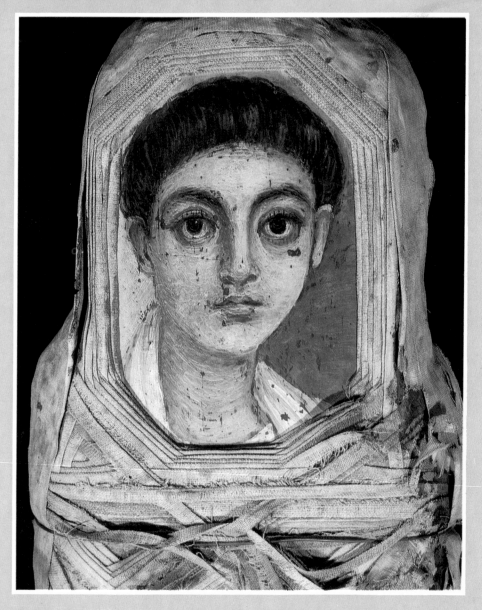

**R**omans prided themselves on their sense of public duty, an essential part of which was to hold public office. There was a clearly defined ladder of public jobs up which the ambitious Roman senator climbed in steady stages. The traditions of citizen-power, or rule by the people, were established in the time of the Republic and the titles and responsibilities of the officials, or magistrates as they were known, lasted in theory throughout the empire. The first emperors were careful to maintain the semblance of elected officials so that the people might still feel that they had some control of their own government. But more and more power was drawn into the hands of the emperor himself and the actual responsibilities of the magistrates fell away almost completely. The jobs nonetheless survived in name because they were useful hand-outs for the emperor to grant to favourites or to withdraw as

He gazes out at us across two thousand years of history. The eyes are curiously compelling. The expression is arresting and haunting. This beautiful painting is on a mummy and it is now in the British Museum. What sort of life did he lead? What caused his death at such an early age?

Stern faced and resolute, these figures from a victory column personify the idealized vision of a Roman. This was how the Romans saw themselves. To the Roman mind, ruling was as natural as breathing. Those who did not share their culture and demanding standards were dismissed as barbarians. How, indeed, could it be otherwise when they belonged to a society that dominated the civilized areas of the western world?

*'Show me a man who isn't a slave; one is a slave to sex, another to money, another to ambition; all are slaves to hope and fear.'*

punishment. Titles, however hollow, always found plenty of aspirants.

The sovereignty of the people was an extremely important ideal under the Republic. The Senate governed Rome on behalf of the Roman people; at least, administrators were drawn from the Senate to govern Rome and the provinces. That is what the famous letters on Roman standards stood for: SPQR (Senatus Populusque Romanus) – The Senate and the People of Rome. The phrase implied that the Senate ruled only in partnership with the people; it was not in any way superior to them. In reality, the senators themselves often felt quite differently about this but the ideal was at least a worthy one.

The Senate was originally a body of men made up of the fathers or heads of the main households, the patricians of Rome. In time they became a mixture of patricians and plebeians, as the Senate was opened up to a wider range of people. The dictator Sulla doubled the number of senators from 300 to 600 in 80 BC and emperors also made appointments to the Senate as they wished. There was, in fact, a qualifying capital requirement of 1,000,000 sesterces before a man could become a senator. Strictly speaking, senators were appointed for life, although it was quite possible for them to be stripped of their honour if they became a nuisance to the emperor. They sat in the Senate House and were expected to remain in Rome and attend all meetings of the Senate. They had lengthy debates about new legislation, how public money was to be spent and other such details of government. Under the empire, they lost most of their decision-making power and became little more than a rubber stamp for the emperor's wishes. The emperor himself continued to speak in the Senate, as if to argue and persuade, but in truth this was only to preserve appearances. Augustus and Tiberius both insisted that they were merely the first among equals in the Senate — but they invariably got their own way.

The top jobs in public service were all elected or appointed by the emperor. The aim of every man was to become consul. There were two each year, appointed for one year of office. One of the great attractions of becoming consul was that the year in which you held office was named after you. So when Julius Caesar shared the consulship with a man called Bibulus, it should have been called the year or consulship of Julius and Bibulus. In fact, Julius Caesar would have nothing to do with Bibulus, so the year came to be known jokingly as the consulship of Julius and Caesar.

Initially the job also held some fairly heavy responsibilities. The consuls were the chief administrators; they spoke first in the Senate and initiated most of the legislation. They also commanded the Roman armies in the field and, by a special vote of the Senate, could be given supreme dictatorial powers in an emergency. Consuls were always accompanied by twelve lictors carrying bundles of rods known as fasces, whenever they went about their official business in Rome. These rods symbolised their authority; the axe which sometimes went with the rods symbolised their right to inflict the death sentence. Those who had already served a term as consul were privileged to speak next in the Senate and were also candidates for appointment as provincial governors, known as proconsuls. Romans believed in making the best use of their mature and experienced citizens in the government of the empire.

The consuls were generally elected from among the praetors, of whom there were eight after the time of Sulla. These were the legal magistrates and were next in importance after the consuls. They could also be appointed to special overseas courts or to courts especially convened in Rome. There was a chief praetor for the city of Rome as well as a chief one for all foreigners and the law itself varied in both cases. They were responsible for ensuring that the legal code was known and kept.

Next came the aediles, or wardens, who had various duties. The name 'aedes' meant 'temple' and they had a certain amount of religious duty but they were also responsible for the games, the markets, various public works and public archives. Their connection between games and religion reminded people of the religious origins of the festivals which the games were intended to celebrate.

The tribunes, who followed, were primarily the champions of the plebeians and so had to be adopted by the assembly of the common people before they could hold office. This requirement was inevitably dropped under the empire and they became just another appointment of the emperor. There was one considerable advantage in being a tribune: your person was inviolate; that is, no one was allowed to seize or kill you. Not surprisingly this was one Republican office that the emperor was extremely keen to claim for himself.

The first step in the career ladder was the job of quaestor, which was where every ambitious young man began. Quaestors were in charge of financial affairs in Rome and in the provinces. There were about twenty in the time of Augustus. Before becoming a quaestor, the careerist would probably have done military service for a few years. In the early days, there were no regular, organised Government Departments. Much of the work of the quaestors, for example, was farmed out to licensed tax collectors who took their own cut of wealth taxes, taxes on the rent of public land, harbour dues, slave sales, death duties or tribute from the provinces. Augustus established proper Departments.

These were the regular jobs. The senators as a whole also elected from among their ranks two censors every five years to conduct a census of the population and to regulate the numbers in the Senate and the numbers of knights – the next class down. Censors were also responsible for public morals. They held office for eighteen months.

There were various other public offices, none of which carried the 'power of command', or imperium, that was vested in the more important jobs. Among these others there were procurators and curators, who were appointed to head special commissions in the provinces, and legates, who were often sent out to help provincial governors. Their duties and those of the magistrates often overlapped and certain responsibilities might be added at the discretion of the Senate or the emperor.

There was, naturally, a good deal of politicking to obtain election. Bribes were forbidden but largesse in the form of feasts was common. A man seeking office relied on his social dependants to back him. Rival candidates were put up by the plebeian and patrician assemblies and by rival clubs or guilds. Political parties became indistinct during the empire: so far as they existed they were remnants of the conservative 'optimates' and the left wing 'populares' of Republican times. Once elected, officials often succumbed to bribes but, on the whole, the empire has a deserved reputation for reasonable and efficient government by its public servants. Organisation was one of the prime Roman attributes. Even the dissolute official could pull himself together to perform his duty, as Seneca, the Stoic philosopher, wrily remarked:

'Let each of us name for himself the people he knows can be trusted with a secret though they can't be trusted with a bottle. I'll give, all the same, one solitary example myself, just to prevent its being lost to human

*'The house where the Senate gathers, though surrounded by the holiest traditions, opens to all, even foreigners, who come with merit.'*

He is the archetypal middle aged citizen of every civilization. The cares of life have creased his brow, he is balding, worried about the latest tax demand, has a family that is making constant demands both on his time and his pocket. He is the 'Average Man', a citizen of Rome but equally a timeless citizen of the middle income bracket.

Across two thousand years of time we can recognize him, sense his problems – and salute him.

memory! . . . Lucius Piso was drunk from the very moment of his appointment as Warden of the City of Rome. He regularly spent most of the night wining and dining in company, and slept from then until around midday, noon to him being early morning; he nevertheless discharged his duties, which embraced the general welfare of the city, with the utmost efficiency.'

Towns in the provinces similarly elected magistrates of various levels and had a council of ex-magistrates, known as the curia, who performed a similar function to the Senate in Rome, although on a smaller scale. Many towns sprang up in territories that had recently been conquered by Rome but few had all the benefits of a colonia. Coloniae were usually founded by discharged soldiers who were given grants of land and expected to settle the area. They were given privileges and tax exemptions to help them start and they remained closely linked to Rome and its customs.

Municipia were very high status towns, already in existence, which earned special charters that gave them all the privileges of Roman citizenship; in other instances they preferred to retain their independent self-government. Rome tolerated this and provided them with another form of charter which gave them the status of allies. Roman officials would make occasional visits to see that everything was in order and that taxes were being paid. In Britain, at one time, there was only one municipium (Verulamium, or St Albans) as against four coloniae.

Governors of new provinces were concerned to 'Romanise' them as peacefully and quickly as possible, by making them accustomed to Roman laws and ways of life, by building Roman towns and by establishing Roman traditions. Tacitus explains how Agricola set about the task in Britain but he ends on a wry note:

'The following winter was spent on schemes of social betterment. Agricola had to deal with people living in isolation and ignorance, and therefore prone to fight; and his object was to accustom them to a life of peace and quiet by the provision of amenities. He therefore gave private encouragement and official assistance to the building of temples, public squares and good houses. He praised the energetic and scolded the slack; and competition for honour proved as effective as compulsion. Furthermore, he educated the sons of the chiefs in the liberal arts, and expressed a preference for British ability as compared with the trained skills of the Gauls. The result was that instead of loathing the Latin language they became eager to speak it effectively. In the same way, our national dress came into favour and the toga was everywhere to be seen. And so the population was gradually led into the demoralising temptations of arcades, baths, and sumptuous banquets. The unsuspecting Britons spoke of such novelties as "civilisation", when in fact they were only a feature of their enslavement.'

Such cynicism about the advantages of Roman civilisation were rare, and not often warranted. Roman governors and local officials set about the task of raising monuments and public buildings with vast enthusiasm and a genuine spirit of gratitude and social goodwill. The best provincial governors were conscientious and energetic. The younger Pliny, as governor of Bythinia, kept up a steady correspondence with the emperor Trajan, consulting with and requesting advice from the emperor. Trajan appreciated this close contact but was not above telling Pliny – occasionally – to get on with the job himself. Provincial governors had a large amount of autonomy. Here is Pliny, anxious to save money, as ever:

*'The Germans are almost unique among barbarians in being content with one wife apiece.'*

Perhaps this character is a street seller. He carries a flagon of wine, a basket and a ham. And somehow he conveys all that perky independence associated with the people of a great city, such as Rome.

'Will you consider, Sir, whether you think it necessary to send out a land surveyor? Substantial sums of money could, I think, be recovered from contractors of public works if we had dependable surveys made.'

But Trajan has his own problems:

'As for land surveyors, I have scarcely enough for the public works in progress in Rome or in the neighbourhood, but there are reliable surveyors to be found in every province and no doubt you will not lack assistance if you will take the trouble to look for it.'

Roman law was a vital element in bringing together the varied nationalities of the empire. The Twelve Tables that had been drawn up in the fifth century BC laid down the penalties for certain basic crimes. These were constantly referred to by lawyers. But a great deal of Roman law was built up from precedent and the accumulated decisions of judges and advisers. The two praetors in charge of the law with regard to citizens and the law with regard to foreigners issued an edict at the beginning of their year of office. This edict stated the way in which they would interpret the law during their year. In many cases the succeeding praetor would take on the edict of his predecessor; sometimes he would issue a new edict that differed slightly. At the same time, he constantly took advice from legal experts who had familiarised themselves with the accumulated edicts of the centuries. This gave Roman law the benefit of wide experience.

In turn, the praefect in charge of foreigners was concerned to find a compromise between Roman law and the customs of the foreigners themselves. There was no point in establishing a law that was totally unacceptable to either party in a dispute. Therefore he had to rise above national considerations, for Rome embraced many nations. The result was that he

Hadrian's magnificent villa at Tivoli is one of the most impressive of all Roman remains. Since its excavation began in the 16th Century the villa's architectural style and adornments have exercised a great deal of influence on design and taste.

The famous villa was probably the most sumptuous and extravagant of all the great Roman villas. It extended for more than a mile over the sloping ground below Tivoli itself.

There was an enormous colonnaded courtyard, a suite of halls, a temple, an island and magnificent statuary. Pillars survive which show that they must at one time have supported a huge central dome.

formulated a universal law that was acceptable to men in general, not to men as nationals of this or that country. As the citizen law blended its experience and wisdom with the universal breadth of the law for foreigners, Roman law became what we might call 'natural' law. That is why it has endured. At various stages, the law was codified. The most famous of these codifications was that ordered by the emperor Justinian, who summed up the precedents of the past in a concise and lasting fashion.

In civil suits a judge was appointed to hear the case; in criminal cases the praetor himself or another magistrate was in charge. Legal experts were to hand in both instances. There were also commissions of enquiry, known as 'quaestiones', to consider some of the thornier specialist crimes. Crimes of treason might be tried by public assembly. Treason trials were alarmingly frequent under Tiberius, when informers were paid one quarter of the accused man's estate! Some honour could be saved by a guilty man if he committed suicide before his trial took place. Since Romans were particularly jealous of their good name, even after they were dead, this was important to them, whether guilty or not. Prison was only for debtors or for those awaiting trial. Apart from capital punishment, which was liberally decreed, there were fines, confiscations, demotion and banishment. Slaves had no legal rights; women had very few. Major cases in the provinces might sometimes be brought to Rome for trial.

Some extreme punishments survived from the superstitious days when priests had been the earliest judges. In his novel *The Golden Ass*, Apuleius describes a case of poisoning:

'The court, with one sole dissentient, was convinced of his guilt and, however tender-hearted they might be, saw no alternative but to sentence him, as the law provided, to be sewn up in a leather sack with four living creatures, a dog, a cock, a viper and an ape, emblems of the four deadly sins, and cast into a river. It now remained to drop their ballots into the brass urn; if this registered a sentence of death the proceedings would be at an end and the condemned man would be handed over to the public executioner.'

Roman citizenship was acquired by birth. It was highly prized. Even when it was extended to other Italian cities, it retained its value, although men from Rome itself always considered themselves vastly superior to those from the 'provinces'. In time, citizenship was granted to whole cities outside Italy at the discretion of the emperor and, eventually, to every free man in the empire. Provincial soldiers were granted citizenship on their discharge, after a certain number of years service. Slaves who had been freed could also be given citizenship and sons born after their fathers had been freed automatically were considered free. To be able to say that you were a free-born Roman citizen was a passport to acceptance anywhere between the Atlantic and Asia Minor, between the Sahara and northern Britain, as St Paul discovered:

'And as they bound him with thongs, Paul said unto the centurion that stood by, Is it lawful for you to scourge a man that is a Roman, and uncondemned? When the centurion heard that he went and told the chief captain, saying, Take heed what thou doest: for this man is a Roman. Then the chief captain came, and said unto him, Tell me, art thou a Roman? He said, Yea. And the chief captain answered, With a great sum obtained I this freedom. And Paul said, But I was free born. Then straightway they departed from him which should have examined him: and the chief captain also was afraid, after he knew that he was a Roman, and because he had bound him.'

'*In the life of man, his time is but a moment, his being an incessant flux, his sense a dim rushlight, his body a prey of worms, his soul an unquiet eddy, his fortune dark, and his fame doubtful.*'

'*Flattery works on the mind as the waves on the banks of a river.*'

'*To refrain from imitation is the best revenge.*'

# The social structure

The traditional division of Roman citizens was into three groups: senators, knights and the third estate, which consisted of everyone else. These were social divisions and they were strictly observed. To be a senator it was not enough just to have the qualifying capital of 1,000,000 sesterces. You had to keep up appearances, in clothes, in slaves, in dinner parties, in public and private generosity; it was not unknown for a senator to be stripped of his rank because he was not keeping up the standards of his class. Such demotion was often at the discretion of the emperor.

Their wealth came usually from estates and property but it was difficult for them to maintain their estates when they were forced to remain in Rome. To make matters worse, they were committed to considerable extra expense if they were elected to one of the magistrate's jobs. A senator serving his term as praetor might also have to pay for a number of games in the circus or amphitheatre to win popular support. This could easily use up several hundred thousand sesterces in his year of office. The wife of one praetor was advised to divorce him before he was elected, for he would certainly be financially ruined by the end of the year. Sometimes senators were forced to beg money from the emperor to keep up their standards. It was even known for them to ask to be stripped of their rank or not to be elected to office because they could not afford the 'privilege'. Senators enjoyed all the advantages of a ruling class, including the trappings – the front seats at spectacles, the purple stripe on the toga, the Republican shoe laced up to the knee. But they paid heavily for their position. Senatorial rank and magisterial office were more often the cause of the ruin of ancient family fortunes than either gambling or drink. Martial portrays a man who has seen better times:

'Accustomed always to sit in the front row in days when to seize a place was lawful, Nanneius was twice and thrice roused up and shifted camp,

Citizens of the empire were strictly conscious of their status but what may seem to us to have been a tightly closed society was in fact extremely fluid. Slaves could gain their freedom and their descendants could themselves become citizens. Under the empire, freedmen could rise to the highest office. Rank and dignity was open to all – by one means or another.

*'Artist, if you plan to paint our daughter be diligent in your art like the bee who finds a sweetness and colour among the flowers high on the rocks of Athens.'*

This man is at the top of the Roman social structure. His rank is denoted by the purple border. A whole system of social etiquette revolved round the toga which was to prove one of the world's most enduring clothing styles. The toga remained the main garment of the upper classes throughout the history of the Empire.

The way in which the toga was draped was also of significance. Rich men had slaves whose main duty was simply the care and handling of the master's toga.

and sat down right between the seats, making almost a third behind Gaius Lucius. Thence with his head buried in a cowl he peers out, and views the show indecently with one eye. Expelled even from here, the wretched fellow passes into the gangway and, half propped up at the end of a bench and allowed small room, with one knee pretends to the knight by him that he is sitting, with the other to Leitus that he is standing.'

The next class, the knights, originated in military service but became a civil distinction. Their qualification under the early empire was a capital of 400,000 sesterces. Membership of the class was not hereditary but might be granted to any free man by the emperor; at first it was confined to noble families, later it was opened to freedmen. They too wore a purple stripe on their toga and had special seats at the spectacles; they also wore a gold ring. Several men were known to wear the ring even though they were not knights. This was forbidden but was obviously worth a try.

Like the senators, they were expected to keep up certain standards of appearance. Senators were elected from the class of knights but the knights often preferred to forgo the distinction than face financial ruin. But they could not escape their own public duties, which included service as advocates, procurators and praefects. Unlike the senators, they were allowed to travel out of Italy as business or desire prompted and so they were altogether a more cosmopolitan crowd. Some were extremely wealthy; others, like Martial, found it hard to make ends meet.

The third estate made up the majority of the population, apart from slaves. Many were very, very poor. They included all those citizens in trade and industry: shopkeepers, merchants and so on. They included the more respectable jobs of teaching and medicine, architecture, engineering and law. They included the small agricultural rent-holders, the clerical posts under magistrates and priests, and the citizens of the army. This class was continually being expanded by slaves who had been freed and had taken up trade or business. Some were very successful; many remained poor and relied for support on the master who had recently freed them.

One of the most curious aspects of the social and economic system in Rome was that of clients and patrons. Huge numbers of people relied on free hand-outs of grain from the State to keep them off the starvation line. These hand-outs, together with the numerous public games, were intended to keep the alarming number of unemployed content. But there were many others in the third estate – and among the knights – who relied on a different sort of hand-out as well. It came from wealthy patrons, who considered it their duty to support their poorer fellows in exchange for certain social obligations. In one way or another, almost everyone was linked together in a complex system of dependency.

The system worked quite simply. Each morning, at daybreak, the patron would hold a levée in the main hall of his house. His clients – the people under his protection and who relied for subsistence on his generosity – would be expected to attend without fail. They hastened from their rooms in the city to pay their respects and chat for a while. Since many clients had several patrons, they might have to rush round two or three houses in different parts of the city. Clients were also expected to turn out if their patrons wished to walk around the city or go on a journey. In return they received regular amounts of money ('sportula') and occasional gifts as well as free meals at their patron's table. On his side, the patron could not afford to be seen without a crowded hall of clients in the morning and without a company of followers when he went out walking. This social snobbery, which often led

patrons to treat their clients in the most contemptuous manner, was tempered by a genuine feeling of responsibility for the less fortunate. The system had its weaknesses but it worked and it lasted.

Martial suffered the agonies of being a client most of his life. Many of his epigrams were written to flatter patrons or to tease money out of them. In one poem he tries to avoid his duties:

'You exact from me gowned service without end; I don't attend, but I despatch to you my freedman. "It isn't the same thing," you say. I will prove it is much more: I could hardly escort a litter, he will carry it. Supposing you get into a crowd, he will thrust them all back with his elbow; my flanks are weak, and a gentleman's. Supposing you tell a story in your pleading, I myself will hold my peace; but he will bellow for you a thrice-redoubled "Bravo". If you have a lawsuit he will pour abuse in stentorian tones; shyness has forbidden me strong language. "So you, though a friend, will give me no service?" you say. Whatever, Candidus, my freedman cannot.'

But when Martial does go to pay his respects to another of his patrons, he finds, much to his indignation, that the man has gone off to pay his own respects to his own patron. It was a never-ending circle:

'I must surmount the track up the hill from the Subura and the dirty

If you were a wealthy, successful Roman citizen you would probably have had a room looking something like this. There are rich mosaics and handsome wall paintings. However spartan the Roman philosophy might have been, in fact their decorative taste tended to be rather florid. There is a rich, almost pre-Raphaelite feel about many of the surviving paintings and mosaics. This is the House of the Vettii, Pompeii.

pavement with its steps never dry, and I can scarce break through the long droves of mules and the blocks of marble you see hauled by many a cable. And – more annoying still – after a thousand exertions, Paulus, when I am fagged out, your doorkeeper says you are "not at home"! Such is the result of misspent toil, and my poor toga drenched! To *see* Paulus in the morning was scarcely worth the cost. A diligent client always has inhuman friends: if you do not stay in bed, you cannot be my patron.'

Finally, Martial despairs of the tiresome round of morning visits:

'At length spare, O Rome, the weary congratulator, the weary client! How long, at levées, among the escort and the full-dressed throng, shall I earn a hundred worthless farthings in a whole day, whereas in a single hour, Scorpus, a winner of the race, bears off fifteen bags of gleaming gold? . . . Do you ask what I long for? To sleep.'

Increasingly, social life and manners were directly related to the style set by the emperor's court. He, too, held a levée each morning, at which gifts were presented to him and petitions made. The atmosphere at these levées varied between fear and friendliness with each emperor. It became traditional for the emperor to greet his friends with a kiss but Tiberius was compelled to stop this habit because there was an outbreak of facial scabs among all those who had been embracing. Caligula offered only his hand or his foot to be kissed but, much to the indignation of the Romans, often insisted on the eastern tradition of prostration. Trajan, on the other hand, seemed perfectly pleasant: according to Pliny he greeted the senators with a kiss when he entered Rome as emperor and gave a personal greeting to many of the senior knights; he was also quick to greet his clients and to show them marks of confidence. The emperor Elagabalus received the Senate in bed!

The emperor's will and character soon dominated the empire. Officials in his household became more powerful than any of the ancient noble families and freedmen were raised to more distinguished positions than knights or senators. It paid an emperor to surround himself with men who relied on him and were indebted to him for their success. But often it was the Greeks who had come to Rome as slaves who were the most efficient administrators. Rome needed the new blood from the provinces to invigorate the social system.

There were many petty facets to the system – the favourites, the boy-lovers, the concubines, the court dancers and mimes. Men fought to get close to the emperor, to become a 'Friend of the emperor' or 'Table companion'. The rewards could be immense in terms of power and money, and these things were important to Romans. But the system also provided great fluidity, as new men were constantly brought in, from lower ranks and from provincials who had often first come to Rome as slaves.

The Roman attitude to slaves was full of paradoxes. Slaves were possessions, like an ox or a dog. They had no rights. They could be bought or sold or punished with death, as their master – or their mistress – wished. Some were treated brutally in the amphitheatre. On the other hand many were treated as part of the family. Thousands – possibly hundreds of thousands – were freed every year to take their proper place in society and in time become Roman citizens. The State and many private citizens relied absolutely on slave labour, which they took for granted, and yet their sometimes ruthless treatment of slaves demonstrated their underlying fear of revolt. There were between 200,000 and 300,000 slaves in Rome at the beginning of the empire, in a population of about one million. It was hardly surprising that a recommendation that slaves should wear a special uniform was turned down

*'Do not waste what remains of your life in speculating about your neighbours, unless with a view to some mutual benefit.'*

*'To pursue the unattainable is insanity, yet the thoughtless can never refrain from doing so.'*

*'If there is a modest one, whose eyes are always cast downward, I am on fire, in a snare, set by her innocent ways. If one is forward and brash, I rejoice that she's not country-simple. I foresee quite a romp in her bed.'*

on the grounds that they would then realise the strength of their numbers. When the gladiator Spartacus had banded together an army of 70,000 slaves in the first century BC, he terrorised Rome for three years until a rift in the leadership brought about his defeat. Six thousand slaves were killed and hung on crosses along the road as a terrible example. Subsequently it was decreed that if any one slave murdered his master every slave in the household should be killed. There were no more major slave revolts.

The slave system was such an integral part of Roman life that there were no attempts to defend the morality of it and few contemporary writers who even discuss it. Seneca was by no means the only Roman with an enlightened and humane attitude to slaves but he was one of the rare contemporaries to take the trouble to protest about their maltreatment:

> 'I'm glad to hear, from these people who've been visiting you, that you live on friendly terms with your slaves. It is just what one expects of an enlightened, cultivated person like yourself. "They're slaves," people say. No, they're human beings . . . strictly speaking, they're our fellow slaves, if you once reflect that fortune has as much power over us as over them. This is why I laugh at those people who think it degrading for a man to eat with his slave . . . We abuse them as if they were beasts of burden instead of human beings . . .'

On the other hand, a slave who began his life in total servitude could end up as rich as Trimalchio, one of the heroes of Petronius' *Satyricon*, whose feasts were famous for their extravagance. For slaves were able to save money and start up in business on their own or on their master's behalf, or work in government departments with positions of responsibility where they might have slaves of their own. It is possible to see the advantages of the slave system, not just to the Romans but to the slaves themselves: the luckier ones acquired an education in civilisation and opportunities for advancement that they would never otherwise have had. Enslavement could, paradoxically, be the first step to freedom.

Slaves came firstly from nations conquered in war. As the empire ceased to expand, they were acquired by piracy and by sale. Children were sometimes sold as slaves and malformed babies or babies of poor families that had been exposed to death were often taken in as slaves. Slavery was also a punishment for severe crimes. And children were born to slavery, if their mothers were slaves.

They came originally from all parts of the empire and they went, not just to Rome, but to every Roman outpost where labour was required. There were Phrygians, Lydians, Cappadocians, Bithynians, Arabs, Persians, Parthians, Alexandrians, Egyptians, Ethiopians, Syrians and Greeks – for a start. Greeks were renowned for their skills but notorious for their morals. Syrians were condemned out of hand by Cicero merely because they knew Greek. Juvenal regarded Syrian music as unendurable. Syrians in the *Satyricon* stole silver plate from the dining room. Spaniards, Germans and Batavians were admired as bodyguards. Thracians were such useful fighters that they were used in the army rather than as slaves. Each nation contributed to the bustling cacophony of language and music in Rome and other major cities. The influx of the East was too much for Juvenal:

> 'Its lingo and manners, its flutes, its outlandish harps with the transverse strings, its native tambourines, and the whores who hang around the race track.'

In the household, Roman luxury and even moderate living depended entirely on the use of slaves, who performed every menial function, from

*'Do unsavoury armpits and bad breath make you angry? What good will it do you? Given the mouth and armpits the man has got, that condition is bound to produce those odours. . . . Apply your reasonableness to move him to a like reasonableness; expound, admonish. If he pays attention, you will have worked a cure, and there will be no need for passion; leave that to actors and streetwalkers.'*

*'I will become a friend of the Emperor and then no-one will dare tread too near.'*

*'I would not dare to defend my absolute absence of morals. No, I own up. I hate what I am and yet, for all my desiring, cannot be anything else.'*

cooking and cleaning to shopping and carrying litters. They wiped up the spittle of the diners; they carved the meat; they learnt off whole books by heart to recite to their masters; they taught the children; they carried messages of business or of love and themselves were not infrequently at the beck and call of the pleasure of their master or their mistress. The upstart Trimalchio had one slave to pick up his handball whenever he dropped it and another standing by upon whose hair he wiped his hands whenever they were wet. Household slaves knew every secret of the family of which they formed a part. It was not surprising that they were kept firmly in their place.

But they went to the theatre and the games; they joined clubs with freedmen; they ran shops often; they took part in the religious observations of the family; they were encouraged to have their own family life in the home. Martial saw clearly the advantages they enjoyed:

> 'You don't realise the cares of a master or the advantages of a slave's life. You sleep well on a rug; your master lies awake on a bed of down. You salute no one – not even your master; he salutes in fear and trembling a number of patrons. You have no debts; he is burdened with them. Do you fear the torturer? He is a martyr to gout.'

According to Martial, therefore, they never knew when they were well off for, not surprisingly, their dearest hope was to obtain their freedom. They gained this by a peculiarly Christian-sounding ceremony, the laying on of hands – or manumission, as it was called. Within certain limitations laid down by the State, any master could set his slaves free either by manumission or in his will. Slaves would be freed as a mark of gratitude after long and faithful service or because the cost of keeping the slave and his family had become prohibitive. In agriculture it was often considered more economical to employ free labour than to use slaves who, although they did not have to be paid, had still to be fed and clothed and had no vested interest in improving the land.

Once freed, the 'freedman' retained a permanent relationship with his ex-master. His master became his patron and he was supposed to show respect towards him whenever he met him. In turn, his master performed the usual duties of a patron: he gave him money, advice and support in his business. Freedmen might rise, through trade and the acquisition of wealth, to become procurators in the provinces, heads of government departments, even consuls. All were keen to show themselves true Romans. They eagerly donated money for public works to immortalise their name and win the esteem of the ranks of free men they had joined. Petronius was able to laugh at the vulgar ostentation of the freedman with his new-found wealth. Martial and Juvenal were less amused. It was too easy to find yourself begging a favour from an ex-slave. Seneca had this advice to give:

> 'Live with your inferiors in just the same way as you would like your superiors to live with you.'

All this seems to cloud the distinctions of social rank in the Roman empire. But the more fluidity there was between the classes, the more tightly those in each class clung to their privileges. No one was more class conscious than the new man. But a senator, the younger Pliny, has the last word on the social order. He wrote to a colleague:

> 'I mean to congratulate you on the way in which you preserve the distinctions of class and rank; once these are thrown into confusion and destroyed, nothing is more unequal than the resultant "equality".'

One place that had no equal was Rome. What was it like to live in the busy heart of such a mingling of nations and people?

*'It is a pauper's household in which the same person has to do the cooking and the dusting and to make the beds.'*

*'How about reflecting that the person you call your slave traces his origin back to the same stock as yourself, has the same good sky above him, breathes as you do, lives as you do, dies as you do.'*

*'You've as many enemies as you've slaves.'*

# The city of Rome

In the first century AD, Rome was the bustling, cosmopolitan centre of the empire. It was also a city of great contrasts. Wealthy patrician senators and knights walked with their slaves and dependants; freedmen merchants spread largesse among impoverished free shopkeepers; slaves had the ear of the emperor but scions of the noblest houses fought in the arena to scrape a living. On the Palatine Hill stood the magnificent palace of the emperor. The Colosseum, the Circus Maximus, the Pantheon (rebuilt completely by Hadrian), the great public baths, temples, gardens, triumphal arches, tombs, statues, the forums and market places at the heart of the city – these embodied the dignity and grandeur of Rome, at which provincials gazed in wonder. But there were also the prostitutes' quarters, the narrow streets of open-fronted shops, the jostling crowds, the perils of the night. The 'Eternal City' may

The cloister-like remains of buildings on the Palatine hill, Rome. The Palatine was part of the original city and the hill was one of the first to be settled. The emperor Augustus was born on the Palatine in 63 BC. Many famous Romans lived on the Palatine including Catiline, Claudius and Crassus, one of the wealthiest of Romans.

sound at times like a marvellous set piece, perfectly proportioned, flawless, unchanging. Underneath the surface, people go about their hectic business: the hammerings and shoutings of construction work, the whisperings of political and sexual intrigue, riots, fires, thunderstorms, dissatisfaction, famine and flood. The first concern of every emperor was to keep the citizens and people of Rome well-fed and well-pleased. It was not always such an easy task.

Suetonius claimed that Augustus had transformed Rome from a city of brick to a city of marble and Augustus himself boasted of his achievements in his 'Res Gestae'. The first emperor initiated a tremendous building programme, lowered the rate of interest for borrowing money, and exploited the superb Carrara marble for the first time on a large scale to embellish the public buildings for which he took on special responsibility. He boasted that he had built more than eighty temples during his reign. The peace and prosperity of his rule ensured that his successors continued the good work. Aristides described in enthusiastic words how Rome was more than the sum of its buildings:

Modern roads sweep past the famous Arch of Septimius Severus. Septimius revived the old idea of the total conquest of Britain and he took personal command of the legions in Britain. He got as far as Aberdeenshire and then his legions were defeated by the combination of bog, forest and guerrilla activity. Septimius Severus died in York in AD 211.

'To you there comes from all lands and seas what the seasons bring forth and the climates produce, what rivers and lakes and the handicraft of Hellene or barbarian make. Whoever, therefore, wish to view all this, must either journey through the whole world or stay in this city. For the work and toil of other folks is ever here at hand and in excess. So many merchantmen come here from all lands during the entire summer and winter, that the city seems a general workshop of the entire world. So many freights from India and Arabia Felix are here to be seen, that it would almost appear as though henceforth the trees of those countries are stripped, and those races must come here to Rome to demand what they need of their own products. Costumes from Babylon and jewels from the depths of barbarian Asia arrive here more in number and with greater ease than they would be shipped from an island in the Archipelago to Athens. In short, all that trade and ships may bring reaches Rome, all that agriculture earns and mines bring to the upper light, and all products of every art, all that is born and grows on earth.'

Rome became the 'inn of the world', an inn, Juvenal assures us, in which it was not cheap to stay: 'nothing is to be had for nothing', he moaned. Rent, food and clothes were all expensive, which was largely why so many relied on the largesse of their wealthy neighbours. But the inn was a meeting place for people and a market for news just as much as for goods. Reports flowed in to the emperor from all parts of the Mediterranean world. They came with messengers of the imperial post; they came with officials returning from a tour of duty; they came with foreign ambassadors and with merchants. Philosophers from Greece, shipowners from Alexandria, barbarian chieftains from the north, slaves from Africa and the East, landowners from Spain, pedlars, money-changers, prostitutes, senators, priests, jugglers, courtesans, clients and tradesmen jostled each other in the streets. Martial reckoned that the whorehouse saw them all:

*'Men who have never known justice have been conquered and then been given rights under your laws. What was only a world, you have made a city. All things have been drawn to you and made good.'*

'You grant your favours to Parthians, you grant them to Germans, you grant them, Caelia, to Dacians, and you do not spurn the couch of Cilicians and Cappadocians; and for you from his Egyptian city comes sailing the poker of Memphis, and the Black Indian from the Red Sea; nor do you shun the groin of the circumcised Jews, and the Alan on his Sarmatian steed does not pass you by. What is your reason that, although you are a Roman girl, no Roman prick has attraction for you?'

A general view of the remains of the Roman Forum. The forum was originally built at Julius Caesar's own personal expense when he was consul – the land alone cost him 100 million sesterces. His building extended the original Republican Forum but in their turn Caesar's buildings were completely reconstructed by Augustus after a fire. The great Forum survived into Renaissance times but today only the outlines of its former glory remain.

*'To count up the glories of Rome is like counting the stars in the sky. The temples of Rome are so fine that the gods themselves might live in them. Streams that flow over my head on arches are grander than even the rainbow's highest arch ... Rivers are channelled within the walls, lakes vanish in the baths, rivers flow in the gardens and the walls echo the sounds of water.'*

Some streets down which the concourse of people swept were broad and handsome; most remained dark from overhanging balconies and obstructed by jars of oil or wine or benches outside the shops. It was cheaper to build up than out. Wooden balconies stretched across the street and people could shake hands from either side. Houses were irregular in height and frontage. Shops were built out into the street with wooden stalls. A crowd at one shop could halt the traffic in the road. Martial sighed with relief when the emperor Domitian forbade stalls in the streets, for the situation had clearly got out of hand, to his mind:

'The audacious huckster had robbed us of all the City, and never a threshold kept within its bounds. You have ordered our narrow streets to expand, and what was but now a track has become a road. No pillar is girt with chained flagons, nor is the praetor forced to walk in the middle of the mud, nor is any razor rashly drawn in the midst of a dense crowd, nor does the grimy cookshop monopolise the whole of the way. Barber, taverner, cook, butcher keep to their own thresholds. Now Rome exists: of late it was a huge shop.'

The over-reaching house created all sorts of dangers for the unwary pedestrian, as Juvenal found out:

'It's a long way up to the rooftops and a falling tile can brain you – not to mention all those cracked or leaky pots that people toss out through windows. Look at the way they smash, the weight of them, the damage they do to the pavement! You'll be thought most improvident, a catastrophe-happy fool, if you don't make your will before venturing out to dinner. Each open upper casement along your route at night may prove a death-trap: so pray and hope (poor you!) that the local housewives drop nothing worse on your head than a pailful of slops.'

He feared the night-time most: young nobles the worse for drink with a crowd of rowdy companions looking for a fight; houses shut tight for the night and silent with no one to hear if you cried out for help; burglars and men with knives lurking at street corners. But when he wished to sleep he found the nights far from silent. Wagons rumbled by in the narrow, winding streets below his lodging window and drovers caught in a midnight traffic jam stood and shouted at each other.

None of these things would surprise the modern city dweller. Why should Rome be more difficult for the emperor to control than any other city? There were many reasons. Rumour and wild reports were only part of the problem. Bad news from the frontier might set the people in a panic. When Varus lost three legions in the Teutoburger Forest, citizens began to pack their bags ready to leave the city in case the barbarian Germans should march on Rome. Augustus had virtually to strip the city of its reserves of manpower to provide hastily organised reinforcements. In so doing he left himself open to the dangers of mob riot. The restless crowd of unemployed and poverty-stricken were never loath to seize an excuse to vent their frustrations. Moreover, fire, flood and famine were very real and recurrent problems which provided excuse and opportunity for vandalism and unrest.

The great fire of AD 64 showed how vulnerable the city was. Tacitus described the scene:

'Whether it was accidental or caused by a criminal act on the part of the emperor is uncertain – both versions have supporters. Now started the most terrible and destructive fire which Rome had ever experienced. It began in the Circus, where it adjoins the Palatine and Caelian hills. Breaking out in shops selling inflammable goods, and fanned by the wind, the conflagration instantly grew and swept the whole length of the Circus. There were no walled mansions or temples, or any other obstructions, which could arrest it. First, the fire swept violently over the level spaces. Then it climbed the hills – but returned to ravage the lower ground again. It outstripped every counter measure. The ancient city's narrow winding streets and irregular blocks encouraged its progress.

'Terrified, shrieking women, helpless old and young, people intent on their own safety, people unselfishly supporting invalids or waiting for them, fugitives and lingerers alike – all heightened the confusion. When people looked back, menacing flames sprang up before them or outflanked them. When they escaped to a neighbouring quarter, the fire followed – even districts believed remote proved to be involved. Finally, with no idea where or what to flee, they crowded on to the country roads, or lay in the fields. Some who had lost everything – even their food for the day – could have escaped but preferred to die. So did others, who had failed to rescue their loved ones. Nobody dared fight the flames. Attempts to do so were prevented by menacing gangs. Torches, too, were openly thrown in, by men crying that they had acted under orders. Perhaps they had received orders. Or they may just have wanted to plunder unhampered.'

In the first century BC the only fire fighters had been teams of slaves. A certain Crassus had his own team with which he hastened to the scene of fires. He would offer to buy the burning house and, if the owner declined, Crassus' men held back. Crassus made steadily lower bids for the house as it rapidly burned down and only when the owner gave in did his men take action to put out the fire. At the very beginning of the first century AD, Augustus organised the first professional fire fighting force, known as the 'Cohortes Vigilum'. There were seven cohorts of 1000 men each, recruited from freedmen and equipped with axes, buckets, swabs, hooks and a few rudimentary handpumps. They remained in force throughout the century and longer but seem

CURIA

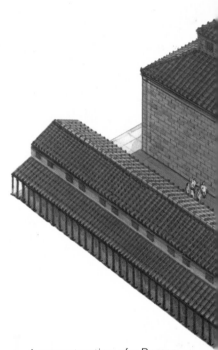

A reconstruction of a Roman forum. In Roman times a basilica was a building designed for public meetings. They were eventually formalised into a central area with aisles or galleries at the side and a raised platform. The curia was a centre for certain formal religious rites and events. The temples shown here would have been dedicated to individual deities. The long arcade contained shops.

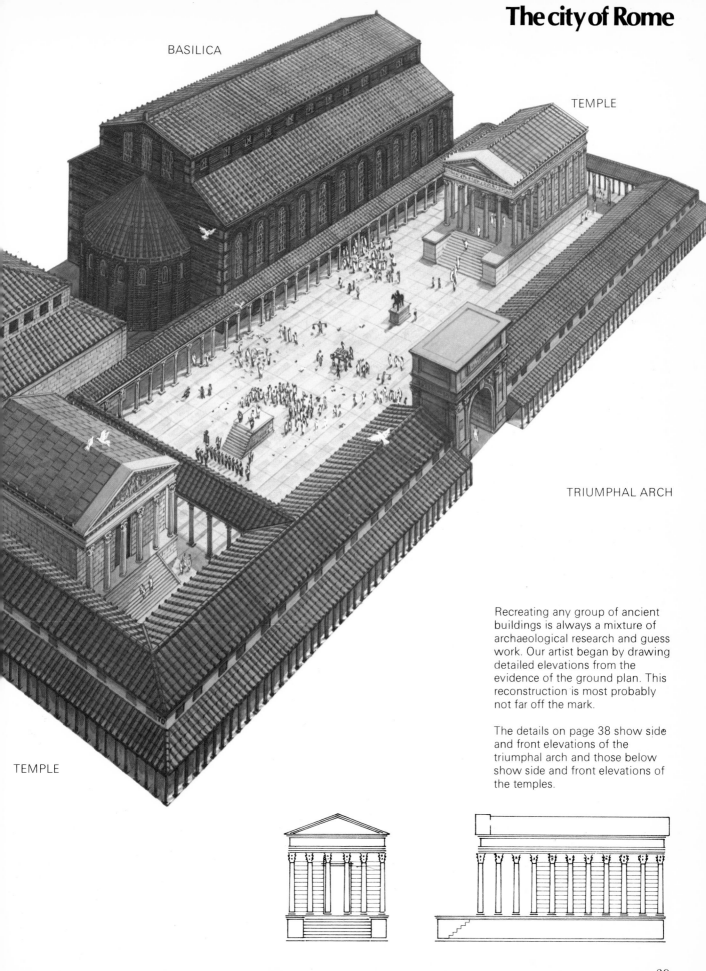

BASILICA

TEMPLE

TRIUMPHAL ARCH

TEMPLE

Recreating any group of ancient buildings is always a mixture of archaeological research and guess work. Our artist began by drawing detailed elevations from the evidence of the ground plan. This reconstruction is most probably not far off the mark.

The details on page 38 show side and front elevations of the triumphal arch and those below show side and front elevations of the temples.

to have been ineffective in AD 64. Nero's fire raged for a week.

The danger of fire was just as great elsewhere in the empire. Lyons was totally destroyed by fire. In Nicomedia, Pliny heard of a fire, fanned by the wind, which spread across wide streets and burned up private houses while the populace looked on idly and made no effort to take counter measures. He learnt that the city had no hand pumps, no proper buckets and no other appropriate instruments for fire-fighting. He wrote to Trajan requesting permission to form a fire brigade. But Trajan refused on the grounds that it would provide a dangerous opportunity for men to group themselves together and become a potential threat to the safety of the State. Rome was always conscious of the need to preserve public order. Any kind of organisation that might lead to political resistance was forbidden.

There was an earthquake five years before the Great Fire and another five years after. There had been three earthquakes in the first half of the century. These, among other reasons, could cause the Tiber to overflow its banks and flood the city. Attempts to drain the river or to control the water that flowed into it were rarely successful. In the worst floods, people became stranded on tops of tenement blocks and could only be reached by boat. There were five floods recorded in the reign of Augustus and two more in Tiberius' reign. Pliny recorded another at the end of the century:

'Can the weather be as bad and stormy where you are? Here we have nothing but gales and repeated floods. The Tiber has overflowed its bed and deeply flooded its lower banks, so that although it is being drained by the canal cut by the Emperor, with his usual foresight, it is filling the valleys and inundating the fields, and wherever there is level ground there is nothing to be seen but water . . . People who were hit by the storm on higher ground have seen the valuable furniture and fittings of wealthy homes, or else all the farm stock, yoked oxen, ploughs and ploughmen, or cattle left free to graze, and amongst them trunks of trees or beams and roofs of houses, all floating by in widespread confusion. Nor have the places where the river did not rise escaped disaster, for instead of floods they have had incessant rain, gales, and cloudbursts which have destroyed the walls enclosing valuable properties, rocked public buildings and brought them crashing to the ground. Many people have been maimed, crushed, and buried in such accidents, so that loss of life is added to material damage.'

The flood waters were likely to find their way into the warehouses and destroy the city's reserves of grain. Famine was a constant threat. There were continuous fluctuations in the amount of corn held in the city at any one time. It was only too easy to miscalculate what was required to feed the population. Sometimes there would be supplies enough for several years: on one occasion Rome was able to send back corn to a starving Egypt. But bad harvests in Egypt, fire or flood in the warehouses, storms which prohibited grainships from landing at Ostia for weeks on end – all these led to high prices, public panic and riot.

The regularity of the corn supply from Egypt and Sicily was essential to the peace of the city. There were historical traditions that had established free hand-outs of corn as the right of every Roman citizen. It was Gaius Gracchus, the reformer, who had taken the first step. He had arranged for every citizen in Rome to receive approximately thirty kilos of wheat a month at a cost that barely covered its cost of production at source. Transport and other costs were subsidised by taxes on the provinces and the price was firmly held down in years of crisis. This did a lot to alleviate the perennial poverty among many

*'Rome has marvels greater than all others; nature herself has made our city great. This is a place of peace and not of bloodshed; honour and fame were granted us by fate. We've made our stand through faith no less than fighting; even our wrath we learn to mitigate.'*

*'I would value a barren offshore island more than Rome's urban heart: squalor and isolation are minor evils compared to this endless nightmare of fires and collapsing houses, the cruel city's myriad perils – and poets reciting their work in August!'*

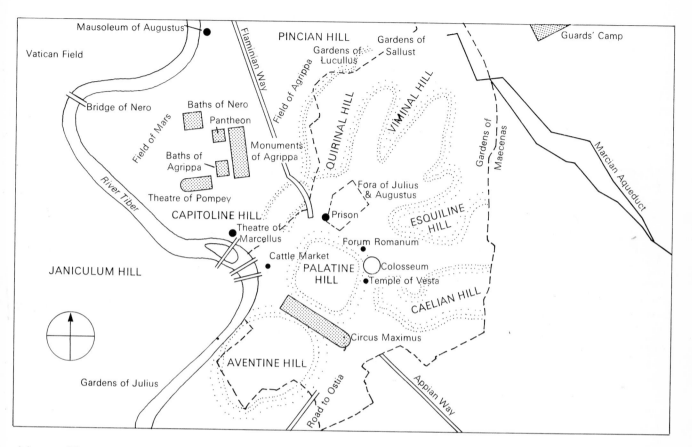

The map is labelled with: Mausoleum of Augustus, Vatican Field, PINCIAN HILL, Gardens of Lucullus, Gardens of Sallust, Guards' Camp, Flaminian Way, Bridge of Nero, Baths of Nero, Pantheon, Field of Mars, Field of Agrippa, QUIRINAL HILL, VIMINAL HILL, Gardens of Maecenas, Marcian Aqueduct, Baths of Agrippa, Monuments of Agrippa, River Tiber, Theatre of Pompey, CAPITOLINE HILL, Fora of Julius & Augustus, Prison, ESQUILINE HILL, Theatre of Marcellus, Forum Romanum, Cattle Market, Colosseum, JANICULUM HILL, PALATINE HILL, Temple of Vesta, CAELIAN HILL, Circus Maximus, AVENTINE HILL, Gardens of Julius, Road to Ostia, Appian Way

citizens of Rome and no one in the opposite party dared to rescind Gracchus' reform after his death for fear of a riot.

Julius Caesar made the hand-out free to more than 300,000 citizens. From then on the number fluctuated but was always controlled to some extent. It remained confined to citizens in Rome and there was an official list of those entitled to this 'dole'. There were, of course, abuses. Many people hoarded their grain and sold it on the black market to others who were not entitled to it. The 'dole' also reached many who, although entitled to it, should, on the apparent evidence of their prosperity, never have received it. But on the whole it was a very necessary counterpart to the 'dole' received by clients from patrons and both forms of 'dole' – public and private – helped large numbers of citizens to survive.

Nero made a bad mistake in AD 68 when the starving population were desperately waiting for a grain fleet from Egypt. Instead of bringing grain, the only ship to reach Italy carried a load of carefully selected Nile-sand for the Emperor's wrestling school. He had to shut himself away for safety from the furious howling of the hungry and frustrated mob. Another time, tons of grain were thrown into the Tiber merely to prove to the nervous citizens that Rome still had ample reserves and that there was no fear of famine. It was a calculated gamble to restore peace: the emperor awaited the grain fleet as anxiously as anyone.

There were other more common city problems. Dust and smoke in the lower quarters gave Rome a heavy atmosphere. Disease spread quickly and Romans were usually complaining about their health. Martial returned from holiday sun-tanned and vigorous and was sure that his friends in the city would not recognise him. But he knew that his colour would soon wear off and

A map of Rome in classical times showing the major buildings and landmarks, roads and hills.

*'An ancestral home needs our presence – and our tears. It is sinful to neglect ruin already compounded by neglect.'*

41

that he would soon be his old white-washed self again. Two serious plagues spread through Rome during the reign of Augustus. There was a great plague in AD 65, a year after the fire, and another terrible one in AD 79, after the eruption of Vesuvius. In the following century there were severe outbreaks of smallpox. It was one of these to which Marcus Aurelius fell victim.

The year AD 5 was one of the worst years for Augustus and for the city of Rome. Every problem came at once. Augustus was already in his mid-sixties and had been emperor for more than thirty years. For a start there were earthquakes, which destroyed a number of cities in the south of Italy. The crops were poor because there was not enough rain in the spring; when harvest time came, heavy storms ruined what was left. The storms caused the Tiber to flood the city and for several days people could get about many parts of the city only by boat. The floods damaged the corn supplies, which were already low from a poor harvest the previous year. Augustus sent commissioners to Egypt to buy extra corn but they were only partly successful: there were shortages there, also. The grain ships arrived late in the year when it was dangerous and difficult to land at the port of Ostia; they had to wait their opportunity.

When the grain did arrive the price was necessarily high and Augustus was forced to distribute large free hand-outs of corn, paid for by himself, to those who were not already entitled to the 'dole'. Then he reduced the numbers of mouths to be fed by sending as many people as he could out of Rome: all the gladiators, all foreigners except teachers and doctors, all slave families and (even!) some slaves belonging to noble families. It was too much for a city already smarting under a new tax recently imposed by Augustus to pay for his German wars. There were riots, there was looting, whole streets were set on fire. It was this that prompted Augustus to organise his professional cohorts of firefighters. Worse still, there were rumours of conspiracy. But Augustus survived the winter and in the spring, when the first grain ships arrived from Egypt, the whole thing blew over.

There were plenty of people only too happy to put up with these drawbacks for the sake of living in the city. Aspiring politicians, ostentatious landowners, fashionable young men and ladies lived there by choice. Merchants, shopkeepers, tradesmen, lawyers, teachers, doctors and craftsmen lived there because Rome was where they could find work and it was their home. Only poets and the rich could enjoy a respite in the country now and then. Martial thrived on the social bustle of the city but at times he was happy to get out of it:

'Schoolmasters in the morning do not let you live; before daybreak, bakers; the hammers of the coppersmiths all day. On this side the money-changer idly rattles on his dirty table Nero's coins, on that the hammerer of Spanish gold-dust beats his well-worn stone with burnished mallet . . . As for me, the laughter of the passing throng wakes me, and Rome is at my bed's head. Whenever, worn out with worry, I wish to sleep, I go to my villa.'

Then he sought simpler pleasures than those offered by the magnificent squalor of Rome:

'A taverner and a butcher and a bath, a barber and a draught board and pieces, and a few books – but to be chosen by me – a single comrade not too unlettered, and a tall boy and not early bearded, and a girl dear to my boy – warrant these to me, Rufus, . . . and keep to yourself Nero's warm baths.'

There were plenty of ordinary people throughout the empire who wished for nothing more or expected much less. Their lives centred on their families.

*'The sea and shore are truly my private Helicon, and endless source of inspiration. You should take the first opportunity yourself to leave the din, the futile bustle and useless occupations of the city and devote yourself to literature or to leisure.'*

*'Venus, you are praised in every corner of Rome's dominion where men live without fetters. The stars, which know all that has been, have never seen a more beautiful Empire.'*

# Life at home

The Romans took family life seriously. It has even been said that they invented it. They certainly gave it an importance that has hardly been matched since. Perhaps we can feel sympathy for their belief in family affection and ties. Now that family life in many countries is being broken down by social and economic attitudes, we may look back to the Roman family with admiration and some regret at times past.

The Romans themselves looked back to the 'good old ways' and grumbled about the decay of family life since the days of the Republic. Even 200 years before the empire, that grand old man Cato was already complaining that things were not as they used to be. He objected to the increasing influence of Greek ideas and attitudes. A good husband, he said, was worth more than a great senator and should never beat his wife or child. Although busy with

The home was very much a Roman's castle. Here he could venerate his household gods and practise the Roman virtues of domesticity. There is a calmness and serenity about this private garden shrine which admirably symbolises the Roman concept of the home.

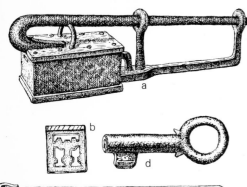

Roman locks were remarkably sophisticated and they were used in heavy wooden doors. The illustration shows a large lock (a) and the end piece (b) of the type of key that would be used with this variety of lock. Other types of keys are shown in figures c and d. The spring of the lock (a) is still in working order.

These particular keys came from Essex, in England. Heavy wooden front doors, embossed with iron and bronze nails and a variety of ornaments survive at Pompeii and Herculaneum. Such a door was discovered at a fort on Hadrian's Wall, guarding a strong room. Curiously, the Romans do not seem to have invented a lock which could be opened from both sides of a door.

public affairs, he took the time to educate his son himself in the old traditions. The good Roman had a duty to his family, which in turn became a duty to a group of families, or clan, and also a duty to the State. The welfare and security of the State rested squarely on the welfare of the family, which was the State in miniature.

The Roman family was a good deal larger than the family we are used to. The household of a prosperous Roman citizen or well-to-do freedman would include not only his wife and children but his slaves and hangers-on. Whatever their different social status, all were part of one family and were ruled over by the head of the household, the 'pater familias'. Cicero described the aged Appius Claudius, who, though blind:

'... yet maintained control of four vigorous sons, five daughters, a great household, and a host of dependants. For instead of inertly capitulating to old age he kept his mind as taut as a boy. He not only directed his home, he ruled it; his slaves feared him, his children venerated him, he was loved by everyone, and beneath his roof prevailed ancestral custom and discipline.'

---

### Respect for Old Age

'So people who declare that there are no activities for old age are speaking beside the point. It is like saying that the pilot has nothing to do with sailing a ship because he leaves others to climb the masts and run along the gangways and work the pumps, while he himself sits quietly in the stern holding the rudder. He may not be doing what the younger men are doing, but his contribution is much more significant and valuable than theirs. Great deeds are not done by strength or speed or physique; they are the products of thought, and character, and judgement. And far from diminishing, such qualities actually increase with age.

'Now I have fought all kinds of wars in my time. First I was a private soldier, then a junior officer, then a commander, and finally a consul. Well, I am not fighting wars any longer, so perhaps I seem to you to be taking my ease. Yet mine is the advice the Senate listens to about which wars to fight and how to fight them.'

(Cicero)

---

Cicero knew from bitter experience what it was like to be torn away from home. At one point in his career his political enemies pulled down his house. He made a speech pleading for his home to be restored and he summed up all that Romans traditionally felt about their homes:

'Is there anything more hallowed, is there anything more closely hedged about with every kind of sanctity than the home of each individual citizen? Therein he has his altars, his hearth, his household gods, his private worships, his rites and ceremonies. For all of us this is a sanctuary so holy that to tear a man away therefrom is an outrage to the law of heaven.'

Family religion and family life were closely bound together and in the early days the head of the family resembled a priest in the degree of his responsibilities. An almost religious respect was shown towards him and towards his ancestors by members of the family and the combined 'genius' or spirit of all the heads of the household from time immemorial was considered to be a very powerful influence on the fortunes of the family. This attitude invested the head of the household with a dignity and authority that would be inconceivable today. It was the source of the power that the individual had within his own family – the 'patria potestas' – a power that gave him the responsibilities of a judge as well as a priest, for it included the right to punish any member of his family by death without reference to the State.

Roman morality was firmly based on family duty and responsibilities. Those well-known Roman virtues of 'gravitas' and 'pietas' were much more than the meaningless words they have become today. Romans believed that even the most trifling matters should be taken seriously and thought about carefully. That was 'gravitas'. They also believed in discipline and the recognition of authority. That was 'pietas'. Another quality was 'simplicitas'. This enabled the Roman to single out that which was important in life; it enabled him to get to the heart of a problem without being side-tracked.

*'Never kiss your wife unless it thunders.'*

In combination with other qualities, these made up what were known as the manners of one's ancestors – the 'mores maiorum' – which were the backbone of the Roman way of life. If that backbone seems at times a little unimaginative and rigid, then perhaps we should accept that a certain degree of inflexibility and 'gravitas' is not a bad thing when you are trying to build a civilisation that is to survive.

All this – the household gods, the wax masks of grandfather and great-grandfather, those weighty virtues – threatens to put the Roman family at several removes from reality. On the contrary, virtues, ancestors and household gods were all very much an active part of the family. Perhaps it is more comfortable to think of the Roman's concern for his ancestors and his household spirits as a concrete expression of the twentieth-century desire to touch the 'life force'. By giving that force shape, the Romans were only being honest about their own sense of wonder and their desire for continuity. They demonstrated a commendable sociability by bringing their gods into their houses and welcoming them into the family.

*'Manliness without ostentation I learnt from what I have heard and remember of my father.'*

Although the man stood firmly at the head of the household, the traditional Roman wife had a position of considerable responsibility, which largely consisted of hard work. The archetypal Roman matron was virtue personified. She ran the home, looked after the earliest education of the children and spun wool. In theory, at least, she had few rights but her importance as a home-maker was never questioned and some of the greatest Romans, including Julius Caesar, were unstinting in the credit they gave to their mothers for the way in which they had been brought up. As in everything else, however, there were changes with Greek influence. The 'good old ways' gave way to irresponsible independence and a measure of emancipation that led to some fairly extravagant behaviour.

*'My mother set me an example of piety and generosity, avoidance of all uncharitableness – not in actions only, but in thought as well – and a simplicity of life quite unlike the usual habits of the rich.'*

There were three forms of marriage. The old religious ceremony was known as 'confarreatio'. The bride and groom exchanged wafers of wheat, known as 'far' and were witnessed by senior priests. There was almost no possibility of divorce so perhaps it was not surprising that this form of marriage gradually died out!

'Coemptio' was more common. It meant 'bride-purchase' but it symbolised the partnership that formed the successful basis of Roman marriage. 'Where you are master,' vowed the bride, 'I am mistress.' ('Ubi tu Gaius, ego Gaia'). The engagement was sealed with a kiss and the gift of an iron ring by the man. The wedding itself had to be held on a 'lucky' day, for the Romans were highly superstitious. The bride had her hair done up in style and wore an orange veil and shoes to match. The veil allowed only the left side of her face to be seen. Her dress was made of white flannel or fine muslin and around her waist there was a woollen girdle which fastened with the 'knot of Hercules' for

A gold ring and two safety pins. The Romans used a lot of pins in their everyday life. Simple pins were made from bronze and bone. More elaborate ones from silver or gold.

Right: Jewellery reached exquisite design standards. These gold ear-rings date from approximately 27 BC.

Gold necklaces were extremely popular with Roman women. This fine and unusual example from Pompeii is made up of a series of beautifully crafted leaf shapes.

good luck. The Romans took their superstitions completely seriously.

The hands of the couple were joined, a sacrifice was made – this was usually a pig – and the marriage contract was read out and signed. This contained the dowry agreement. A procession of guests (most of whom attended purely as a social obligation) then accompanied the bride and groom to their home, where the bride rubbed oil on the doorposts and hung up a garland of wool. She also brought three copper coins, one of which she gave to her husband, the other two to the household gods. In return, her husband gave her a symbolic offering of fire and water to show that she now had control over his home. The day was rounded off by an excellent feast and the couple were sent off to bed.

It was the third form of marriage that steadily became the popular one. This was roughly equivalent to our common law marriage. It was known as 'usus'. There was no ceremony. The couple were deemed to be married when they had lived together for a year. But the woman could escape the usual authority of a husband by ensuring that she spent at least three nights of the year away from his home. She thus retained the status that she had before they began living together. There were several advantages to this. A wealthy divorcee or widow could retain control over her own money. Or a widow of senatorial rank (women took on the rank of their husbands) could enjoy a relationship with a freedman, whom she was not officially allowed to marry.

Marriages were frequently arranged. There were even professional brokers. But no doubt every well-meaning person leant a hand when it came to setting up a good match. Pliny described the merits of a prospective husband with enthusiasm in one letter. But Apuleius turned a request for advice on the matter neatly to his own advantage. On a visit to Tripoli, a friend explained that he was worried that his widowed mother would make an unsuitable re-match. Apuleius took a look for himself and found her attractive and wealthy. The family were most upset when he married her but in the court case that followed he was acquitted.

Divorce was fairly common under the empire. A man could divorce a woman if she was childless, if she became ugly or merely if she argued too much. If she committed adultery, he could sentence her to death. A woman, on the other hand, could only divorce her husband if he deserted her, if he joined up as a legionary or if he became a prisoner. Cato bemoaned the double-standards of morality that prevailed even in the Republic:

> 'If you should take your wife in adultery, you may with impunity put her to death without trial. If you commit adultery or indecency yourself, she dare not·lay a finger on you and she has no legal right to do so.'

If her husband died, the wife had to wait between ten and twelve months before she could remarry.

The increasing importance of the dowry complicated the matter of divorce and often made it less attractive to the husband. Fathers and fathers-in-law still played a large part in their married children's lives. The larger the dowry, the more reluctant was the father of the bride to throw it away on a short and wasteful marriage. It was therefore agreed that, in the event of divorce, the dowry would be paid back to the bride's father. A rich father would certainly know how to get his daughter a divorce – and thereby retrieve the dowry – if the girl complained that her young husband was playing around with slaves or other girls or boys. Juvenal could think of nothing more fraught with problems than a rich wife and Martial declared that a rich wife would soon turn him into a wife's maid.

Some women became independently wealthy by gaining control of their own dowry. This could be done if she divorced when her father was already dead. Theoretically her dowry was then looked after by an agent but in fact he acted almost exclusively under her direction. Roman society of the first century AD was plagued – or pleasured – by rich and idle women, who had little else to do but join the men's banquets and mix with them at the circus and theatre. The more intelligent took a keen interest in literature. But these were, of course, the exceptions in society. Many women worked hard to keep their houses and often to help their husbands in their business.

There were those, like the censor Metellus, who thought that marriage was not worth the trouble, if only it was possible to live without wives. But he recognised that, though life with them was hard, life without them was harder still. Juvenal saw both sides of the problem:

> 'Marry a wife and she'll make some flute-player or guitarist a father, not you.'

But the errant husband might also be at fault:

> 'To bounce your neighbour's bed, my friend, to outrage matrimonial sanctity, is now an ancient and long-established tradition.'

What every man feared was the dominant wife. Tacitus recognised a terrible example in a German tribe:

> 'Bordering on the Suiones are the nations of the Sitones. They resemble them in all respects but one – woman is the ruling sex. That is the

This relief shows a typical family scene which suddenly 'bridges the gap' and brings Roman life-in-the-everyday very close to us. Father is reclining on his couch, mother is cradling her baby. Human life – ordinary, simple human life – has changed little over the centuries that separate us from this Roman 'family hour'.

This new-born baby is being bathed in a basin by a midwife. In Roman times the baby was not accepted into the family until it had been seen by the father.

measure of their decline, I will not say below freedom, but even below decent slavery.'

Cato sensibly acknowledged that this had already happened in Rome:

'All men rule their wives, we rule all men – and who rules us? Our wives.'

There was only one course of alternative action: not to marry at all, if you could afford to ignore Metellus' words. Many thought it was better to content themselves with a mistress and avoid the awkward embarrassment of children by an easily obtained abortion. As Juvenal said:

'Our skilled abortionists know all the answers.'

It was only too easy to spread scandal about the wives of rich and important men. The satirists seized on them with relish. From many accounts, Rome was a Pandora's box of sexual delights – of pretty actors, pliable slaves, heroic gladiators and charioteers. Even the emperors did not remain untouched. Augustus was forced to banish his daughter Julia because of her promiscuous behaviour. Claudius remained unsuspecting for years that his young wife Messalina was deceiving him at every opportunity. Caligula took the matter into his own hands and prostituted his sisters.

Beneath the surface there were many happy marriages. The respect with which men had held their wives in the early days of the Republic was still common. Sentimentality was not a Roman characteristic but Pliny revealed genuine affection for his wife Calpurnia:

'At this moment I particularly want to be with you; I want to believe the evidence of my eyes and see what you are doing to look after your little self, whether in fact you are enjoying to the full the peace and the pleasures and the richness of the place. Even if you were strong your absence would still disquiet me. For when you love people most passionately it is a strain and a worry not to know anything about them, even for a moment . . . I beg you therefore all the more earnestly to be kind to my fears and to send me a letter, or even two letters, every day. While I am reading it, I shall worry less; when I have finished it, my fears will return.'

With some pride, he noted that she seemed equally devoted to him and to his work:

'She is highly intelligent and a careful housewife and her devotion to me is a sure indication of her virtue. In addition, this love has given her an interest in literature; she keeps copies of my works to read again and again and even learn by heart. She is so anxious when she knows that I am going to plead in court and so happy when all is over . . . She has even set my words to music and sings them, to the accompaniment of her lyre, with no musician to teach her but the best of masters, love.'

But we only obtain from contemporary writers an impression of upper class marriage. There was no literary Hogarth or Breugel to caricature the poor and the outcast, both free and slave. It is the poor themselves who have left what evidence we have, on their tombstones and memorials. There we can find many honest appreciations of marital virtue. The commonest praise is given in the simple initials 'SVQ' ('sine ulla querella') – Without a Quarrel. 'She was dearer to me than life', reads one epitaph. Another says, 'I am waiting for my husband'. A third celebrates eighteen years, three months and thirteen days of marriage to 'a virtuous wife and a careful housemistress', with whom 'I have lived without any complaint'. An imperial slave summed up the virtues of his wife:

'She was the patron saint of my home, my hope and my life. Her wishes were mine; her dislikes mine. None of her secret thoughts was concealed

The balcony of the Trellis House at Herculaneum. Although well preserved, the house is built of humble materials – rubble masonry which is held together by a mixed framework of wood, reeds and cane. It seems that good building material was scarce in this neighbourhood. Lava stone was used to pave the streets.

*Martial wrote many tags for hosts to give away with presents to guests at dinner parties. Some of the presents were very expensive, some were very simple.*

from me. She was a busy spinner, economical, but generous to her husband. She did not delight in eating, save with me. She was a good counsellor, prudent and noble.'

Another epitaph leads us on to the children in the family: 'To Graxia Alexandria, a woman of exemplary chastity who fed her sons at her breast.' It was not strange that her husband found it worthwhile to mention this characteristic above all else. It became increasingly rare for a woman to bother with the upbringing of her children in the days of the empire. Slaves were commonly used as wet-nurses.

Augustus was concerned at the amorality of Rome and even more concerned at the decreasing birthrate among the upper levels of society. The wealthy were not interested in having children. A rich childless couple could enjoy the flattery and admiration of legacy-hunters. If necessary, they preferred to adopt a mature son rather than go through the discomfiture of bringing up their own. Augustus feared race suicide and instituted measures intended to encourage large families. All men still unmarried at twenty-five and all women still unmarried at twenty were penalised. There were rewards for those with more than three children. Pliny recommended a friend:

'He has several children, for here too he has done his duty as a good citizen, and has chosen to enjoy the blessings of a fruitful marriage at a time when the advantages of remaining childless make most people feel a single child a burden. Such advantages he has scorned.'

But Augustus' measures were remarkably unsuccessful. By the time that Pliny was writing, at the end of the century, the rewards that were offered had merely become another privilege to be handed out by the emperor for whatever service he liked. Pliny himself was one of those to benefit:

'I have no words to tell you, Sir, how much pleasure you have given me by thinking me fit for the privileges granted to parents of three children . . . Still more now do I long for children of my own!'

A father acknowledged the legitimacy of his child and his own responsibility for it by lifting it ceremoniously in his arms. On the eighth or ninth day the child was purified and given its name. If it was a Roman citizen, its birth had to be registered within thirty days. The death rate among babies was high. Deformed children and baby girls were exposed to die in Republican days and the custom continued to a lesser extent even during the empire. Romans needed strong male children to carry on their traditions. Girls were considered an encumbrance. Despite this harsh attitude, there is evidence from inscriptions on tombstones that parents were quite as fond of their children as we might be and found considerable satisfaction in having children despite the prevailing irresponsibility so deplored by Augustus. Pliny was deeply sorry when his wife finally had a miscarriage.

Whether the mother herself or nurses and slaves looked after the children, the household scene would not be complete without cradles, pet dogs or birds (cats were less common) and toy animals made of bronze, pottery or wood. Jointed dolls were also made of wood. There were dolls' houses, toys to pull along the ground, hoops, rag dolls, rattles, hobby-horses, see-saws, hand-balls and even tiny carts pulled by mice.

There were also fairy tales, not so different from today's. They began 'Once upon a day' and the best ones had princesses 'too beautiful for words', who had to undertake three tasks. In one tale, she had to pick out millet from a pile of grain but the ants came to help her; then she had to pull out the tufts from the wool of the wild, golden-fleeced sheep but the reeds came to her rescue; finally she had to fetch the miraculous water from the dragon's well but the

*A bra or bandage to make breasts firm: 'Compress the swelling breasts of my mistress that there may be something for my hand to seize and cover.'*

*(Gift tag)*

The wealthiest Roman houses enjoyed underfloor central heating but most Romans relied on open or closed stoves, which were often elaborately decorated, like this domestic brazier.

49

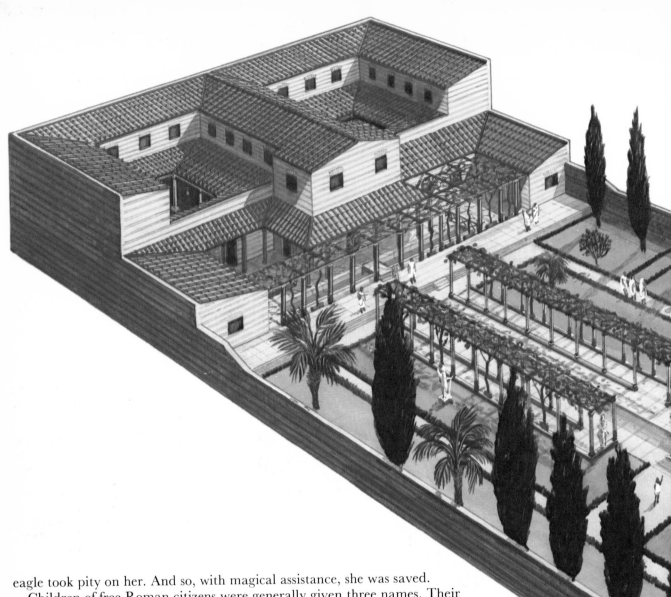

eagle took pity on her. And so, with magical assistance, she was saved.

Children of free Roman citizens were generally given three names. Their first name, or 'praenomen', was their own personal name, which was usually abbreviated when it was written. Lucius, Marcus and Titus were typical praenomen. Gaius was abbreviated with a 'C' from the days when they had no letter 'G'. The second name, or 'nomen' was the clan, or 'gens', name. Each family belonged to a group of families, which the Romans called a gens and the heads of the households met together frequently to discuss important issues. The gens name would be inherited by the son and taken on by his wife. Julius, Claudius, Livius, Porcius and Tullius were only a few of some of the well-known Republican gens. The third name, or 'cognomen', was either the same as the father's or used especially to differentiate father from son or from another person of similar name. This was usually a nickname or a name given to mark a particular honour or trade. Just as Mr Smith or Mr Baker or Mr Short became common names, so the Romans had 'Faber', which meant 'Smith' or 'Carpenter', and 'Flaccus', which meant 'flabby'. Scipio Africanus was the conqueror of Africa, just as we have Montgomery of Alamein. Sometimes a fourth name, or 'agnomen', would be added.

Boys wore a knee-length tunic or toga with a purple band around the edge if they came from an upper class family. This was the toga 'praetexta'. The boy discarded this when he reached manhood and wore the plain white toga 'virilis'. At the same time he also took off the lucky charm, or 'bulla', that he had worn around his neck since he was born. Girls dressed more or less like their mothers but they wore a somewhat longer tunic known as a 'stola'.

All clothes were fairly simple. Men also wore the knee-length under-tunic, over which the free citizen of Rome wore the heavy toga. The female equivalent of the toga was the 'palla'. This differed from the toga mainly in the way in which it was wrapped around the body. You did not so much get into your toga or palla as wind it around you. Women also wore a band, or 'fascia', around their breasts. Their fashions did not change with seasons and extravagance could only be displayed in the colour or texture of their clothes. It was considered ostentatious to change your clothes too often merely to display the extent of your wardrobe. Martial noticed that one nouveau riche

Not a particularly splendid Roman villa but nevertheless a handsome and commodious residence. The sort of average out-of-town residence of a prosperous Roman within commuting distance of the city. Note the carefully arranged and very formal garden with its long trellis of vines and its covered waterway. Romans became quite self-conscious about making their villas fit into the surrounding landscape.

changed his dinner costume eleven times in the course of one dinner party! A comfortable coloured robe called the 'synthesis' could be worn at dinner.

When it was cold, loin cloths might be worn beneath the tunic and cloaks worn over the toga. Augustus suffered greatly from the cold and invariably wore several tunics beneath his toga. Cloaks became quite flamboyant. The moralists insisted on greys or browns but scarlet was popular with the young nobles and hyacinth was not unknown. This cloak was called the 'lacerna'. The thick, coarse 'paenula' was a much more sensible cloak made of natural wool or leather for craftsmen and those who had constantly to be out in the cold. Travellers often wore a cloak with a hood. The military cloak was known as the 'sagum'. 'To put on the sagum' became a phrase for going to war; 'to take off the sagum' meant peace.

The mass of people had no such variety. They worked in a loin cloth if it was hot and otherwise they wore a tunic gathered at the waist. They were lucky if they had a cloak of any kind when it was cold. Clients relied on the generosity of patrons to obtain second-hand cast-offs. Martial was quick to complain if the cast-offs were threadbare!

Etiquette allowed no divergence from the norm. Tacitus observed that:

'The front edge of the tunic should come a little below the knee; in the back, to the middle of the knees. For below this point it is the dress of a woman; above, that of a centurion.'

Horace complained that people laughed at him if any under garment showed beneath his tunic or if the folds of his toga fell unevenly.

The emperor wore a purple toga. Senators wore a broad purple stripe around the edge of the normal white toga. The narrow stripe was the mark of a knight. As in many things, the increasing ostentation of fashion wore away many subtle distinctions and no doubt there were plenty who tried to get away with adornment of a kind that they were never entitled to. The privileged must be constantly vigilant to preserve their marks of favour.

Although most clothes were white, the Romans had plentiful sources of dyes, from plants and minerals. The Tyrian purple from the shell-fish known as murex was the most highly prized dye, and the one that was used for the edging of togas. The wool was usually dyed in the fleece rather than when it had been spun and woven.

In the early days of the Republic all clothes were spun and woven at home on distaff and spindle looms. A basic blanket was made of wool or flax. This might be square, rectangular, circular or semi-circular. It was then cleaned, bleached, combed, shrunk and softened. In time most of this work was done by the fuller. We will look more closely at his trade in the next chapter.

Imported Egyptian linen was of fairly low quality. Cotton was used more for sails and awnings than for clothes. Eastern silk was extremely expensive and considered an effeminate luxury; clothes that were made of silk woven with linen or cloth were considered little better. Wool remained the most common material but several yards of woollen toga draped around a man was no light burden. Martial sighed with relief at the end of the day when he got

The balcony of the Samnite House, at Herculaneum, with its Ionic columns, has an open side, shown in silhouette in this picture. The railings continue the decorative motif of the interior balcony or loggia – an architectural style which continued into Renaissance times.

home and could relax in his tunic. It is a remarkable compliment either to the adaptability of the toga or to the dogged perseverance of the Romans that the toga lasted for almost a thousand years. Certainly the Romans were not to be tempted to trousers. They were thought fit only for barbarians.

Hair styles provided a better chance of display, at least for women. The upper-class woman had a slave hairdresser at home; men usually went out to the barber. Fashions for women changed frequently and were usually set by the emperor's wife and the ladies of the court. The severe, conservative style of the Republic was to have the hair tied back in a bun and fixed with a pin. Ringlets were much more popular and could be most becoming. A young girl looked best in a simple hairdo but fashionable wives and widows preferred to pile up their hair in extravagant confections, according to Juvenal:

> 'See the tall edifice rise up on her head in serried tiers and storeys! See her heroic stature – at least, that is from in front: her back view is less impressive; you'd think it belonged to a different person. The effect is ultra-absurd if she's lacking in inches, the sort who without stilettos resembles a sawn-off pigmy, who's forced to stand on tiptoe for a kiss.'

Ovid once called on a woman who was caught by such surprise that she put on her wig the wrong way round. He sympathised with the problems of baldness and grey hairs:

> 'There is nothing graceful about becoming bald. Snatched by age, our hairs fall like autumn leaves torn by a chill wind from the trees. When woman's hair turns white, she dyes it with German herbs and seeks by artificial means a colour which is better than any which is natural. She has a mass of hair – all bought.'

Blondes and redheads were much in vogue. Batavian foam was used to make the hair fair; fat and ashes to make it red. Combs might be of ivory, wood or tortoiseshell.

On the whole men were clean shaven, except for philosophers and those in mourning. The fashion for shaving came in about the third century BC and

*An earthenware chamber-pot: 'While I am called for by a snapping of the fingers, and the home-born slave lingers, oh, how often has a pillow been made my rival.'*

*(Gift tag)*

Another view of the Samnite House. This shows the atrium, or entrance hall. Light came from the hole in the ceiling which also allowed rainwater to collect in a pool below known as an impluvium.

continued until the time of Hadrian. From then on beards became fashionable again and several emperors sported a smart growth.

Young men would sometimes wear beards to prove they had style. These would be carefully curled, nothing like the rough, straight beards of the Republic. The poor shaved less often because they could not afford to. For those who had the money, a visit to the barber was an important daily routine. We shall meet some barbers when we go round the shops.

Hair styles changed so frequently among women that one sculptor made a detachable scalp for the head of his subject, so that the style on the statue could be changed to match the current style of the lady. Since the emperor's favourites changed almost as fast, another sculptor, unable to keep up with the pace of demand, was in the habit of carving a common body on to which could be grafted the latest popular head, which could be changed quickly when the face fell from favour. Some men seemed more worried about losing their hair than their heads. They were prepared to apply almost any remedy to hang on to the last few strands: from marrow fat to the excrement of rats! Women's body hair was another matter altogether. It was considered most undesirable and was removed – painfully – with pumice stone. Facial hair was often removed with an application of pitch and resin – the only alternative for men to the agony of shaving.

Good teeth were an important aspect of health and beauty and children were encouraged at an early age to brush their teeth regularly in the morning before going off to school, even if they only used their fingers and clean water. Toothbrushes were available and so were tooth-powders and special herb-scented sweets to perfume the breath. Martial thought these were useless:

'That you may not smell strongly of yesterday's wine, Fescennia, you devour immoderately Cosmus's pastilles. That snack discolours your teeth, but is no preventive when an eructation returns from your abysmal depths. What if the stench is stronger when mixed with drugs and redoubled the reek of your breath carries farther? So away with tricks too well known, and detected dodges, and be just simply drunk!'

The blackened teeth characteristic of the poor were considered most unseemly among the rich. If your teeth were bad, it was better to keep your mouth shut. Even to laugh, when your teeth were black, too long or irregular, could be the ruin of you. False teeth were made from ivory or bone or even from a form of cement paste.

Sitting before her dressing table, the Roman lady had an array of scent bottles and lotions to apply to her skin. The healthiest face creams consisted of milk and flour. She washed in water scented with perfumes. Lanolin from sheep's wool was used as a skin lotion and make-up was available in the form of white lead or chalk and rouge. Martial complained that each was as bad as the other: the chalk ran in the rain and the rouge melted in the sun. Juvenal found the whole process absurd:

'There's nothing a woman baulks at, no action that gives her a twinge of conscience once she's put on her emerald choker, weighted down her ear-lobes with vast pearl pendants. What's more insufferable than your well-heeled female? But earlier in the process she presents a sight as funny as it's appalling, her features lost under a damp bread face-pack, or greasy with vanishing cream that clings to her husband's lips when the poor man kisses her – though its all wiped off for her lover. She takes no trouble about the way she looks at home: those imported Indian scents and lotions she buys with a lover in mind. First one layer, then the next: at last the contours emerge till she's almost recognisable.'

Two elaborate hair styles – one formidably so, as befits a matronly figure. Both men and women curled and oiled their hair. The idea of the oil was to encourage hair growth.

Here, in an elegant room off the central courtyard of her home, an upper class Roman is having her hair dressed by a bare-footed female slave. The girl is using a comb made from ivory or bone and her mistress is sitting in a wicker chair. A second attendant takes a sidelong look at the various unguents on the marble topped, bronze-legged table with its moulded stags' head supports. The floor is of polychrome marble, a popular style of flooring in a wealthy Roman home.

There was a wide variety of scents on the dressing table, although Cicero disapproved of them. There were, too, lipsticks, powder compacts and mirrors made of highly polished metal. Eye-shading and beauty patches were all part of the fashionable girl's armoury.

But when you came down to it – as Martial usually did – beauty that was only lotion deep soon rubbed off. If Fescennia, poor girl, had a problem with her breath, then Thais had a much worse problem. Martial pulled no punches in comparing her body odour to a smashed crock of urine, a he-goat that had just coupled, the breath of a lion, an old hide dragged through the street by a dog, a rotten egg or stinking fish:

'In order craftily to substitute for such a reek another odour, whenever she strips and enters the bath she is green with depilatory, or is hidden behind a plaster of chalk and vinegar, or is covered with three or four layers of sticky bean flour. When she imagines that by a thousand dodges she is quite safe, Thais, do what she will, smells of Thais.'

Martial was unkind, since men used scents quite as much as women. Balsam and cinnamon were among the most popular. It was well-known that the emperor Domitian's favourite, Crispinus, smelled stronger in the morning than two funerals!

Whatever the better-off Romans did to patch up their wrinkles and make themselves supposedly presentable, they did at least have a commendable interest in personal hygiene. Public health and plenty of water were considered essential. The large number of brilliantly engineered aqueducts proved this. Rome had fourteen in the end, bringing supplies of fresh water from springs that were often many miles from the city. Men and women, rich and poor, went every day to the public baths. Public lavatories were easily available and were flushed clean by running water. (Only the rich had private lavatories.) This and all other waste water ran into the vast subterranean sewers, the famous Cloaca Maxima that had been the main drain of Rome since the sixth century BC.

*Dentrifice (made of ashes of dogs' teeth mixed with honey, according to Pliny, or of pumice): 'What have you to do with me? Let a young maid use me: I am not wont to polish purchased teeth.'*

*(Gift tag)*

*Frieze coverlet: 'Your coverlet of wool is bright with purple brocade. What is the use of it if an aged wife freeze you?'*

*(Gift tag)*

*'You've been a good girl, Nippy, for a slave, giving good service in the stealthy night, adroit in brushing my hair or setting my waves, tipping me when I might not, when I might.'*

## Painted Ladies

'How long, old Madam, will you
           carry on
This monstrous racket, which your
           patient lord
So obviously can't afford?
Your lease of life is nearly done,
Yet, midst the golden girls you
           play and ply,
A blot on their bright galaxy,
Forgetting that what Pholoe may do
Is less acceptable in you.
Your daughter, now, is at the age

To storm a bachelor's chambers,
           and rampage
Like a daft Maenad with a
           tambourine;
Poor darling, she's in love, and so
Must be allowed to play the wanton
           roe!
For you, 'tis time to quit the scene,
The red rose in the wig, the violins,
The red wine drained; for at your
           age, you know,
A body stays at home and spins.'

*(Horace)*

Washed, powdered and dressed, with her hair done up, any self-respecting girl had still to adorn herself with the odd piece of jewellery before she went out. She would not be satisfied with the simple decorations of the early Republican days. There were rings and bracelets, pins of gold and ivory, earrings, ankle-rings, necklaces, hairpins and ornamental brooches of silver inlaid with precious stones. The diamond was not the girls' best friend in Roman times. Diamonds were occasionally worn in rings but no way had yet been found to cut them properly. Pearls, emeralds, beryls, opals and the sardonyx for seal-rings were all much favoured. Imitation jewellery was common and, according to Pliny, a highly profitable business. The Romans were expert at making imitation emeralds out of common glass.

Pearls were the greatest extravagance of the time. Rome received most of the exported pearls of Alexandria, from the fisheries of the Persian Gulf and the Indian Ocean. There were no pearls for the poor but Roman barmaids had a reputation for wearing gold chains around their necks. Perhaps they were gifts from lovers or admirers. It was just as well to have your capital resources about your person.

The lady was now ready to dine. Dinner parties were among the wealthy Roman's greatest pleasures and feasts offered varied forms of entertainment, which we shall meet later. But average daily fare was quite a different story. The poor relied on wheat which they would boil up into a stew with sauces and bits of vegetables, fish or meat – if they could afford the extra. In the old Republican days, even noble families did not always eat meat; the poor could only get it at festivals when the rich might hand out the flesh of slaughtered animals. The hero of *The Golden Ass* was delighted when:

> 'the baker's wife prepared a supper grand enough for a priest's banquet, carefully decanting vintage wine and cooking up a delicious ragout of tender wheat and thick gravy.'

On another occasion, his mistress, the nubile slave girl Fotis, was:

> 'preparing pork-rissoles for her master and mistress, while the appetising smell of haggis-stew drifted to my nostrils from an earthenware casserole on the stove.'

There could be three meals a day but the first two were quite light. Breakfast, or 'ientaculum', consisted of bread and honey with, perhaps, some

*A bedroom lamp: 'I am a lamp, privy to the pleasures of your couch: you may do what you will, I shall be silent.'*

*(Gift tag)*

Private baths at Conimbriga. This picture shows the six-sided hypocaust or underfloor heating system.

The ingenuity of the Roman glass maker is admirably shown in these superb jugs. The one on the left was found at Urdingen in Germany. The jugs date from approximately 200 AD. Note the snake thread decoration. The jug on the right is made in the shape of a gladiator's helmet and was found at Cologne.

The bowl (insert) shows great delicacy of design and dates from the first century. It is now in the British Museum.

dates and olives. There might be a glass of wine in which to dip the bread. Milk was only drunk by children and by invalids. The bread for the poor was very coarse but wealthier Romans preferred pure white bread.

Lunch, or 'prandium', might include some eggs, with bread and cheese. If there was a visitor, it could become a full-blown meal, with fish, meat and watered-down wine. Seneca preferred:

'Dry bread, no need of a table, no need to wash my hands afterwards.'
The main meal of the day was dinner, or 'cena', which was eaten at about the ninth or tenth hour, after the day's work was done and the baths had been visited – that would be the middle or late afternoon, depending on the time of year. Guests would change into slippers and there would be three main courses. The hors d'oeuvre, or 'gustus', would be salads and shell-fish, followed by a drink of honey and wine known as 'mulsum'. Then the meat courses would follow. Pork was probably the most common meat. There was a great variety of poultry in addition to such domestic fowls as chickens and geese: for a feast, there would be doves, pheasants, partridges, thrush, peacocks and even ostriches. It was reckoned that there were nearly a hundred kinds of fish to choose from, if you could afford them. Cato complained that some fish were so expensive that a single one might cost as much as a cow. This might be compared to the expense of a good cook, who was said to cost as much as a horse!

## Kitchen Gardens

'Yet here among the thorns he grew a kitchen garden, and all round white lilies, vervain and the slender poppy, rivalling wealth of kings, and coming home late every evening, loaded up his store with home-grown feasts. He was the first to pluck the rose in spring, the apple in the autumn, and when grim winter broke the rocks with cold and halted flowing water with its ice, he was already gathering the flowers of tender irises.'

(Virgil)

*'She was Latin but remained a German in her pretty face, blue eyes and blonde hair.'*

The meat course was known as 'lena'. The fruit course that followed was called simply 'second tables', or 'secundae mensae'. There were some delicious dishes, sweetened with honey. Cane sugar was only used for medicine. Wine was usually served after the meal. In the early days women were discouraged from drinking wine altogether, unless it was well watered down, but this stricture was dropped during the empire. Greek Chian was popular and so were Italian Falernian, Nomentanum, Setian, Caecubium and Albanum. Martial and Pliny both thoroughly enjoyed their wine and Pliny was something of an expert on vintage wine. One of the best vintages was nearly 200 years old by Pliny's time and was probably undrinkable. Horace preferred the simple supper:

'I make my way home to a plate of minestrone with leeks and peas. My supper is served by three boys; on a slab of white marble stand two cups and a ladle, beside them a cheap bowl, an oil-flask and a saucer – all of Campanian ware.'

But Juvenal liked the healthy country supper:

'Now here's what we're going to have – all homegrown produce, nothing bought in the market. First, a plump kid from my farmstead at Tivoli, the pick of the flock, that's never cropped grass, or nibbled low-sprouting

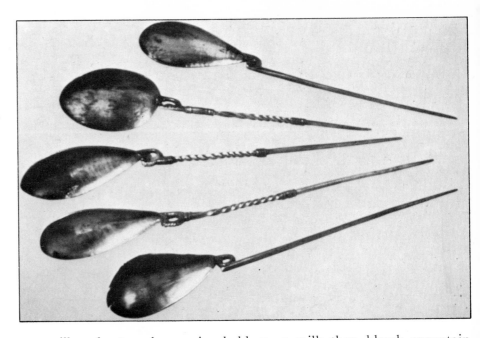

Spoons came in a variety of shapes and sizes. They were made from wood, bronze or silver. Here is a collection of silver spoons, of excellent workmanship.

*'The more I think of it the more sure I am – to have an old wife and a rich one is to say goodbye to slumber. It's a positive torture to go to bed.'*

*A young slave: 'May I have a boy with a cheek smooth with youth, not with pumice, for whose sake no maid would please me.'*

*(Gift tag)*

willow-shoots, whose veins hold more milk than blood; mountain asparagus, picked by my bailiff's wife, after she's finished her spinning; big straw-packed eggs still warm from the nest, and the pullets that laid them, and grapes preserved for six months, but as fresh as when they were gathered.'

For those who wanted to cook for themselves, or to make sure that their cook knew what he was doing, there was an authoritative Roman cookery book written by a wealthy gourmand called Apicius. In fact Apicius was a little excessive in his habits and gestures – he committed suicide when he discovered, to his dismay, that he had only ten million sesterces left from his original fortune. He could not face penury. It was observed that many a Roman could have lived most comfortably off the interest alone of such 'penury'. Despite this, some of Apicius' recipes are worth a try:

### Chicken with milk and pastry sauce

'Braise the chicken in "liquamen" (sauce), oil and wine, to which you add a bouquet of fresh coriander and onions. Then, when done, lift it from its stock and put into a new saucepan milk and a little salt, honey and very little water. Set by a slow fire, crumble pastry, and add gradually, stirring continually to prevent burning. Put in the chicken whole or in pieces, turn out on a serving dish, and pour over the following sauce: pepper, lovage, origan, add honey and a little "defrutum" (mead) and cooking-liquor. Mix well. Bring to the boil in a saucepan. When it boils thicken with cornflour and serve.'

### Rissoles

'Put in a mortar pepper, lovage and origan; pound, moisten with "liquamen" (sauce), add cooked brains, pound thoroughly to dissolve lumps. Add five eggs and beat well to work all into a smooth paste. Blend with "liquamen", place in a metal pan and cook. When it is cooked turn out on a clean board and dice. Put in mortar pepper, lovage, origan; pound, mix together; pour in "liquamen" and wine, put in saucepan and bring to the boil. When boiling crumble in pastry to thicken, stir vigorously, and pour in the serving dish over the diced rissoles; sprinkle with pepper and serve.'

The peristylum or central courtyard of the House of the Vettii at Pompeii. This is the best preserved of all the peristyles. The house was built by two rich merchants at a late stage in the ill-fated town's life. The House of the Vettii was, above all, a secluded house, unlike most of the Pompeiian dwellings. The ground floor rooms fronting on to the streets were not – as was a common practice – converted into shops. They had no entry into the street and were used as store rooms and living rooms.

More than half of this splendid house's total area was devoted to the peristylum and the vast triclinium or dining room. This dining room was magnificently decorated with a wide variety of themes showing everyday crafts and pursuits. The house contained frescoes of mythological subjects – Bacchus and Ariadne, and Hercules strangling the serpent.

Apicius admitted that no guest would be able to tell what the ingredients were when he ate the final dish but he was boasting. The Romans were keen on hiding the real taste of meat, fish or poultry by strong sauces and liberal sprinklings of herbs. In one of the comedies of Plautus, a cook complains that men eat herbs that even the cows would not eat; that they season herbs with more herbs; and that they destroy their intestines with a variety of herbs that no one dare mention, let alone eat!

Wine and oil were stored in earthenware jars and the dishes of the poor were also made of earthenware. There were fine pottery or even silver dishes for the rich and beautiful decanters and goblets of coloured glass. Gold was very ostentatious. But Romans had little time for plates: they ate straight from the dish and from the table, using their fingers and, sometimes, a spoon. Knives and prongs were used only in the kitchen. There were bowls of water and sponges and napkins for mopping up and for cleaning the table between courses.

The range of cooking utensils included ladles, baking pans, pastry moulds, earthenware pots and sturdier cauldrons and frying pans made of bronze. There were special enclosed water heaters. Pots were often stood directly over the fire on tripods or gridirons, for frying and grilling. Small brick ovens were used for baking but boiling and frying were more common. Charcoal or wood were used for the fire.

There were no proper chimneys and, until the end of the first century AD, Romans rarely had windows with glass. After that glazing became more common. Light also came from a hole in the roof of the main hall, or 'atrium'. This hole had originally been intended to let out the smoke of the fire and to collect water in a pool below.

The best examples of houses that we still have come from Pompeii and Herculaneum, the two towns that were swallowed up by the eruption of Mount Vesuvius in AD 79, but these houses were probably typical of many wealthy homes throughout the empire and similar examples have been found in Britain and elsewhere. The basic plan turned the house away from the street and made the atrium the centre of activity. The shallow pool in the middle of the atrium was called the 'impluvium' and was often used as a

*A cook: 'Insufficient is his art alone for a cook: I would not have his palate that of a slave; a cook ought to possess the taste of his master.'*

*(Gift tag)*

goldfish pond. It was in the atrium that the patron held his morning reception for his friends and clients.

The rest of the rooms in the house surrounded the atrium. The dining room, or 'triclinium' (there were three couches on which people reclined around three sides of the low table), was often brightly painted, with mottoes on the walls:

'Let the slave wash the feet of the guests and dry them and remember to place a linen cloth over the cushions that are on the couches.'

The study, or private room for the master and mistress of the house, was known as the 'tablinum'. There were also bedrooms and lavatories off the atrium. The bedrooms were generally quite small and wealthy men and women often slept in separate rooms.

Larger houses had an extension known as a 'peristylum'. This was a courtyard surrounded by columns which provided a covered walk. The peristylum might be cultivated as a garden. There would be more rooms around the peristylum and the family might well occupy these, leaving the rooms around the atrium for office space. The rooms facing the street were often let out as shops or used by the family as their own retail outlet for produce from their country villa. Many Romans with enough money to have a pleasant town house relied on land ownership for their income, although many were not able enough to turn their land to a profit.

Occasionally a second floor was built over part of the house. The blocks, or islands ('insulae'), of apartments in which most people lived often rose several storeys. Even in the third century BC, there were three-storey blocks and, by the second or third century AD, there were five and six storey blocks. Augustus put a limit of about twenty-five metres on apartment blocks to stop developers getting out of hand. A single block would be about 300 or 400 metres round each side. It represented quite a contrast to the private houses of the wealthy. The rooms were small, they were often rented at exorbitant prices, fires were common and there was no water or lavatory. Juvenal was extremely indignant:

'We live in a city shored up for the most part with gimcrack stays and props: that's how our landlords arrest the collapse of their property, papering over great cracks in the ramshackle fabric, reassuring the tenants they can sleep secure, when all the time the building is poised like a house of cards. I prefer to live where fires and midnight panics are not quite such common events. By the time the smoke's got up to your third-floor apartment (and you still asleep), your heroic downstairs neighbour is roaring for water and shifting his bits and pieces to safety. If the alarm goes at ground level, the last to fry will be the attic tenant, way up among the nesting pigeons with nothing but the tiles between himself and the weather.'

If the apartment dweller wanted water he had to climb all the way down to the communal tap at street level. The private house had its own supply. Water was drawn off in narrow pipes from the main supply pipes that ran from the city reservoirs. Rates had to be paid for private supplies of water and many citizens tried to tap the main pipe surreptitiously or to slot in a larger private pipe than they had paid for. There were various other ruses to increase the pressure of the water supply but occasional searches were made by officials to check on any tampering or misappropriation.

If the apartment dweller wanted warmth or heat for cooking, he used a small portable stove. This was quite a valuable possession but it could have a mind of its own. One proud owner, finding that he was completely unable to

Dentistry in the ancient world was alive to the possibilities of false teeth. This primitive 'bridge' device was made from gold. The roots of 'dead' teeth were sawn off and then riveted on to the band or 'bridge'.

Examples of glass work from Roman provinces. Sophisticated glass work was produced in many different places throughout the empire.

A gold armband in the form of a serpent and a silver one with decorative ends.

fan the thing into life, was advised by his friend to wait till the summer and use it as a refrigerator! There were also stoves in the rooms of the rich but the wealthiest houses had underfloor central heating. This was known as the hypocaust. The floor was supported on short columns and a wood-fed fire in a neighbouring chamber spread heat through the space. Sometimes the walls, too, had spaces up them through which the heat rose. The same method was used to heat the public baths.

Apart from the charcoal-burning stove, the poor had little furniture. Their bed was no more than a shelf along the wall. Martial listed the total possessions of someone preparing for a move: a bed with only three legs, a table with only two, a lantern, a bowl, a cracked chamber pot, a jug and a filthy brazier. Even the rich had few pieces of furniture but they were usually good pieces. The dining couches were often the most valuable, inlaid with rare woods and with ornate, curved, bronze legs. The wooden table was normally square but might consist of the complete cross-section of a tree. We know that Cicero indulged in considerable extravagance when he bought a citron-wood table that was worth anything between half a million and one million sesterces.

There were few chairs and only the best would have arms. Stools were more common. It was a mark of great respect to ask someone to sit down. Wooden beds were raised well off the ground and their woollen or straw-stuffed mattresses were held up on leather webbing or on ropes. There would have been one or two blankets for covering, although the toga would often have

This lamp is made from bronze and is in the form of a dog's head. The more expensive variety of bronze lamps – of which this British Museum specimen is a fine example – were frequently made in curious and very beautiful shapes. They have been found in the form of dolphins and some have handles decorated with leaves. In other cases the handles take a serpentine form and culminate in a serpent's head. Oil was an expensive commodity even in Roman times and so the receptacles for oil used in lighting were given appropriately handsome shapes.

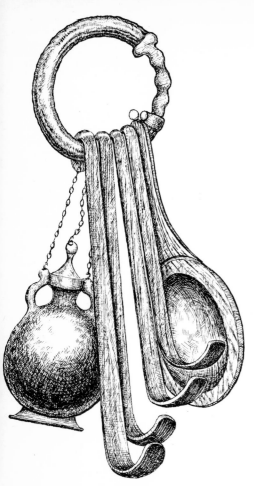

A sophisticated Roman's personal toilet equipment. The ring holds a small oil flagon, a selection of strigils for scraping oil from the skin after the bath and a scoop or oil pan.

*A tucker: 'I shrink from big-breasted women: hand me over to some young girl, that my linen may enjoy a bosom of snow.'*

*(Gift tag)*

been sufficient, and there would almost certainly have been a brightly coloured coverlet. Pillows, filled with wool, could become very lumpy.

Small tables to hold glasses or ornaments were often beautifully decorated with delicately curved legs. They were made of bronze. There were also sideboards, a few cupboards and, sometimes, a bookcase. The shrine of the household gods was kept in the atrium and there would certainly be several busts and statues dotted around the main rooms of the house. Lampstands were often one of the most ornate pieces of furniture but these were rare. Oil was expensive and most Romans went to bed when it got dark and got up when it was light. The cheapest form of lamp was a primitive shape made of pottery and filled with oil, with a wick sticking out of the narrow end made of linen, papyrus or oakum. Olive oil, sesame oil, nut oil and fish or castor oil were all used – and were all expensive. One reason for this was that all were regarded by the poor primarily as food. In Britain, for example, only a small proportion of the imports of oil could be spared for lighting. Torches or candles could be used as an alternative: these were made of tallow fat rolled around a twisted wick. There were no street lamps but some shops might stay open in the evening and provide light on the streets from the lamps on their counters. Caligula and Domitian lit up their late-night gladiatorial shows with torches. Nero used Christians.

During the day – and perhaps in the evening, too – Romans liked to walk or sit outside, in their private gardens if they could afford them, in the public gardens if they could not. Gardens were a great source of pleasure to most Romans. The villa garden and the garden in the peristylum were formal affairs with box hedges, statues, paved walks, fountains, bay trees and roses. Vines and ivies gave the casual touch, and an aviary with doves the touch of class. There would often be another shrine to the household gods.

Paintings in the house often showed false windows with realistic garden scenes. These were painted directly on to the wall. The Romans saw a painting as an essential component of the room itself and there were bold, bright, stylish and subtly beautiful murals in all the best houses. There were also framed paintings hung in porticos and easel portraits of the emperor were sent round the provinces. One scene in the *Satyricon* is even set in an art gallery. The Romans loved colour and decoration in the home.

The best examples of paintings came from Pompeii. There are frescoes of subjects ranging from mythology to landscape, portraits, still-life and architecture. One of the earliest fashions was to use coloured stucco to imitate marble streaking. Pigments were made from earth colours, mineral colours and plant and animal dyes. The background of the picture was painted directly into the gypsum or lime plaster on the wall, so the artist had to work fast before the plaster dried. Details in the painting were added afterwards – such as figures – and the pigment for these was mixed with water or egg-white to form a tempera finish.

The architectural style of painting resembled the back-cloth to stage scenery and included visual tricks of perspective such as half-open doors and corners that looked real and that must have delighted the Romans. Rural scenes next became popular – shepherds, groves and wildlife; panels of fruit and birds in still-life. There were larger-than-life figures, heroic and romantic figures, and figures that appear almost impressionistic, described by a few bold strokes of the brush. Even children are at times successfully and realistically portrayed.

Some of the portraits are the best paintings of all. Citizens of Pompeii look out from their rooms across 1900 years, clear, confident and full of character.

## Housekeeping Account

*This conscientious account of a housewife's outgoings in AD 1 shows the comparative prices for some of the everyday things she had to pay for. It comes from the eastern end of the empire and was originally given in 'drachma' and 'obol'. One drachma was the equivalent of one denarius and one obol was the equivalent of one-sixth of a denarius:*

| January/February | Drachma | Obol |
|---|---|---|
| Cloak | 10 | |
| Turnips for preserving | 1 | 2 |
| Hire of copper vessel for dyeing | | 2 |
| Salt | | 2 |
| Entertaining guest for meal | | 4 |
| Myrhh for burial of Phna's daughter | | 4 |
| Wax and stylus for children | | 1 |
| Pure bread | | $\frac{1}{2}$ |
| Lunch and beer for the weaver | | 3 |
| Leeks for weaver's lunch | | 1 |
| A pigeon | | 1 |
| Grinding wheat for flour | 1 | 2 |
| Asparagus for dinner at fuller's feast | | $\frac{1}{2}$ |
| Cabbage for boy's dinner | | $\frac{1}{2}$ |
| Milk for the children | | $\frac{1}{2}$ |
| Birthday garlands | | 2 |
| Pomegranates for the children | | 1 |
| Toys for the children | | $\frac{1}{2}$ |

This cylindrical silver pyxis, or box, shows hunting scenes which could represent Mithras in pursuit of evil and death since the box – and the strainer – were both found in the wall of the London temple dedicated to Mithras. They date from the late third or early fourth century AD.

A young lawyer and his wife stand side by side to have their portrait painted. Another young girl stands patiently with her pen raised to her lips as if about to chew on it. Portraits were done in mosaic tiles as well. A tired, middle-aged woman looks up sympathetically from a bedroom floor.

Mosaics were made up from small pieces of marble, tile or precious stone. The earliest mosaics were simply made from variegated natural pebbles; later mosaics were made with cut cubes laid in a bed of cement. There were large mosaics in geometric designs that covered the whole floor and smaller, carpet-like mosaics with borders that provided pictures underfoot. Not all were quite so small. The famous Battle of Issus mosaic that shows the struggle between Alexander the Great and King Darius III of Persia measures more than fifteen square metres.

Illustrations were often chosen that were appropriate to the room in which they were laid. In a dining room there was a mosaic representing the unswept floor after a dinner party, with shells, the stones of fruit and bits of bread littered untidily about. Bathroom mosaics showed scenes of fish: one includes about twenty different kinds of fish and shows a battle between an octopus and a giant lobster. A mosaic at Pompeii shows a dog, with the words 'cave canem' – beware of the dog! There were similar paintings by the doorman's niche. A mosaic at Lisbon was accompanied by a written warning not to damage it with a scratchy broom! Brothels, if they did not rise to mosaics, were decorated with invigorating murals to stir the imagination – and the activity – of clients.

*A sunshade: 'Accept a sunshade to subdue the overpowering heat; even though there be a wind (when the public awnings would be furled), your own awning will cover you.'*

**(Gift tag)**

The Roman house is much more lively and colourful than we might at first have imagined. There are bright scenes on the walls and strange creatures on the floors. No room ever seems empty when there are statues and busts in every corner and painted portraits round about. The smell of cooking, the scent of perfume; blue and green glass, a bright cloak, a boxful of jewellery spilling over the marble surface of a small table; green shrubs in the garden glimpsed through an open door on a warm day and the fresh sparkle of a fountain; children playing round the pillars – it is not hard to understand what Cicero felt at the loss of his home.

Pliny described the pleasure he found in his Laurentine villa, twenty-seven kilometres from Rome – just close enough to reach for the night after a day's work in the city:

> 'The house is large enough for my needs but not expensive to keep up. It opens into a hall, unpretentious but not without dignity, and then there are two colonnades, rounded like the letter 'D', which enclose a small but pleasant courtyard. This makes a splendid retreat in bad weather, being protected by windows and still more by the overhanging roof. Opposite the middle of it is a cheerful inner hall and then a dining room which really is rather fine: it runs out towards the shore, and whenever the sea is driven inland by the south-west wind it is lightly washed by the spray of the spent breakers. It has folding doors or windows as large as the doors all round, so that at the front and sides it seems to look out on to three seas, and at the back has a view through the inner hall, the courtyard with the two colonnades, and the entrance-hall to the woods and mountains in the distance.'

There is a bedroom with opposite windows to let in both the rising and the setting sun, sunny corners that are protected from the winds, a library with shelves for all his books, another bedroom for the winter with a raised floor and pipes for hot steam to circulate at a controlled temperature, bath rooms, oiling rooms, rest rooms, a swimming pool from which you can see the sea, a ball court, a dining room, a driveway encircled by box-hedges and rosemary, a garden with mulberries and figs, a terrace where you can smell the violets, a covered arcade which can be closed down on whichever side the wind is blowing from, and his favourite room – a sun-parlour which he had built especially, with folding doors to an alcove just large enough to hold a couch and two armchairs:

> 'It has the sea at its foot, the neighbouring villas behind, and the woods beyond, views which can be seen separately from its windows or blended into one. Next to it is a bedroom for use at night which neither the voices of my household, the sea's murmur, nor the noise of a storm can penetrate, any more than the lightning's flash and light of day unless the shutters are open. This profound peace and seclusion are due to the dividing passage which runs between the room and the garden so that any noise is lost in the intervening space. A tiny furnace room is built on here, and by a narrow outlet retains or circulates the heat underneath as required . . . When I retire to this suite I feel as if I have left my house altogether and much enjoy the sensation.'

Pliny hoped by this description to entice his friend Gallus to come from the city and join him. Romans lucky enough to have fine homes were not only keen to display them but genuinely welcomed guests. The home was a place to be treasured but it could also be shared. Romans did not like to cut themselves off. They were used to sharing the bustle of everyday work and activity.

*An earpick:* '*If your ear is troubled with a persistent itching, I give you an instrument appropriate to such vagaries.*'

*(Gift tag)*

*Skin-scrapers:* '*Pergamus sent these; scrape yourself with the curved blade: the laundryman will not so often wear out your towels.*'

*(Gift tag)*

# VI

# The working day

An olive crusher made from the lava of Vesuvius and designed to separate the pulp of the olives from the stones. The two wheels are linked by a wooden cross-piece. The wheels themselves rotate round an iron pin fastened in the hollow lava basin.

**H**orace knew all about job dissatisfaction:
'How is it, Maecenas, that no one is content with his own lot – whether he has obtained it by an act of choice or taken it up by chance – but instead envies people in other occupations?'

On the other hand, Cicero envied almost no occupation and, as a free man, was opposed to all trade. He wrote to his son advising him not to degrade himself by becoming a hired workman, who has no creative skill and whose wages are the badge of servitude. The mechanic in his workshop and the merchant in his store-room were both to be despised, said Cicero; so too were fishmongers, butchers, cooks, poulterers, perfumers, dancers and performers of all kinds who appealed purely to the pleasure of the senses. Other free men condemned undertakers, tax farmers, cleaners of the main drains, auctioneers

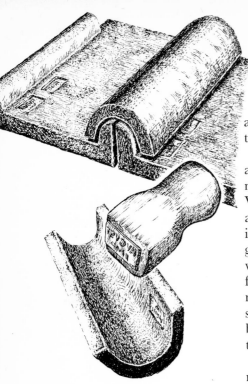

This drawing shows how Roman roof tiles were fitted together. Many tiles were stamped with the maker's mark, an example of which is shown here. Apart from these curved and flanged tiles used for roofs, tiles were also made in larger sizes for drains and in box shapes to let into walls for the hot air from the hypocaust or heating system. Other and much smaller tiles were made for floors and arranged in attractive patterns.

*'And now the perch, delight of our tables! Only you can be ranked with the mullet . . . The pike is cheap and sold in shops that stink with the rank odour of his frying flesh.'*

and town criers. Undertakers and town criers were even forbidden by law to try for election to city offices in Caesar's time.

Architects, physicians, lawyers and orators of almost any kind were approved by Cicero. Architects became so respectable and so numerous that many of them were totally unfit for their work. One of the greatest of them, Vitruvius, who wrote a book on architecture that became a model for the architects of the Italian Renaissance, complained bitterly of the number of incompetents under Augustus. Sculptors and painters, however, were generally despised, although there were exceptions. They rated on a level with firms of interior decorators or stonemasons, which was what they were in fact. Considering how much the Romans owe them for perpetuating their memory – for a great deal of what we know about the Romans comes from stone inscriptions and works of art – this was a little unfair. Musicians fared better. Actors were greatly disapproved of, unless they became the darling of the ladies.

A friend of Juvenal's, called Umbricus, bitterly complained that there was no longer any room in Rome for decent professions:

'They don't show any profit. My resources have shrunk since yesterday, and tomorrow will eat away more of what's left . . . So farewell Rome, I leave you to sanitary engineers and municipal architects, men who by swearing black is white land all the juicy contracts just like that – a new temple, swamp drainage, harbour works, river clearance, undertaking, the lot – then pocket the cash and fraudulently file their petition in bankruptcy.'

There were, of course, other ways of making a living. At a pinch, it was even known to make a bit on the side by training birds to sing or speak. One impoverished shoe-maker tried to sell a raven to the emperor Augustus, having trained it to praise him. Augustus refused the gift. There were, he said, quite enough people already singing his praises. So the shoe-maker trained the bird to say, 'All my trouble's gone for nothing', and sold it for an excellent price.

It was all very good for the well-off Roman to condemn manual labour and trade, while he concentrated on public service, the army or running his estates. There were, after all, slaves to do the menial work. But not all Romans were well off and there were jobs that had to be done. In the earliest days many of these were done in the home – baking, cloth-making, hair-cutting, the forging of weapons and tools. But as the Romans became more sophisticated, these jobs became more specialised, along with many others, and Rome divided itself into two societies: those who worked in trade and those who worked in the 'public good'; with the coming of the empire, there were also those who worked in government departments.

Whatever the work, the day began at dawn. Shops were open in the morning and the late afternoon, for even shopkeepers went to the baths after lunch. Public men worked during the morning and stopped at lunchtime; they spent the afternoon, until dinner, at the baths or meeting and talking in other public places. Only busy lawyers worked on during the afternoon.

Women stayed mostly at home. The poor did what little housework there was to be done and often helped their husbands in their shops or went to the baths. The wealthy received guests or visited friends. There were few women in trade – the occasional secretary or clerk, one or two rare teachers and doctors, midwives and nurses, seamstresses and hairdressers. They were all regarded with considerable suspicion and were probably forced to work because they had no other means of living, unless they became prostitutes.

The wealthy sent slaves to do their shopping for them; in any case, it was often the men who did the shopping, particularly for things like furniture.

The house of the rich man burst with energy in the early morning. Slaves with buckets, cloths, feather dusters and brooms, with sponges on the ends of poles and with step-ladders, cleaned out every corner of the house ready for the arrival of guests and clients. They swept the floor with brooms of palms and twigs twisted together and they scattered sawdust on the floor and then swept it away with the dirt. Juvenal watched the hectic scene:

'If a visitor is expected, then none of your household's idle. "Get the floors swept," you shout, "Burnish the columns, fetch down those spider webs up there. You, clean the silver plate, and you, the embossed vessels." Hark at the voice of the master, standing over them, whip in hand. You're all of a dither, poor creature: your friend's eye might be offended by a dog's turd in the lobby, or some splashes of mud down the covered colonnade – things that one small slave-boy could fix with a bucket of sawdust.'

At crack of dawn, impoverished clients struggled into their togas and shoes and hastened along the streets in the half light bumping into tradesmen and slaves as they opened up their shops. When they reached their patron's door, they had to beg entrance from a doorkeeper who was only half awake himself. But everyone had to earn a living in some way and, even if Juvenal and Martial objected to the indignity of it, at least some people made a profit from the morning's work, as Juvenal was quick to notice:

'When the consul himself tots up, at the end of his year, what the dole is worth, how much it adds to his income, how are we poor dependants to manage? Out of this pittance we must pay for decent clothes and shoes, not to mention our food and the fuel for heating. But plenty who can afford a litter still queue up for their bob-a-day; some husbands go the rounds with a sick or pregnant wife in tow, or better (a well-known dodge) pretend she's there when she isn't and claim for both . . .'

The conscientious man of leisure then pursued a busy round of social engagements. Pliny paused for a moment to consider whether they were

*Rich dainties: 'Get up: already the baker is selling to boys their breakfast, and the crested fowls of dawn are crowing on all sides.'*

*(Gift tag)*

Shop units in the Via Biberatica, known as Trajan's Market, in the very heart of the commercial centre of ancient Rome. These shop fronts are among the best-preserved specimens of their kind. Apart from their usual day-to-day 'shopping' function, the shops were also used to distribute foodstuffs to the people. They are built on different levels on the hillside in large, step-shaped structures in an attempt to avoid landslides. Their survival is a tribute to their design and placing.

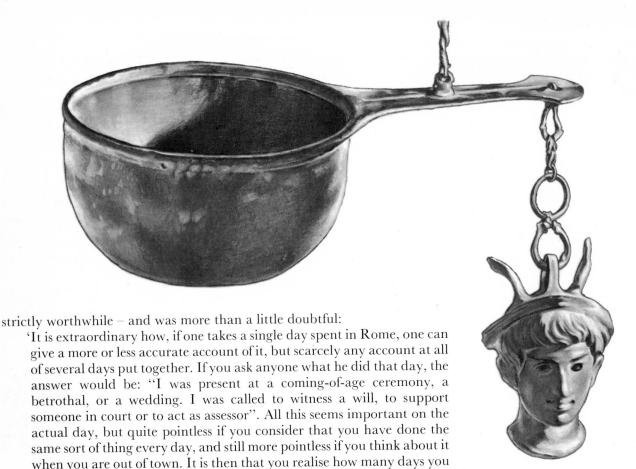

This beautifully designed weighing apparatus has a cup for the goods to be weighed and the counter-balance is an ingeniously carved head. The Romans seem to have taken infinite trouble with the decoration of these everyday objects.

strictly worthwhile – and was more than a little doubtful:

'It is extraordinary how, if one takes a single day spent in Rome, one can give a more or less accurate account of it, but scarcely any account at all of several days put together. If you ask anyone what he did that day, the answer would be: "I was present at a coming-of-age ceremony, a betrothal, or a wedding. I was called to witness a will, to support someone in court or to act as assessor". All this seems important on the actual day, but quite pointless if you consider that you have done the same sort of thing every day, and still more pointless if you think about it when you are out of town. It is then that you realise how many days you have wasted in trivialities.'

Several of the functions that Pliny mentions – the witness, the court and the assessor – involved legal matters. Lawyers were far from idle. They had to scrape up cases just as hectically as young lawyers must today. The legal profession was one of the most respectable of all and the class of lawyers supplied a good many of the magistrates in the city because their cases, argued in public, gave them an excellent chance to publicise their own merits as public speakers. Young men learnt the skills from older, more experienced lawyers. Talented oratory was important and dramatic pleading was often necessary to win over the jury, or 'judices'. There might be as many as fifty judices, especially chosen from among the ranks of the upper classes – a splendid audience for the aspiring politician. Not all lawyers addressed the court. The weighty tome of accumulated wisdom and learning that constituted the law necessitated legal experts whose job it was to advise the barrister. These experts received fees. Other lawyers made do with gifts, which often made them a good deal richer. Juvenal picked out a few who were not so lucky:

'How about barristers then? How much do you think they extract from all their work in court, all those bulging bundles of briefs? They talk big enough – especially when there's a creditor listening, or, worse still, some dun with a weighty ledger comes nudging them in the ribs, and makes trouble about a bad debt. Then they huff and puff like a bellows, pump out tremendous lies, spray spittle all over themselves – yet if you look at their incomes (real, not declared), you'll find that a hundred lawyers scarcely make more than one successful jockey.'

At the other end of the social scale was the tradesman, whose toil was largely honest and whose profits were generally a great deal lower. Many

*'Look at the big ships crowding our seas and harbours: we've more men afloat than ashore now. Wherever there's hope of profit, our merchant fleet will venture.'*

The bakery shown here served the town of Pompeii. The millstones used by the baker can be seen in the background.

*'"Come on, cast off!" cries the merchant who's bought up a load of grain or pepper. "This overcast sky, this gathering blackness is nothing to worry about – just summer lightning." Poor devil, before the night is ended he may find himself in the water, waves surging over him . . .'*

The shops themselves were generally small and run by a family, who lived behind or above the shop. There were no windows on the ground-floor, only shutters which opened up to reveal the whole front of the shop along the pavement or roadside. The shopkeeper sat on a high stool behind the counter and the customer usually stayed on the street side of the counter: you did not often go *inside* a Roman shop. A clerk – or sometimes the shopkeeper's wife – would enter the accounts and purchases on a wax tablet. Cloth and other goods were often hung from the ceiling. There were cup measures for wine and in some shops there were various sizes of cup-like indentations on the counter surface for measuring quantities of produce. The form of scales used by the butcher – and others – was called a steelyard and is still in use today. The butcher held a horizontal rod by a hook attached to the rod closer to one end than the other. The lump of meat was hung from the shorter end of the rod and a weight, in the form of a little head, was moved along the other end until it balanced the meat and the rod remained horizontal. By reading off the mark on the rod where the weight was placed, the butcher could tell the shops were self-supplying units and had to make what they sold: the baker, the confectioner, the perfumer, the carpenter, the metal-worker, the tanner, the shoe-maker and the jeweller, for example. Perishable goods came in from market gardens outside the city. Carts were only allowed to bring in produce at night. Bulk produce, such as timber and stone, were usually brought in by water to the nearest port, where they were stored by merchant middlemen in warehouses from which retailers received supplies. As the city of Rome became decreasingly self-supporting, her reliance on imports became greater and greater and Ostia and Puteoli flourished as vital harbours. Imported goods such as wine and grain were hauled up the Tiber from Ostia to Rome in barges pulled by slaves or oxen.

weight of the meat. Butchers also sold some extremely good sausages.

The baker was one of the most important tradesmen in the street or market. He did his own milling and baking behind the shop. There were small hand-mills, consisting of two flat stones, one on top of the other, with a handle on the top one, but the more common type of corn-mill was made of one hollow, hour-glass-shaped stone which fitted over another conical stone. The upper stone had a beam through its waist, which was turned either by slaves or by a donkey. The grain was poured in through the funnel-shaped top and the flour came out through a channel at the bottom. It was then stored in large earthenware jars and the baking was done in a clay oven heated by charcoal or wood. Some loaves were baked in special patterned moulds. There were a few water-mills for grinding corn on a large scale but these were usually owned by the State. The stone used for the corn mills and wine presses in Pompeii and Herculaneum was lava stone from nearby Vesuvius.

The fuller also received regular calls from most families. He cleaned, mended and refurbished everyone's clothes. Once the cloth had been made up into its basic shape, it was usually sent along to the fuller to be cleaned, bleached, combed, shrunk and softened. These could be pretty unpleasant tasks, which the Roman preferred not to do at home. Of course, if the garment was for a slave, then only the cleaning was considered necessary. For this, instead of soap, the fuller used carbonate of soda, potash or fuller's earth, an alkaline clay. He bleached the cloth by hanging it over wickerwork frames and burning sulphur beneath. This was extremely bad for the lungs, as the man in *The Golden Ass* discovered when his lover hastily concealed him inside such a cage.

*A basket: 'I have come, a barbarian basket, from the woad-stained Britons; but Rome now prefers to call me her own.'*

*(Gift tag)*

A collection of Roman building tools, some of which have a remarkably 'modern' and familiar look about them.

In this collection we have a chisel, a hammer head, a mason's square for squaring up stones and a small pick.

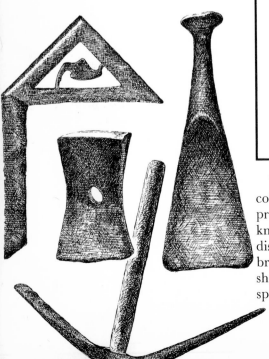

## Weighing and Measuring

*Juvenal warned against 'an out-at-elbows official inspecting weights, giving orders for the destruction of short-measure pint pots'. These are some of the common weights and measures he might have been checking on, with their approximate equivalents:*

| | |
|---|---|
| Libra (a pound weight) | approx. 330 grams |
| Modius (for wheat, salt, etc.) | approx. 9 litres |
| Hemina (for liquids) | approx. $3\frac{1}{4}$ litres |
| Pes (one foot) | approx. 32 centimetres |
| Passus (one pace) | approx. $1\frac{1}{2}$ metres |
| Mile (1000 passus) | approx. 1500 metres |
| Iugerum (approximately the area that one yoke (iugum) of oxen could plough in one day) | approx. 2500 square metres (5/8 acre) |

This was not the only 'occupational hazard' that the fuller suffered. Urine collected daily from the public lavatories was used as a 'chemical' in the process of mattening and thickening the cloth which the fuller trod and kneaded all day long. Not surprisingly, he suffered from a variety of skin diseases. After this, the cloth was pulled out with teasels or hedgehog skins to bring up a nap which was then sheared off to produce a smooth surface. The shearings were used to stuff pillows and cushions. Finally the cloth was sprinkled with water sprayed from the fuller's mouth. It was then ready to be made into a garment, or worn again as good as new. No one had to fear losing their buttons at the fuller's, for buttons and buttonholes were hardly ever used. Brooches were the common form of fastening.

The barber, too, received frequent calls from his customers. He was such a gossip that sometimes the calls lasted rather long, as Martial found out:

'While at command he was going over the same hairs, guiding his hand by the judgement of the mirror and smoothing the skin and making a second thorough clip of the close-cut hair, my barber became a bearded man himself.'

But Martial had had worse experiences than that:

'He who does not wish to descend to the underworld should avoid barber Antiochus. These scars on my chin, if you can count them, may look like those on a boxer's face but they were not caused that way nor by the sharp talons of a fierce wife but by the accursed steel and hand of Antiochus. The he-goat is the only sensible animal; by keeping his beard he lives to escape Antiochus.'

At all costs, though, it was essential to avoid the female barber who lived in the poor quarter:

'A female barber sits just outside at the entrance of the Subura, where the blood-stained scourges of the executioners hang . . . But that female barber does not crop you, I say. What, then, does she do? She skins you.'

In case it might be thought that Martial had a thing against barbers in general, it should be noted that iron razors were not the easiest implements to handle for the daily shave, which was why many Romans preferred the pitch and resin hair-removing lotions. Customers at the 'tonstrina' waited their turn on benches and sat on a stool in the middle of the room to be attacked by the iron scissors. There were curling irons for dandies who wanted to cut an extra dash.

The wine shop and the tavern were two more good places for gossip. You took your own jug to the wine shop to be filled with a measuring cup from one of the large jars behind or beneath the counter. Sometimes the jars had to be propped up outside the shop as well. There were plenty of taverns, especially at Pompeii. They were often rooms, like shops, rented from a large house or block of apartments with street frontage. There were kettles for heating up the wine on a cold day, marble counter tops and the usual graffiti: two men are playing dice; one says 'I've won' but the other protests 'It's not a three, it's a two.' Other graffiti by thirsty customers demand 'full wine jars' for the scribbler. Inn signs displayed messages and pictures no different from today: at the sign of the three jars! Some taverns sold 'pub food' as well but under certain emperors this was restricted because it encouraged rowdies to stay out late and terrorise the streets.

Many men preferred to drink at their clubs. These 'guilds' or 'collegia', as they were known, were strictly non-political and were carefully licensed and vetted. They were predominantly for particular trades or groups of trades and enabled the members to get together for dinners and to share the expenses of memorials and burials. There were plenty of bye-laws; there were entrance fees; and there were elected officials who were expected to produce generous gifts to the collegia. A wealthy patron was usually adopted and his own generosity would be recognised by statues and memorials erected by the collegia in his name.

The collegia were not like the guilds of the Middle Ages, for they did not attempt to organise apprentices, to maintain standards of work or to guarantee any right to work. If they could scrape together enough money, the

A millstone driven by a donkey. The mill had a lower stone which served as an axle and an upper stone which revolved and ground the grain. This impression is a reconstruction of mills found at Pompeii, adjacent to the bakery.

*'Idleness gradually develops a strange fascination of its own and we end by loving the sloth that at first we loathed.'*

members would build their own dining hall or temple, where they could hold their meetings; if they were lucky their home-town might even donate money for that purpose. Banquets were very splendid and gave tradesmen the chance to taste the good-life. The system was morale-boosting and made all the members feel worthy citizens. Election as an official gave to an ordinary tradesman a pride quite as great as that enjoyed by a patrician who achieved high public office. We know this from the pride with which collegia offices have been inscribed on members' tombstones. Even slaves could become members of a collegia, with their master's permission.

Most workers of identifiable trades formed their own collegia and often took over the greater part of a single street. Specialised crafts seceded from the main collegia and formed their own units; their numbers were often sufficient for a whole street to be named after them. Besides bootmakers, for example, there were sandal makers, slipper makers, ladies' shoemakers. The bakers' union was divided into a variety of special pastry unions. Copper smelters were also divided – into those who made pots, candelabra, lanterns, weights, helmets and shields. Even the restoration of works of art in metal were divided into modellers, polishers, chisellers and gilders. All this helped to give the Roman that all-important sense of belonging, of identification.

Shopkeepers were a very conservative lot, for if there was a riot of any sort they were the first to suffer. An excited crowd on its way to the amphitheatre or circus could do a lot of damage and if the mob was in an angry mood the shops were the first buildings to be fired. They therefore backed the emperor and were the first to celebrate his birthday; they decorated their shops at festival times and closed them down in times of national mourning. Strikes were exceedingly rare and did not usually stretch to confrontation.

Just as tombstones give us a good idea of what many Romans did, so they also give us the best pictures of some of the tools that the craftsmen used: the smith with his hammer, the carpenter with his rule and adze, the cobbler on his bench. Builders, carpenters and stonemasons seem always to have been busy. It was commonly recognised that no sooner had any Roman bought a new house than he started to pull it down again to rebuild it in accordance with his own tastes.

Stonemasons used hammers and chisels, patterns, measuring sticks, squares and compasses, bow drills and double-handled saws. They carved statues and busts and tombstones as well as shaping columns and cutting stone for building blocks. The carpenter also had wedges, planes, spansaws and augers, set squares, dividers and levels – almost everything that the modern carpenter still uses. Gaul is particularly rich in tombstones illustrating these instruments.

Many workers in trade and industry were slaves and, often, they held down quite important jobs. They might even own a shop of their own and have their own slaves, who were known as 'vicarii'. Slaves carried out business deals on behalf of their masters, acting as agents or wholesalers, and were allowed to sign contracts and carry out their own business dealings with their master's permission. If they went broke, their master was responsible for their debts.

By using their spare time to make deals on the side, slaves could build up a certain amount of money – known as 'peculium' – which in theory still belonged to their master. If they were subsequently freed, they used it as a capital sum to get them started in their own business. They might add to this 'peculium' with small gifts from their master and from his guests. Although most of the retail shops were run by freedmen, in many cases they were merely carrying on with what they had learnt as slaves. Even innkeepers were

A tavern scene. Mine host – the man in blue – is clearly involved in a discussion with a customer. The soldier might be on leave or about to join his legion in a remote part of the empire. The holes in the counter are for wine jars. Food was also available. The walls are decorated with tavern scenes – notice the amphora or wine-jar motif. This could be seen through the open entrance by passers by and took the place of a modern inn sign.

Across the street a woman in a butcher's shop is weighing out meat for a customer on a steelyard. Her husband is jointing meat with a cleaver.

A weight similar to that shown on Page 70 but this time the counterbalance shows what is possibly the head of an emperor or some heroic figure – note the laurel wreath round his head.

sometimes slaves. One young innkeeper, in his epitaph, begs to be forgiven by any traveller whom he has cheated and claims he did it only to help his father. He commends both his father and mother to the travellers concerned. There seems to have been little or no rivalry between freedmen and slaves working in similar jobs. Perhaps this underlines their awareness that there was only the whim of their masters between slavery and freedom.

State slaves were bought by the state or city or town and paid for out of public funds. They were used for public works, road-making, aqueducts, buildings, even for guarding temples and in religious ceremonies. Pliny reported to Trajan that in one town under his control slaves were being used to guard the prison – a measure of considerable trust. Sometimes the emperor's private slaves would be used on public works, if the emperor was keen to get some praiseworthy undertaking finished quickly. Slaves were also employed in government departments such as the treasury and the corn supply – partly because the Romans deplored clerical work but also because Greek slaves were undoubtedly much better at it.

Some slaves made their fortune in merchant trading. There were great profits awaiting those prepared to risk importing cargoes in the winter months when the seas were dangerously rough. There were bankers and money-lenders to provide backing, although at times these activities were limited by imperial decree which had to be circumvented by complex systems of barter or lending in kind. A form of insurance could be arranged for cargo vessels in which loans provided for the trip were repaid with interest if the cargo arrived safely. But many preferred to put their faith in the gods or the stars. They consulted priests and astrologers for a suitable time to sail and provided gifts or sacrifices to the appropriate gods in advance.

Petronius described the rise to fortune of the ex-slave Trimalchio:

'I came from Asia as big as this candlestick. In fact every day I used to measure myself against it, and to get some whiskers round my beak quicker, I used to oil my lips from the lamp. Still, for fourteen years I was the old boy's fancy. And there's nothing wrong if the boss wants it. But I did all right by the old girl too. You know what I mean – I don't say anything because I'm not the boasting sort. Well, as heaven will have it, I became the boss of the house, and the old boy, you see, couldn't think of anything but me. That's about it – he made me co-heir with the emperor and I got a senator's fortune. But nobody gets enough, never. I wanted to go into business. Not to make a long story of it, I built five ships, I loaded them with wine – it was absolute gold at the time – and I sent them to Rome. You'd have thought I ordered it – every single ship was wrecked. That's fact, not fable! In one single day Neptune swallowed up thirty million. Do you think I gave up? This loss honestly wasn't more than a flea-bite to me – it was as if nothing had happened. I built more boats, bigger and better and luckier, so nobody could say I wasn't a man of courage. You know, the greater the ship, the greater the confidence. I loaded them again – with wine, bacon, beans, perfumes and slaves. At this point Fortunata did the decent thing, because she sold off all her gold trinkets, all her clothes, and put 10,000 in gold pieces in my hand. This was the yeast my fortune needed to rise. What heaven wants, soon happens. In one voyage I carved out a round ten million. I immediately bought back all my old master's estates. I built a house, I invested in slaves, and I bought up the horse trade. Whatever I touched grew like a honeycomb. Once I had more than the whole country, then down tools! I retired from business and began advancing loans through freedmen.'

'*The hills of the Moselle stretch themselves down the slopes of Bacchus like a yeoman's bow. The landsmen are gay as children playing while the hard-working farmer happily labours in song on the brow of the hill.*'

Everyday workmen's tools for the Roman carpenter. A pair of pliers and a double-headed axe in excellent states of preservation.

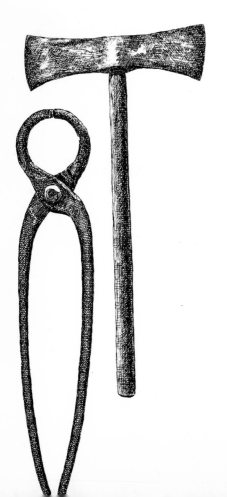

The expedient adopted by Trimalchio's master of making the emperor co-heir in his estates was a sensible one and a common practice among the wealthy. If it was overlooked, the emperor might well feel slighted and seize the entire estate, regardless of the dead man's will.

On the whole, Greeks were much better traders than Romans. They sailed around the Mediterranean and through the Persian Gulf to India and even China. They benefited enormously from Roman rule which enabled them to sail in relative safety unimpeded by protective trade barriers. The uniform system of currency and the availability of common banking procedures also helped the flow of trade. Wine, amber, glass and metalwork changed hands in trade with the northern countries of Europe and Gaul. Luxury goods, ivory and perfumes, pepper and pearls and silks came from the east. The annexation of Egypt after the battle of Actium provided a route through the Red Sea across to India. A group of merchants was reported to have reached China in the time of Marcus Aurelius. Vast amounts of grain came from Egypt, so did carpets and fine linens. Spain and northern France produced coarser cloths. The finest metalwork came from near Capua. Marble came from Greece and Italy. The transportation of heavy items was limited by the prohibitive cost of hauling it from one part of Europe to another. If there was any possibility of using a river or sea route, it was taken at once, but large items could easily double their price on the journey. This encouraged produce on a local level.

The production of glass and pottery became well-developed and the various popular types were spread all over Europe by merchants. The reddish-brown gloss of the Samian pottery was one of the most popular. The potters often stamped their names on their work, so it is possible to trace the movement of the craft. Samian ware began in Italy, where it was largely made by slaves, and moved to Gaul and subsequently to the Rhineland and Spain. The coarse North African pottery was also popular and a good deal cheaper.

There were several centres for glass manufacture: Syria, Egypt, Cologne, Belgium and northern France. Before glass-blowing was discovered in the first century BC, glass vessels were either wrapped around a core to produce the required shape or the molten glass was poured into a mould. Scenes of

The ruins of the forum, with its basilica, at Pompeii. In the background is Vesuvius, the smoking giant which destroyed the city.

*The confectioner: 'A thousand toothsome shapes of handiwork that hand will construct for you; for him alone labours the frugal bee.'*

*(Gift tag)*

gladiators and chariot races seem to have been much admired on these moulded glasses: they were picked out in relief. There was plenty of decoration on later glass, as well. Some jugs were shaped like bunches of grapes, some had designs cut into them, some were gilded, many were in beautiful greens, blues or reds.

A great many people – most of them slaves – were employed on construction work, ship-building and in industries such as mining. Conditions in the mines were appalling, although some of them had pit-head baths. Spain was famous for its silver mines; gold was mined also in Spain and in southern France and Wales; tin was mined in Cornwall; copper was mined in Spain and Italy.

When quarrying for stone, the Romans cut their blocks almost perfectly from the face of the quarry so that the minimum amount of finishing was required. Carrara marble was being mined as long ago as the first century BC and various types of marble were used for decoration and surfacing in temples, public buildings, baths, private tables and for statues. It is almost certain that many marble statues were painted originally. This may seem criminal to us but it would have made the traditionally classical figure look a great deal more lively and cheerful. In general, quarries and mines were owned by the State and run by procurators or leased to contractors.

The Romans were highly skilled construction engineers and invariably planned things on a large scale. The fourteen aqueducts that supplied Rome ran a total of about 400 kilometres. At one point the Pont du Gard, near Nîmes, has three tiers of arches reaching up to 50 metres. The aqueduct at Carthage runs for 150 kilometres through tunnels and over arches. These aqueducts were not an invention of the Romans; they had been used by many earlier civilisations. But the Romans achieved them on a grander scale.

Aqueducts were paid for by the city, though often with the help of private benefactors. Part of the expense was paying for the land over which they went. Surveyors worked out the appropriate route, allowing for a regular slope all the way from the source of the water to the large reservoirs within the city. In certain cases they made use of the principle that water will find its own level – the aqueduct would be taken down a steep slope and sharply up the other side to a level not quite so high. Tunnelling was usually done by digging shafts downwards and working from them; afterwards, the shafts were used for servicing the channels. Occasionally they were dug from either end. There is one recorded instance where the surveyor's plans were not strictly followed and the two digging parties from either end missed each other.

When Frontinus left his job as Govenor of Britain and became the chief water commissioner at the end of the first century AD, he did a tremendous

*'Riches so hardly come by cost still more anxiety and care to preserve: the guardianship of a fortune is a wretched chore.'*

Large and elaborate lifting equipment was needed in the construction of the vast Roman aqueducts and other major structures. Workers treading on the spokes of a vast wheel – rather like a treadmill – provided the lifting power which hoisted huge blocks of stone by ropes and pulleys to the top of the lifting beam.

## Daily Work

*'The first and the second hour wearies clients at the levee, the third hour sets hoarse advocates to work; till the end of the fifth Rome extends her various tastes; the sixth gives rest to the tired; the seventh will be the end. The eighth to the ninth suffices for the oiled wrestlers; the ninth bids us crush the piled couches. The tenth hour is the hour for my poems, Euphemus, when your care sets out the ambrosial feast.'*

*(Martial)*

*'How nice it is to watch the oarsmen row their boats together in the middle (of the Moselle) weaving makeshift pageants on the water. They circle in and out and build a dance which touches the sedge growing by the shore. The bargemen run from bow to stern like boys playing their summer games and the farmer rests his back and gaily watches these feats of skill, on the river's flat surface.'*

job of reorganising and repairing the system of aqueducts. He then wrote a book about his work. He boasted that he had enormously improved the health of the citizens of Rome and the cleanliness of the city by making large amounts of water available but he was no doubt the bane of many private householders because it was he who clamped down on illicit tapping of the main supply. However he pointed out that the emperor had increased his grants for private water supplies to such an extent that anyone could now afford water without the anxiety of being caught and punished for obtaining it illegally. Frontinus concluded that the construction of the aqueducts was a job 'worthy of the greatest care' because they were 'the main evidence of the might of Roman power'.

The Romans were also experts in the construction of bridges, viaducts, dams, massive harbour walls, lighthouses and large public buildings. They were helped by the use of slave labour, concrete and the arch and vault, which enbabled them to span greater distances than those achieved by previous engineers. The brick and concrete arch was one of the greatest contributions that the Romans made to building. Brick was used as a basic frame and was filled in with concrete so that the whole thing set solid. Wooden forms were used to get the shape of an arch or domed roof. The concrete structure was then faced with brick, stone or marble. Not all bricks were rectangular. It was common to cut them in the shape of an isosceles triangle, with their bases lined

Nîmes must have been one of the wealthiest of all the Roman towns in Gaul. Its famous amphitheatre is the best preserved in France. The equally celebrated Pont du Gard is a three-tiered aqueduct which towers some fifty metres above the Rhône.

A pair of cutters and a long nosed pair of pliers, which might have be found on any workman's bench over the last 2000 years. In fact, they belonged to a Roman.

*Ivory money-boxes: 'To fill these money-boxes with anything but yellow money (gold) is unfitting: let cheap wood carry silver.'*

*(Gift tag)*

along the outside of the wall and their points inwards, so that from either side of the wall they pointed inward like teeth. The centre was then filled with concrete or rubble and mortar.

Although the arch enabled greater distances to be spanned than the straight lintel of the Greeks and although it also provided greater strength, upright pillars and lintels were still used, partly because the Romans often employed Greek engineers and architects. They also borrowed the Greek style of columns – Ionic, Doric and Corinthian – and strove to outdo the Greeks in the splendour of their buildings.

Cranes for raising the huge blocks of stone were powered by giant treadwheels, inside which slaves kept up a steady foot-slog. These tread-wheels, together with the water-mills, were the main sources of mechanical power. Although the Romans knew all about cogwheels, pullies, levers and pumps, their technology was very limited. The capstan principle was occasionally used to drive wheels for raising water and there is even a reference to a paddleship in which oxen were used to drive the paddles from a capstan. But there is no evidence that the ship was ever produced.

Most of the technical knowledge of the Romans was already known by the Greeks, the Egyptians, the Persians or even the Assyrians. Rather than turning their practical genius to invention, the Romans seem to have limited themselves to modest refinements of old techniques and a basic grandeur of scale. Slave labour has been blamed as the main reason for this lack of development. It certainly contributed. With plenty of manual labour available, there was no incentive to discover other forms of power. Any alternatives would have caused mass unemployment and a vast social problem. The slaves themselves had little interest in improving existing methods of production and the civil servants who ran the State businesses through the slaves were mainly concerned in keeping their noses clean rather than trying to be clever and inventive.

The most inventive people were the Greeks of Alexandria. These included the renowned Archimedes, Hero and Ctesibus, who all worked in Alexandria about the third century BC and produced several potentially useful inventions which were never put properly into practice. For example, they discovered that air expanded when heated but they made use of this source of power only to produce mysterious gimmicks such as temple doors that were opened without any apparent human aid. Hero also made a steam turbine that caused a ball to revolve very fast on a pivot – but he failed to develop the concept.

On the other hand the water pump was developed in various ways – to pump water, in fire engines and for water organs. There was also a water clock, which Vitruvius admitted that he borrowed from the Alexandrians. This consisted of a water tank which dripped water at a constant rate into a reservoir in which there was a float on top of which stood a shaft. The upper end of the shaft had a row of teeth which rotated a cogwheel as the float and shaft were forced up by the inflowing water. The cogwheel was fixed to the back of a hand which indicated the hour on a dial. There were sundials, too. Several sundials have been found at Pompeii. Portable sundials, although heavy, could be carried by slaves and set up wherever convenient.

Vitruvius also described a hodometer, which was sometimes used for the accurate measurement of distances. This box-like object had a wheel that was rolled along the ground; as it revolved, it turned a number of cogs that eventually let fall a pebble into a reservoir. The pebbles fell at regular intervals and were added up at the end of the journey, so that the distance could be gauged. The cogs also turned dials, so that more precise measurements could be read off between the falling stones.

An important 'scientific' instrument was the groma, used by the surveyor to make sure that roads, streets and walls were at right angles. This simply consisted of two sticks fixed at right angles on a pole. A plummet was suspended from each of the four points of the two sticks to ensure that the sticks were held absolutely horizontal. The surveyor then sighted along one stick and used the other to determine the accurate right angle.

The Roman system of numbers was not conducive to scientific progress or higher mathematics. It was unwieldy, to say the least. The abacus, with its rods and beads, was widely used; so were counting boards, divided into columns and used with counters. Some counters found at Pompeii show pictures of hands with various numbers of fingers held up to indicate the number of the counter. Finger counting was very common. However brilliant they were at engineering, the Romans were not scientists or mathematicians. The truth was that their hearts lay more in the land, from which they had traditionally derived their living and which continued to be an important part of their economy and their way of life and work.

*'This is good Greek work, not that of some pap-eating barbarian jerry-builder. See how well the doors fit . . .'*

## Telling the Time

*The Roman hour did not remain the same length of time throughout the year. Whatever the season, the period of daylight was divided into twelve hours. Therefore a Roman hour varied from about three-quarters of a modern hour in winter to about one-and-a-quarter modern hours in summer. That was in Rome itself. The length of the hour differed the further north or south you went.*

*Our modern abbreviations – a.m. and p.m. – come from the Latin 'ante meridiem' and 'post meridiem', before and after the middle of the day. The Romans referred to the First, Second, Third, Fourth hour and so on. They did not try to divide the hour into minutes and, on the whole, were not very accurate about time. Sundials and water-clocks confused the issue by trying to divide the day into equal parts throughout the year. Seneca said that it was easier to find agreement between two philosophers than between two water-clocks.*

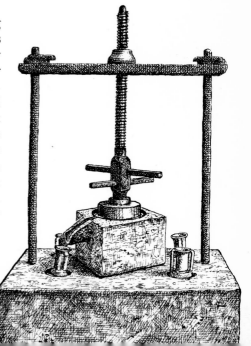

An ingenious oil press for pressing olives. The oil trickled out of the spout into the small receptacles as the press was turned.

Cicero referred to the 'unbelievable amount of enjoyment' that farming brought him in old age and both Pliny and Horace found enormous satisfaction in their farming villas. The poet Tibullus harked back to the early days of Rome, when farmers tilled their own small plot to provide enough for their wants:

'I'll be a real farmer and sow the soft-stemmed vines in their season, and stout fruit trees with a practised hand. Never, my hopes, desert me, but always offer heaped-up harvests, and supply the rich must in the brimming vats – because I am respectful of every lone tree trunk in the plough-land that holds a wreath of flowers, and every old cross-roads stone; and whatever the harvest that each new season produces, the first fruits are laid up for the farmer-god . . . A small crop is enough; enough indeed to rest on a mattress, if I can, and refresh my limbs on my familiar bed. How pleasant to hear the unbending gales from the bedroom, holding my mistress in my unwarlike arms . . .'

But Tibullus spoke of a romantic ideal. Land was a political pawn and the basis of wealth for many Romans. The great estates, known as 'latifundia',

A scene at the baker's shop in Pompeii. But in this case the man behind the counter is probably an official who is giving away bread free to gain popular support for the forthcoming local elections. Electioneering was a cut-throat business in Pompeii and the walls of the town were often covered in propaganda slogans.

A loaf of bread found in the ashes of Pompeii. This loaf was baked one thousand nine hundred years ago. The baker has gone to some trouble to make his loaf look as attractive as possible.

The cutler had a wide variety of knives and other cooking implements. This relief shows a Roman cutler proudly displaying his wares. Some knives had bone handles, others wooden handles.

The poultry shop. The Roman shopkeeper tended to make his shop very much a family affair. His wife often worked with him in the shop – just like the small shopkeepers of today.

that had grown up during the Punic Wars and that had swallowed up many of the small land-owners had not been broken up by the attempted reforms of the Gracchi brothers. But the interests of the landlords lay less in the land itself than in the opportunities it provided for prestige and political advancement in Rome itself. Stewards were left to run the estates.

These stewards were often slaves, who had no particular interest in making the maximum profit out of the estate, provided they satisfied their master; it was easy to obscure laziness with talk of crop-diseases and bad weather. There was no long-term farm policy and the farmland suffered in consequence. Old soldiers who were pensioned off with land grants also sought a short-term income in preference to long-term land improvement. Long gone were the old Republican days when Cincinnatus was called from his plough to become dictator in a national emergency and, having re-established the security of the State in sixteen days, returned at once to his ploughing, where the real work was to be done.

Of course, there were many estates that ran efficiently and profitably, and there were several writers on farming that were required reading for the conscientious. The earliest of these was the book *On Agriculture* (De Re Rustica) by the stern old censor M. Porcius Cato. This hotch-potch of useful information was based on his own experience. It shows no particular love of the beauty of the landscape but it is packed with details on olives and vines, cattle and their ailments, labourers, land-purchase, building construction, fig-trees, lime-kilns, pruning, oil-presses, pests, seasonal activities and household clothes. Another writer of a book of the same title was Varro, who died at about the same time that Augustus became emperor. He was clearly much kinder to his slaves than Cato and had a real feeling for the Italian rural traditions but his book is no more than a miscellaneous selection of odd bits of collected information.

The vogue for encyclopedic works of information continued into the reign of Tiberius. Celsius wrote on agriculture as well as medicine and a variety of other topics. And in Nero's reign, Columella wrote yet another book *On Agriculture* in which he attacked absentee landlords and included a vast number of assorted bits of advice: how to set up a hen-house; recipes for pears; the advantages of a white sheep-dog to distinguish it from a wolf at twilight and dawn; and many useless but entertaining cures. Most of our knowledge of Roman farming comes from these writers and from surviving mosaics, particularly from villas in north Africa.

The most important crops were cereals, vines and olives. Stock farming became increasingly widespread because it could often turn in greater profits and sheep could be grazed on the less fertile upland areas. Apart from one or two examples of simple reaping machines, in which a cart with knives at the front edge was pushed through the corn by oxen or asses, there was virtually no farm machinery. Slaves were used universally. Spades were made either entirely of iron or of wood with an iron shoe fitted over the tip. There were also mattocks, two or three different kinds of hoes, and sickles. Ploughing was usually done by oxen. Ploughs for lighter soil had only a plough-share but a coulter, or knife, was placed in front of the share to help break up heavier ground. But even after several ploughings, clods of earth still had to be broken up with mattocks and hoes.

Seed was sown broadcast, by hand, just as it continued to be sown until the end of the last century and even into this century. The corn was generally scythed by hand. Straw was used for thatching and for animal litter. The crop was threshed by the trampling of horses or by a wooden sled studded with

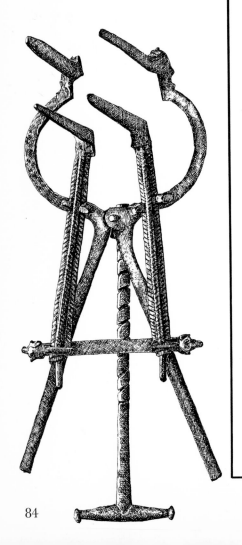

Not, as one might imagine, some instrument of torture – although its application may well have been extremely painful. This drawing shows a Roman speculum used for gynaecological purposes. The instrument shows a considerable degree of manufacturing sophistication and therefore the type was probably not in wide use. Used for internal inspections of the vagina, it closely resembles its modern counterpart.

## Price-fixing – Diocletian's Edict

*In AD 301, the emperor Diocletian tried to hold down inflation by fixing maximum prices for a variety of goods throughout the empire. He was not very successful. Here are just a few of the goods he listed. Some of the prices and quantities have been made approximate so that they relate more easily to each other. All prices are in denarii:*

| | |
|---|---|
| Wheat | 11 d. per litre |
| Barley & Rye | $6\frac{1}{2}$ d. per litre |
| Lentils | 11 d. per litre |
| Rice (cleaned) | 22 d. per litre |
| Salt | 11 d. per litre |
| Wine (various types) | 16–60 d. for just over one litre |
| Beer (various strengths) | 4–8 d. for just over one litre |
| Oil (various types) | 24–80 d. for just over one litre |
| Honey (various types) | 16–80 d. for just over one litre |
| Pork & Lamb | 36 d. per kilo |
| Beef, Mutton & Goat | 24 d. per kilo |
| Ham | 60 d. per kilo |
| Lucanian sausage | 30–48 d. per kilo |
| Sea fish | 48–72 d. per kilo |
| River fish | 24–35 d. per kilo |
| Cheese | 24 d. per kilo |
| Pheasant | 125 or 250 d. each |
| Goose | 100 or 200 d. each |
| Chickens | 60 d. a pair |
| Eggs | 1 d. each |
| Cabbage & Lettuce | 0.4 or 0.8 d. each |
| Peaches | 0.2 or 0.4 d. each |
| Patrician shoes | 150 d. a pair |
| Soldier's boots (no nails) | 100 d. a pair |
| Military saddle | 500 d. each |
| African cloak | 500 d. each |
| Dalmatian tunic (unmarked) | 2000 d. each |
| Hooded cloak, Laodicean | 4500 d. each |
| Four-wheeled wagon with yoke (excluding ironwork) | 1500 d. each |
| Transport of wagon load (550 kilos) | 20 d. per mile |
| Transport of donkey load | 4 d. per mile |

### Wages

| | |
|---|---|
| Farm labourer | 25 d. with keep per day |
| Stone mason & Carpenter | 50 d. with keep per day |
| Mosaic worker | 50 or 60 d. with keep per day |
| Barber | 2 d. per customer |
| Scribe | 20 or 25 d. per 100 lines |
| Elementary teacher | 50 d. per month per boy |
| Rhetoric teacher | 250 d. per month per boy |
| Fuller | 175 d. for cleaning one new hooded cloak of Laodicea wool |

nails, which was repeatedly drawn over the grain. The best seed was kept for sowing the following year's crop.

Wheat was preferred for bread, although barley was an equally important crop. Emmer, oats and spelt were also grown but were a good deal coarser. Emmer was more often used for the bread made by the poor. Barley was also used for animals and for beer. Certain writers recommended alternating cereal crops with vegetables. Broad beans were commonly eaten both by men and by animals. Cabbage was highly recommended for the greater benefit of the constitution. Italy was quite unable to keep up with the demands of Rome for grain and so Rome received most of her supplies from Sicily, North Africa and Egypt.

Olives were useful because the trees needed little attention. They were knocked off the trees with a long stick and put through an oil-mill to produce a pulp and then through an olive-press. The oil was stored in large earthenware jars. Grapes were more trouble because the soil around the vines had to be looked after carefully. Foot-treading was common but there were also wine-presses. Reasonably good wine was stocked for up to five years before being drunk. The Romans were largely responsible for the spread of viticulture in Europe and areas such as Moselle, the Rhine, Beaune and Nuits-St-Georges were soon under cultivation. Pliny kept a careful eye on his own vineyards:

'As for me, at this very moment I am gathering in the grape harvest, which is poor but better than I had expected, if you can call it "gathering" to pick an occasional grape, look at the press, taste the fermenting wine in the vat, and pay a surprise visit to the servants I brought from the city.'

Needless to say, not all wine-producers were purists. There were plenty of complaints about merchants mixing their wines with all manner of herbs to disguise their taste or lack of taste and, in the process, producing something

Above: The House of Diana at Ostia. This typical tenement building had balconies although these were often purely decorative. Upstairs apartments were reached by steps leading from the ground floor between the shop units. The House of Diana is one of the best examples of this type of building. It is made of unfaced brick.

Above left: Lifting holes in the huge granite blocks used in the construction of the Segovia aqueduct.

even more obnoxious than the original. They also observed the age-old trick of watering them down, as Martial noted:

'The crop of the vineyards has not everywhere failed, Ovidius: heavy rains have been profitable. Coranus has made a hundred jars – of water.'

Sheep were important because the Romans relied so much on wool for their clothes. They were also used for milk and cheese; so were goats. Their manure enriched the soil. Sheep flocks might be as large as a thousand. Cows were less favoured for their milk but their meat was popular in the north, their hide could be used for leather and they were sometimes even used instead of oxen for draught-work. Generally, oxen drew the ploughs and carts; donkeys were used for short-haul work and for the mills. Oxen, pigs and sheep were all used for sacrifices.

There were plenty of hens, geese and ducks, tended by boys and old women. Seneca went to have a look at a battery-farm:

'Poultry that are being reared for the table are cooped up in the dark so as to prevent them moving about and make them fatten easily; there they languish, getting no exercise, with the swelling taking possession of their sluggish bodies and the inert fat creeping over them in their magnificent seclusion.'

Villas with large estates would have a number of outbuildings, including barns, baths and slave quarters. Cato, who was an enlightened farmer in many respects, regarded the slaves on his estate as little better than the oxen and sold them off as soon as they were beyond useful work. Columella complained that slaves did not work the land as well as free men – there were still many free peasants on the land, of whom we hear almost nothing.

Columella also had a great deal to say about the ideal treatment of slaves on a large estate. He writes about keeping them occupied with indoor tasks in the winter so that they don't get bored; he suggests that their clothes are checked regularly; and he advises the teaching of specialised skills – the ploughman, for example, should not be too tall in case he grows tired too soon, whereas the oxen-driver should be large and impressive, with a bull-like voice, to keep the oxen in order; the goatherd should be nimble enough to lead his herd through the mountain paths, whereas the shepherd should follow his flock gently and quietly. It was important that the farm bailiff had certain qualities. The most

*'Wickedness is the cheapest thing you can find around here. You can pick a peck of it for nothing.'*

Below right: This particularly fine and elegant mosaic forms the ceiling of a vault at Santa Constanza, Rome. It dates from the fourth century and is a highly stylized interpretation of the grape harvest. Mythical birds and nymphs form the background design motif.

More examples of Roman glass work. These fine specimens are from the provinces and date from the first to the fourth century AD.

## Slaves on a Country Estate

*Writers on farming disagreed on the number of slaves that were needed to work a country estate. These are probably average numbers for the first century BC:*

a) *240 Roman acres of olive groves required thirteen slaves: a foreman, a housekeeper, a muleteer, a swineherd, a shepherd, three cowherds and five labourers.*

b) *100 Roman acres of vineyard required fifteen slaves: a foreman, a housekeeper, a muleteer, a swineherd, a cowherd and ten labourers.*

c) *One slave was required for every eight Roman acres, which should take him forty-five days to dig over: four days digging per acre, plus thirteen days for illness, bad weather, idleness and carelessness.*

*(Varro)*

This relief from a Roman tomb shows a butcher in his shop. Judging from the quantity of meat bones found on Roman shop sites, the butcher must have carried out a good trade despite the relatively high cost of meat.

essential qualification was a wife – she should not be too good-looking, in case the bailiff never went to work, nor too ugly, in case he never returned home. She had almost as many duties as her husband and her authority was only slightly less.

The farm described by Columella would have been a large estate but there were many small farms with only a few slaves. The little farm that Horace owned, that was considered a model of its kind, was worked by eight slaves. In such a case, there would have been much more of a family relationship between master and slaves, just as there would have been in the less ostentatious private houses in town.

Most of the writers of the day found their country villas and farms, if they were lucky enough to have them, a sanctuary from the bustle of city life. Seneca also saw the country as a great benefit to his health:

'I expect you're keen to hear what effect it had on my health, this decision of mine to leave? Well, no sooner had I left behind the oppressive atmosphere of the city and that reek of smoking cookers which pour out, along with a cloud of ashes, all the poisonous fumes they've accumulated in their interiors whenever they're started up, than I noticed the change

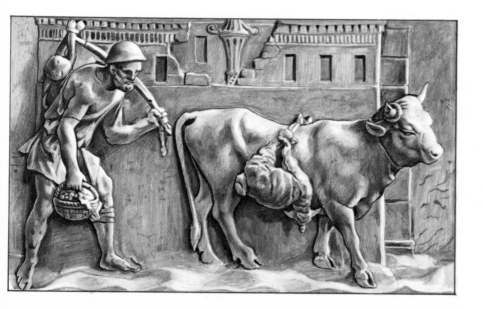

Like all the great ancient civilisations, Rome and its empire was an agricultural civilisation. We tend to think of the magnificent cities and temples when we think of Rome but this whole urban structure was based on vast armies of peasants who laboured in the fields to provide food for the masses in the cities.

There is a timeless quality about this first century relief. He is driving his cow down the road, past the wayside shrines. He may well have been a small independent farmer although he was more likely to have been a tenant farmer.

in my condition at once. You can imagine how much stronger I felt after reaching my vineyards.'

Health was an important pre-occupation among both the working and non-working Romans, for life-expectancy was a good deal shorter than it is today. There were a handful of good doctors but many quack ones and, although the Romans showed some proficiency in surgery, they showed little in making cures, which were still bedevilled by superstitions and old wives' tales. The cult of the Greek god of healing, Asclepius, was adopted by the Romans under the name of Aesculapius, to whom they built many temples and who was symbolised by a snake. The army, not surprisingly, cultivated worship of the god assiduously.

Army hospitals were probably the best there were, although the first hospitals for the poor began in temples. There was, for example, an island in the middle of the Tiber on which a temple to Aesculapius had been built. Sick and worn-out slaves were dumped on the island to save anyone the bother of looking after them. Suetonius recorded that the emperor Claudius decreed that all slaves on the island should be freed and in time this island temple became one of the first Roman public hospitals. Military hospitals throughout the empire were highly organised and spread Roman knowledge of surgery. Trajan's column shows illustrations of blood-letting and bandaging. Broken and dislocated bones could be dealt with and amputations were common. But anaesthetics consisted only of such painkillers as mandrake and poppy – and probably alcohol – and many must have died under the shock of treatment. A great deal of surgical equipment has been found at Pompeii, including forceps, scissors, tweezers, clamps and probes.

What the Romans did know about medicine came largely from the Greeks and the writings of Hippocrates in the fifth century BC. Dioscorides added a lot of useful information about drugs and medicinal plants in the first century AD and Galen's twenty-one surviving volumes on biology and medicine that were written in the second century AD were the main source for all medical practice for nearly a thousand years. Celsius, on the other hand, contributed little more than a collection of facts as varied as those he produced on agriculture. He did, however, refuse to believe that illness derived from divine wrath and he rejected the practice of vivisection on human beings. He also refused 'to be moved by the screams of the patient into greater haste or less cutting than the case required'.

Although Celsius tried to shrug off many superstitions, he recorded the continued use of powdered liver of fox to cure asthma and of lizard's dung and pigeon's blood as purgatives. There were many other, equally revolting cures, and many remedies that included some remarkably unscientific thinking. Cato believed he could cure a sick ox by giving it three grains of salt, three laurel leaves, three rue leaves and various other triple portions for three days, while both the patient and physician fasted; it was important, he added, that the drug was administered while both patient and physician were standing upright. The Elder Pliny was convinced that the herb dittany had the power to extract arrows. This had been proved, he said, when arrows that were embedded in stags had become loosened when the animals ate the herb. A cure for cuts in the *Satyricon* mentions 'cobwebs soaked in oil'.

Eye diseases seem to have bothered the Romans very much. There were many opticians to treat conjunctivitis, opthalmia and cataracts with a range of drops and ointments. Special eye salves were made up for particular ailments and have been discovered in stick form. Stamps have also been discovered that were used to stamp the sticks with the name of the ailment for

*'Stick to the good old ways, my boy, and do as I tell you. I hate to see a good man corrupted by the filthy, perverted manners that pass for morality nowadays.'*

Roman medical instruments – 'uvula' forceps with toothed grips, a short and blunt probe and a narrow surgical knife. The point was probably used for cutting fine areas of skin.

which they were intended. The sticks were generally dissolved in water to be applied. They also suffered badly from toothache, which was why they were so concerned with keeping their teeth in good order. There were no fillings; the only remedy was extraction. Tonsils could be removed; hernias could be operated on; and cosmetic surgery was available: surgeons could remove the brand marks on slaves. Childbirth was treated robustly by midwives.

---

## Roman Money

*New coins were introduced from time to time and the value of all coins was affected by inflation. The silver 'denarius' and 'sestertius' were two of the most common and manageable coins; the copper 'as' was used for small change; the gold 'aureus' became increasingly useful as the 'denarius' lost its value. The first coins were bronze but many had to be melted down for use in the Punic Wars. In 213 BC, the silver 'denarius' and 'sestertius' joined the old bronze 'as'. The gold 'aureus', the copper 'as' and the 'quadrans' all came in with the empire and the 'sestertius' reappeared now in bronze.*

| | | |
|---|---|---|
| 1 aureus | = | 25 denarii |
| 1 denarii | = | 4 sesterces |
| 1 sestertius | = | 4 copper as |
| 1 copper as | = | 4 quadrans |

*It is almost impossible to compare the value of Roman money with modern money, because of constant inflation. But one pound sterling or approximately two American dollars would be roughly equivalent to between 5 and 10 sesterces when this book is published.*

---

*'The necessity of letting my farms is also becoming urgent and giving a good deal of trouble, for suitable tenants can rarely be found.'*

*Ploughing in Tuscany: 'Then come the meadows and cornfields, where the land can be broken up only by heavy oxen and the strongest ploughs, for the soil is so stiff that it is thrown up in great clods at the first ploughing and is not thoroughly broken until it has been gone over nine times.'*

If you were wealthy, the doctor came to your house; if you were poor, you went to his. The doctors were usually freedmen or slaves and had certain privileges. They were, for example, exempt from paying taxes. Doctors were employed by towns and by the guilds, or collegia, to attend their poor. Training became increasingly organised and young doctors would go to the main centres of learning to acquire their knowledge. Part of this training was the inevitable doctor's round with the students. Martial bitterly complained that by the time he had been pawed by the frozen hands of a hundred apprentices he most certainly had contracted the fever that he might well not have had at the start. Inevitably, too, there was great rivalry between the various schools of medicine, as Pliny discovered:

'Hence those wretched quarrelsome consultations at the bedside of the patient, no consultant agreeing with another . . . hence, too, that gloomy inscription on monuments: it is the crowd of physicians that killed me.'

A doctor was judged by results and a good bedside manner was a marvellous asset, as Galen knew well. A doctor, he said, must not stay too long or too short a time and, above all, must not get his patient angry or excited. Doctors should not make speeches at the bedside that bored the patient and they should not reek of garlic or onion. Galen prided himself on being able to diagnose what was wrong with the patient without asking him and he never once made a wrong diagnosis. Usually, the diagnosis was simple: the patient was either in or out of love. Celsius was more cautious. He felt that a doctor should take a few elementary precautions before he took on a new case:

> 'In the case of external injuries, it is beyond everything imperative upon a medical man to know which are incurable, which are difficult to treat and which are easier. For the wise doctor's duty is, first, to decline handling a patient ill beyond the possibility of recovery, and so avoid the appearance of having killed one who was already cut off by his own fate; next, where there is serious apprehension – falling short, however, of absolute hopelessness – to inform the relatives of the person in danger that hope is beset with difficulty, so that, if his skill is baffled by the malady, he may not produce the impression either of ignorance or of deception. But, just as this is the fitting attitude for a wise man, so on the other hand it is worthy of a charlatan to magnify a trivial case in order to produce the impression of a greater achievement.'

The use of herbs and sensible diet were the greatest marks of progress in Roman medicine. Galen was quite convinced that, apart from the infirmity of love, most chronic cases of infirmity merely required a slimming diet, without any need for medicine. There was a special imperial store of herbs and physicians often cultivated their own. Galen emphasised that doctors should be able to prepare their own drugs and not rely on ready-mixed potions. He himself collected ingredients from all over the empire and was continually being sent rare materials from distant provinces. Galen also had an interest in another source of supply for research: he was frequently to be found at the amphitheatre ready to take advantage of the cut-open bodies of gladiators to further his knowledge of anatomy. Like Celsius, he thought vivisection unnecessary but seized the opportunity afforded by these 'natural' incisions.

Grateful patients still gave more thanks to the gods than to the doctors. There were plenty of gods besides Aesculapius who governed various aspects of the body and any number of ailments. The goddess Febris, or Fever, had three temples in Rome, for example. Among many other gods, there were Uterina, who guarded the womb; Lucina, the goddess of childbrith; and Fessonica, who governed lassitude. It was a common practice for people to bring images of, for example, a mended limb to present at the appropriate temple. A macabre assortment of anatomical parts have been discovered in recent years.

There was, unfortunately, no remedy against old age. Those who were lucky – or unlucky – enough to live over the age of forty or fifty suffered the same sort of disappointment in failing health that we suffer still. Juvenal looked ahead with dread:

> 'Old men all look alike, all share the same bald pate, their noses all drip like an infant's, their voices tremble as much as their limbs, they mumble their bread with toothless gums. It's a wretched life for them, they become a burden to their wives, their children, themselves; the noblest and best of them become so loathsome a sight that even legacy hunters turn queasy. Their taste buds are ruined, they get scant pleasure from food or wine, sex lies in long oblivion – or if they try its hopeless; though they labour all night long at that limp and shrivelled object, limp it remains. What can the future hold for these impotent dodderers? Nothing very exciting.'

Whatever your cares and ailments – old age, declining powers, the failure of your crops, bad business, a hard day at the office, the insufferable noise of the city – Horace had the only proven answer:

> 'For sound sleep: take an oil massage; swim across the Tiber three times; before retiring ensure the system is thoroughly soaked in strong wine.'

*Scarecrow Priapus:*
*'A god I am, the terror of thieves and birds. Thieves are deterred by the weapon in my hand and also by the red stake projecting obscenely from my crotch. The birds are an absolute pest but the reed stuck in my head frightens them off and stops them settling on the renovated gardens.'*

*'What is no good for the hive is no good for the bee.'*

# VII

# Travelling

H orace found healthy sleep from a swim in the Tiber and a soaking in wine but Seneca found a good health cure was a trip in a sedan chair, even though it was a little tiring:

'I've just this moment returned from a ride in my sedan chair, feeling as tired as if I'd walked the whole distance instead of being seated all the way. Even to be carried for any length of time is hard work, and all the more so, I dare say, because it is unnatural, nature having given us legs with which to do our walking, just as she has given us eyes with which to do our own seeing. Soft living imposes on us the penalty of debility; we cease to be able to do the things we've long been grudging about doing. However, I was needing to give my body a shake up, either to dislodge some phlegm, perhaps, that had collected in my throat, or to have some

The Roman road – symbol of an empire that depended on the biggest network of roads built by any of the ancient civilizations. This road and arch at Djemila in North Africa are typical examples of Roman engineering. Their roads were built to last – and last they *did*.

thickness, due to one cause or another, in my actual breathing reduced by the motion, which I've noticed before has done me some good.'

Quite apart from shaking up the body, Seneca found that litter-travel was excellent for intellectual pursuits, for reading, dictating, speaking or listening. Juvenal thought it had many advantages:

'If a business appointment summons the tycoon, he gets there fast by litter, tacking above the crowd. There's plenty of room inside: he can read or take notes, or snooze as he jogs along – those drawn blinds are most soporific. Even so he outstrips us: however fast we pedestrians hurry we're blocked by the crowds ahead, while those behind us tread on our heels, sharp elbows buffet my ribs, poles poke into me . . . here's the great trunk of a fir tree swaying along on its wagon, and look, another dray behind it, stacked high with pine logs, a nodding threat over the heads of the crowd.'

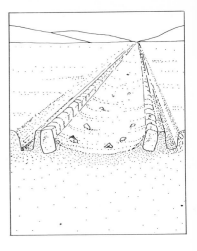

This was the way the rich man travelled, born aloft by his slaves or drawn in a carriage, accompanied by his retinue of clients, who groaned under the additional expense of any protracted journey with their patron. Seneca watched one of these cavalcades:

'Nobody travels now without a troop of Numidian horsemen riding ahead of him and a host of runners preceding his carriage. One feels ashamed not to have men with one to hustle oncoming travellers off the road and to show there's a gentleman coming by the cloud of dust they raise. Everybody nowadays has mules to carry his crystal ware, his myrrhine vessels and the other articles engraved by the hands of master craftsmen. One is ashamed to be seen to have only the kind of baggage which can be jolted around without coming to any harm. Everyone's pages ride along with their faces smeared with cream in case the sun or the cold should spoil their delicate complexions; one is ashamed if there is no member of one's retinue of boys whose healthy cheeks call for protection with cosmetics.'

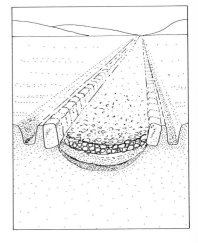

But travel for most people was a much more hardy business. The poorest walked, whatever the distance. The lucky ones rode on horseback, without stirrups. There were four-wheeled, four-horsed 'raeda', that could hold several people and were fairly slow and ponderous. The two-wheeled, two-horsed 'cisium' was faster and lighter and there was a variety of other light chariots. Ox-wagons had solid wheels but spokes were used on the faster vehicles.

The fastest method of travel on the roads was by the Cursus Publicus, the imperial post instituted by Augustus. Suetonius described the advantage of the system:

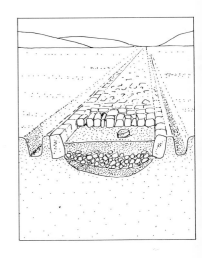

'At the beginning of his reign he kept in close touch with provincial affairs by relays of runners strung out at short intervals along the highways; later, he organised a chariot service, based on posting stations – which has proved the most satisfactory arrangement, because post-boys can be cross-examined on the situation as well as delivering written messages.'

Relays of horses were supplied every ten to twenty kilometres and there were inns every thirty or forty kilometres where grooms and wheelwrights could attend to the carriage. The average distance covered by the messengers in twenty-four hours was eighty to a hundred kilometres. The burden of paying for the horses and repairs fell on the local community.

This convenience was for official despatches only; any other use required a special permit. Private letters were sent by friends or by private couriers. On one occasion Pliny had to explain to Trajan:

The stages of a typical Roman road. Stage one began with a thorough survey of the terrain. The line of the road was then marked out with stakes and, as far as possible, the road took the shortest – and hence the straightest – route. A ditch was dug and the kerbstones laid on each side of the ditch. Then a deeper ditch was dug between these stones and this was filled in with stones and other suitable hard core. The top layer consisted of large, flat, stones, rising in a slight curve towards the centre so that rainwater would drain off into the ditches.

*A padded-saddle: 'Take, hunter, the housing of a nimble steed, for from a bare-backed horse piles are wont to spring.'*

*(Gift tag)*

'Up to now, Sir, I have made it a fixed rule not to issue anyone a permit to use the Imperial Post unless he is travelling on your service but I have just been obliged to make an exception. My wife had news of her grandfather's death and was anxious to visit her aunt. I thought it would be unreasonable to deny her a permit when promptitude means much in performing a duty of this kind.'

The inns available for ordinary folk were pretty rough and most preferred to stay with friends, if they had any in the area. Wealthy men brought elaborate tents with them, or slept in their carriages, or had their own houses at regular intervals along any route they were accustomed to take frequently. There were milestones every thousand paces (approximately 1500 metres), that recorded the nearest towns and the name of the emperor in whose reign the roadwork had been done. We can trace the various stages of repairs on the roads as all repairs were recorded on new milestones which again gave the emperor's name.

The roads themselves were a major engineering achievement and have proved to be one of Rome's most lasting monuments. They brought together people of many nationalities and languages and enabled rapid travel between the ends of the empire. The smooth-running of the empire depended to a large extent on the efficiency of this communications network, despite the rude comment of one historian who remarked that Roman roads were nothing more than walls buried in the ground. The Romans were by no means the first civilisation to create a comprehensive road system. Greek and Persian roads were often almost as good, if not better. But the sheer immensity of the distances covered by the Roman roads makes them remarkable.

Slaves, prisoners, soldiers and gladiators were all involved in the construction of the roads. The expense was usually born by the State with contributions from cities and towns through which the road passed. We learn from one surveyor that:

'Public highways constructed at State expense bear the names of their builders and they are under the charge of administrators, who have the work done by contractors; for some of these roads, the landowners in the area are required, from time to time, to pay a fixed sum.'

Whatever the advantages of a link with the rest of the world, perhaps landowners had as deeply rooted objections then to the newest highway as they do today.

The poet Statius described the construction of a road at the end of the reign of the emperor Domitian, in AD 95:

'The first task here is to trace furrows, ripping up the maze of paths, and then to excavate a deep trench in the ground. The second comprises refilling the trench with other material to make a foundation for the road build-up. The ground must not give way nor must bedrock or base be at all unreliable when the paving stones are trodden. Next, the road metalling is held in place on both sides by kerbing and numerous wedges. How numerous the squads working together! Some are cutting smooth outcrops of rock and plane great beams. There are those binding stones and consolidating the material with burnt lime and volcanic tufa. Others again are working hard to dry up hollows that keep filling with water or are diverting the smaller streams.'

This is one of the few actual descriptions we have of Roman road-making. We can analyse that the foundations were made of layers of sand, stone and pebbles; the kerbing was to hold the slabs of stone, or metalling, in place. But roads were not always paved. Paving was only necessary in towns and on the

This splendid marble relief shows the harbour at Ostia about 200 AD. Neptune can be seen holding his trident – a symbol of the sea which we retain today. A small boat is taking goods to the large vessel. Behind the vessel can be seen the lighthouse built by Claudius in 50 AD.

way into towns, partly to allay the dust and because of heavy use, and on important highways that received constant wear.

The roads themselves were built in lengths of a thousand paces or so at a time and it is sometimes possible to discern the slight change of alignment as a new strip begins: Roman roads are not as continuously straight as their reputation credits. But, wherever possible, the surveyors took the shortest, straightest possible line. Important roads would be about ten to twelve metres wide, including draining ditches on either side. Other roads would be one half or even one quarter of the width. Roads built over marshy areas were constructed on a wooden framework for support. Embankments were used to raise roads or to protect them on either side. The most famous of all Roman roads is the Via Appia, which was begun in 312 BC and extended to Brindisi in 264 BC. It was unpaved then. The earliest paving of which we know was in 174 BC. Roads of strategic importance were maintained by the army and towns developed along these roads from the nucleus of the army fort that was originally built to protect the roads.

There were contemporary maps of Roman roads throughout parts of the empire but they were generally stylised. The Peutinger Table – a Mediaeval copy of a Roman road map – distorts the geography of the empire into an unrecognisably elongated shape. This may have been exceptional or it may have been a common ploy to make the map easier to handle. Most long-distance travellers would have used written lists of towns with distances marked between them. In some major towns columns were erected which listed the distances to all the neighbouring towns – and some far-distant towns. The 'itineraries' or hand-lists may have been copies of these.

Horace had to take a long and vexatious journey to Brindisi and Tarentum one year, for a special commission. The distance from Rome to Brindisi was about 544 kilometres and the journey took Horace and his companions about two weeks. The most frustrating part that he records was near the beginning, when he had to take to a barge to be towed through a swamp:

> 'I declared war on my stomach because the water was quite appalling and waited impatiently as the other travellers enjoyed their dinner. Now night was preparing to draw her shadows over the earth and to sprinkle the heavens with glimmering lights when the lads started to shout at the boatmen, who replied in kind. "Bring her over here!" "How many hundred are you going to pack in?" "Whoah, that's enough!" While the fares are collected and the mule harnessed, a whole hour goes by. The blasted mosquitoes and the marsh frogs make sleep impossible. The boatman, who has a skinful of sour wine, sings of his distant loved one, and a traveller takes up the refrain. Weariness finally gets the better of the traveller and he nods off. The lazy boatman lets the mule graze; he ties the rope to a stone and lies on his back snoring. When the day dawns we realise the barge is making no progress. This is remedied when a furious passenger jumps ashore, seizes a branch of willow and wallops the mule and the boatman on the head and back.'

Later on the journey was enlivened by another accident:

> '. . . we went straight to Beneventum, where the fussy host very nearly burnt his house down while turning some skinny thrushes on the fire. For Vulcan fell out sideways through the old stove, and his darting flame instantly shot up to lick the roof overhead. Then, what a sight! Greedy guests and frightened servants snatching up the dinner and all struggling to put out the blaze.'

Later still, Horace was foolish enough – he admits himself – to stay awake till midnight, 'waiting for a girl who broke her promise'. But like all good travellers he reached his destination in the end.

Because of the nature of the empire, with Rome at its centre, there was always a great deal of travelling to be done. Embassies came from all over the empire to see the emperor; officials came back home to report on events in the farthest provinces; important legal cases were brought to Rome for trial; merchants and tradesmen came to Rome to make their fortune; slaves were brought there, whether they liked it or not. And so, too, there was travel outwards from Rome – soldiers, governors, officials, businessmen: they all spread the influence of their home-countries through the increasingly cosmopolitan empire.

But there were some severe dangers in travelling, as Apuleius recorded in *The Golden Ass*:

> 'We crossed the wooden mountain and the plain on the other side and as the evening shadows lengthened on our road we reached a thriving town. The authorities requested us not to continue our journey that night, or even the following morning, because the district was over-run by packs of enormous wolves, grown so bold that they even turned highwaymen and pulled down travellers on the roads or stormed farm-buildings, showing as little respect for the armed occupants as for their defenceless flocks. We warned that the road we wished to take was strewn with half-eaten corpses and clean-picked skeletons and that we ought to proceed with all possible caution, travelling only in broad daylight . . .'

Apuleius refers again to the dangers of wolves in another passage and recommends travellers to walk together in groups.

Representations of Roman ships are few and far between. Mostly they are confined to a few reliefs and mosaics. This five-oared galley figures on a coin. Neptune's trident can be seen at the back.

*'I will write long poems about cities graced by the silent channels of this River Moselle. I will tell of fortresses built for war but now converted to granaries. I will tell of rich men on either shore and how the river parts the fertile fields.'*

The army was meant to provide police protection against brigands but it was not always effective. There were brigands even in Italy itself during the first two centuries AD. In the following century, under the emperor Severus, one famous bandit terrorised a large part of the country at the head of 600 armed men. His name was Felix Bulla. Many people sympathised with him and were prepared to conceal him when necessary and advise him on shipments of goods or the travel plans of the rich. Once, he entered the town and rescued two of his men who had been condemned to the lions. Another time, he captured a centurion who had been sent out to rout him, shaved his head and sent him back to Rome with the message that if masters treated their slaves better there would be no more robbers. This early 'Robin Hood' was finally betrayed by his mistress and captured while asleep in a cave.

Pirates were also common at sea, until Pompey made a clean sweep of them. At one point when he was quite young, Caesar himself was captured by North African pirates and detained by them. He swore to them that when he was ransomed he would return and kill the lot, which amused them greatly until he did just what he had promised!

It was often a great deal quicker to travel by ship. Seneca recalled the excitement of the arrival of ships from Alexandria:

'Today we saw some boats from Alexandria – the ones they call the mail packets – come into view all of a sudden. They were the ones which are normally sent ahead to announce the coming of the fleet that will arrive behind them . . . The whole of Puteoli crowded on to the wharves, all picking out the Alexandrian vessels from an immense crowd of other shipping by the actual trim of their sails, their boats being the only vessels allowed to keep their topsails spread.'

There were two main types of sea-going craft, the 'ponto' and the 'corbita'. The corbita had a rounded hull from which the stem and the stern rose up in arcs; the keel of the ponto projected in front of the stern post. The ships generally had square sails and were steered by a paddle either side of the stern. We know that the ship St Paul sailed in to Rome held more than 270 passengers as well as grain. Lucian described a grain ship nearly 55 metres long and up to 1500 tons. The largest 'floating palaces' may have held as many as 1000 passengers. The greatest monster of all was built at Caligula's orders to transport the obelisk for the Vatican Circus; it ran almost the entire length of one side of the harbour of Ostia and carried as ballast a vast amount of Egyptian lentils!

Puteoli and Ostia were the two main ports for Rome. Goods might also be landed at Brindisi or at Tarentum and then sent overland to the city. The journey from Puteoli to Alexandria could take as little as twelve to fourteen days. The journey straight across to North Africa – to Carthage, for example – took about five or six days. The first thing to greet the traveller on arrival at Alexandria was the great lighthouse – the Pharos – whose fire, reflected by mirrors of polished metal, could be seen seven or eight miles out to sea. The Pharos was built in 280 BC. There was another big lighthouse at the mouth of the Tiber, four storeys high. Caligula had one built at Boulogne that was reputedly nearly three times as high and two more were built on either side of the harbour at Dover. One of these still survives in part.

The Mediterranean can brew up quite a storm and the Romans found that the only safe period for travel was between about April and September. Even during those months, passengers often preferred to take a ship to Corinth (about four or five days sail from Puetoli) and travel over the isthmus to join another ship to Asia Minor, rather than round the stormy southern tip of the

A section of the Via Appia, which was called by the poet Statius 'the Queen of Roads'. The first section, from Rome to Capua, was built by the censor Appius Claudius, at the end of the fourth century BC. Julius Caesar and several subsequent emperors improved and extended it, eventually, to Brindisi. The first few kilometres of this most famous of Roman roads was lined with the tombs of Rome's most important citizens.

*Paelignian wine: 'Paelignian wine-growers send you turbid Marsic wine. Do not drink it yourself, but let your freedman do so.'*

*(Gift tag)*

Boar hunting was a popular pursuit in the ancient world. This mosaic of a hunt comes from Sicily. The clothes and face of the huntsman suggest a North African origin or influence.

Peloponnese. Some small ships were actually hauled on rollers by slaves across the isthmus. Caesar made plans to cut a canal through the narrow neck of land and Nero himself dug the first spadeful of earth for his own planned canal but neither came to anything.

Wherever possible European waterways were used for the transport of goods and people. The army, in particular, relied heavily on river transport for quick movement of large numbers of troops. The writer Ausonius described a journey by river up the Moselle: he went from forest to open farmland and was greeted with shouts and jokes by the workers in the fields and by small boys in dinghies; his river boat disturbed local fishermen and he passed the occasional wealthy-looking villa. At one or two points there were stone or wooden bridges to take a main road across the river but more often there were ferries. There was other traffic on the river – sailing boats and heavy barges, organised by bargees who had their own specialist guilds for each particular boat craft.

Beyond the boundaries of the empire, the Romans were less sure of themselves. Apart from one or two outstanding figures, they were not great explorers. Pomponius Mela, who wrote about the end of the first century AD, still believed that the world was a sphere and that the land on the sphere was completely surrounded by water; what little he knew about the Earth in general, he almost certainly took from Greek sources. His geography relied on coastal surveys but, even so, he mistakenly believed that the Danube flowed into the Adriatic. He seized any chance to describe the beauties of a cavern or other natural marvel and enlivened his book by descriptions of ancient battlefields. He recorded the existence of headless men with faces on their chests, of birds that shot their wing feathers like arrows, of African tribes who cursed the Sun both at its rising and setting, and of a well that brought on a fatal laugh. He regarded the Atlantic tides with amazement and, though he realised that they might be caused by the Moon, he asked also whether they might not be the action of the Universe, with its heaving breath, or the result of a cavernous hole in the ocean floor, into which they sank and from which they rose.

Mela was particularly vague about central Europe, which was strange since the area was of great importance to the army. He described Britain as triangular in shape, which was just how Caesar had described it nearly 100 years earlier; later Tacitus described it as diamond-shaped. Both Caesar and Tacitus thought that Spain lay west of Britain and that the Pyrenees ran north-south. A hundred years after Mela, Ptolemy of Alexandria wrote one of the most knowledgeable geographies of the time, basing his maps on the reports of merchants and Roman officials. But even Ptolemy's world was limited. His boundaries in the north were the oceans beyond Britain, northern Europe and the unknown lands in the north of Asia; to the south, he imagined there were unknown lands enclosing the Indian Ocean and his knowledge of Africa did not stretch beyond Libya and Ethiopia; he did not know what lay beyond India and the borders of China to the east; and westwards there was only the great ocean.

Some Andalusian sailors brought back reports of the lushness of the island of Madeira and there were strange stories of satyrs with red tails who attacked women in the Canary Islands. Only one general crossed the Atlas mountains but his expedition came to nothing. Nero sent soldiers to discover the source of the Nile: they went up the White Nile, failed to reach their destination, and came back with stories of dwarfs with two mouths and no ears and of monstrously distorted men. Tales from India were richer and more enticing –

A vigorous interpretation of a two-horse bronze chariot or 'biga', found in the River Tiber at Rome. It dates from the first century AD.

lush vegetation, a land of pleasure, a people who loved festivals – but Roman merchants rarely went inland beyond the ports along the coast. In the north, although Britain was circumnavigated, the 'icy regions' were best left alone. Tacitus wrote that it was rumoured you could hear the sun splash into the sea at night.

Two men besides Ptolemy contributed much to Greek and Roman geography. One was Eratosthenes of Cyprus, who lived in the third century BC. He worked out systems for measuring the earth and for treating geography as a more mathematically precise subject; he even suggested the circumnavigation of the globe. The other was Strabo, who lived in the first century BC. He drew maps using projection and prided himself on having travelled as far as any man. He had been east to Armenia, north to the Black Sea and south to the frontiers of Ethiopia.

India was probably the farthest point to which regular sailings were made for trade. A Greek called Hippalus discovered the regularity of the monsoon winds, which enormously helped seasonal sailings to and from India and the Red Sea. By the time of Augustus there were as many as 120 ships a year sailing to India. The island of Ceylon was discovered accidentally by a tax collector blown off course while sailing around Arabia.

On the whole Romans preferred what they already knew. The empire was large enough without pushing their noses into the cold or hot regions. Britain was disliked for its fogs. Asia Minor was continually threatened by drought. Deep wells made parts of North Africa fertile that are barren now but the sand quickly crept back in time of war and waste. The Alps and the Pyrenees were much greater barriers than they are today from the south – from the north, invaders seemed to find them far easier. Romans liked the gentle warmth of Italy and complained bitterly during a period of protracted cool damp during the second and third century BC. Even so, Rome could become too hot in the summer and then was the time to leave for the country villa or go abroad.

Young men travelled to widen their education; old men travelled for their health; tourists went on pilgrimages to shrines and sanctuaries and famous places. Seneca did not believe in a word of it:

'What good has travel of itself ever been able to do anyone? It has never acted as a check on pleasure or a restraining influence on desire; it has never controlled the temper of an angry man or quelled the reckless impulse of a lover; never in fact has it rid the personality of a fault. It has not granted us the gift of judgement, it has not put an end to mistaken

*'Who the first inhabitants of Britain were, whether natives or immigrants, is open to question: we must remember we are dealing with barbarians.'*

A more elaborate chariot than the one shown on the opposite page. This is a four-horse chariot and might more aptly be described as a carriage or 'coach'.

attitudes. All it has ever done is distract us a little while, through the novelty of our surroundings, like children fascinated by something they haven't come across before. The instability, moreover, of a mind that is seriously unwell is aggravated by it, the motion itself increasing the fitfulness and restlessness. This explains why people, after setting out for a place with the greatest of enthusiasm are often more enthusiastic about getting away from it; like migrant birds, they fly on, away even quicker than they came . . . Travel won't make a better or a saner man of you . . . All this hurrying from place to place won't bring you any relief, for you're travelling in the company of your own emotions, followed by your troubles all the way . . . Travelling doesn't make a man a doctor or a public speaker: there isn't a single art which is acquired merely by being in one place rather than another. Can wisdom, then, the greatest art of all, be picked up in the course of taking a trip? Take my word for it, the trip doesn't exist that can set you beyond the reach of cravings, fits of temper, or fears. If it did, the human race would be off there in a body.'

Despite this salutary advice, the Romans were keen tourists within the cosy confines of the Mediterranean world. For short trips out of Rome, the rich hastened down to the Bay of Naples, stretching out below Vesuvius. There was Naples itself, full of famous faces; there was ill-fated Pompeii; there was the Sybil's grotto at Cumae; there was the island of Capri; and there was the popular resort of Baiae. Men like Virgil were glad to leave Rome completely and work in Naples; others retired there to farms and villas. The southern part of the bay, later ravaged by the eruption, was covered in vineyards and fields half way up the mountain. There were other resorts on the eastern coast, at places like Tarentum: some were favoured for their coolness, some for their warmth; some were bearable for only part of the year, some had a continuously mild season.

Of all these places, Baiae had the worst reputation for high living. In its early days, the fashionable considered it unhealthy during the mid-summer months but its attractions soon overcame this and people flocked there throughout the summer. There was off-shore boating; there were lovers' walks; there were places to sit quietly and places to drink late. Every writer had something to add about the town. One said that old men renewed their youthful spirits there and maidens became fair game for everyone. Another called it the home of vice. Women flocked there to wound men's hearts and relieve themselves of their virtue.

*'The Britons readily submit to military service, payment of tribute and other obligations imposed by government, provided that there is no abuse. . . . They are broken in to obedience, but not as yet to slavery.'*

'Besides the dogs bred in
Sparta and Molossus, you
should also raise the breed
that comes from Britain
because this dog is fast and
good for hunting.'

## The Eruption of Vesuvius

*The mountain of Vesuvius stands a little back from the Bay of Naples, which in
Roman times was full of popular resorts and busy harbours and dotted with
villas. The volcano erupted in August, AD 79, and destroyed the two towns
immediately below it: Pompeii and Herculaneum. The elder Pliny, author of an
encyclopaedia on science and natural history, was in command of a fleet in the Bay
at the time of the eruption. His nephew, the letter-writing younger Pliny, wrote to
Cornelius Tacitus, the historian, to describe the events of those terrible few days.
Anxious to get a closer look at the umbrella-shaped cloud that rose up from the
volcano, the elder Pliny ignored the falling ashes and sailed across the Bay to a
point on the shore quite close to Vesuvius:*

*'Meanwhile on Mount Vesuvius broad sheets of fire and leaping flames blazed
at several points, their bright glare emphasised by the darkness of night. My uncle
tried to allay the fears of his companions by repeatedly declaring that these were
nothing but bonfires left by the peasants in their terror, or else empty houses on fire
in the districts they had abandoned. Then he went to rest and certainly slept, for
as he was a stout man his breathing was rather loud and heavy and could be heard
by people coming and going outside his door. By this time the courtyard giving
access to his room was full of ashes mixed with pumice stones, so that its level had
risen, and if he had stayed in the room any longer he would never have go out. He
was wakened, came out and joined Pomponianus and the rest of the household
who had sat up all night. They debated whether to stay indoors or take their
chance in the open, for the buildings were now shaking with violent shocks, and
seemed to be swaying to and fro as if they were torn from their foundations.
Outside, on the other hand, there was the danger of falling pumice-stones, even
though these were light and porous; however, after comparing the risks they chose
the latter. In my uncle's case one reason outweighed the other, but for the others it
was a choice of fears. As a protection against falling objects they put pillows on
their heads tied down with cloths.*

*'Elsewhere there was daylight by this time, but they were still in darkness,
blacker and denser than any ordinary night, which they relieved by lighting
torches and various kinds of lamp. My uncle decided to go down to the shore and
investigate on the spot the possibility of any escape by sea, but he found the waves
still wild and dangerous. A sheet was spread on the ground for him to lie down,
and he repeatedly asked for cold water to drink. Then the flames and smell of
sulphur which gave warning of the approaching fire drove the others to take flight
and roused him to stand up. He stood leaning on two slaves and then suddenly
collapsed, I imagine because the dense fumes choked his breathing by blocking his
windpipe which was constitutionally weak and narrow and often inflamed.
When daylight returned on the 26th – two days after the last day he had seen – his
body was found intact and uninjured, still fully clothed and looking more like
sleep than death.'*

(*Younger Pliny*)

'God made the country and
man made the town.'

Farther afield, the sights of Greece lured many travellers, just as people
from the Americas today tour Europe to see the origins of their civilisation.
Greece had decayed much since its wars with Rome in the first century BC
and possibly that very decay lent its buildings an added attraction. Romans
gazed in wonder and admiration at the beauties of Athens; they passed
through Corinth, a bustling entrepôt for east and west; they visited the shrine
of Aesculapius at Epidaurus, where sightseers and patients lay in the shade of

the spreading grove and looked on the great ruins with a sense of awe.

Many of the Aegean islands were too barren for Roman tastes but they visited Lesbos, Chios, Samos and Rhodes to the east. Rhodes was by far the most popular. It had been considered one of the greatest cities in Greece until it was devastated by an earthquake in AD 150. There was a harbour crowded with ships from all over the Mediterranean; there was an acropolis covered with gardens and parks; there were broad streets, walls with fine towers and innumerable statues, many of which remarkably survived the earthquake.

Ilion, on the mainland of Asia Minor, had a contested reputation as the site of the original Troy and Romans flocked there to be gulled by guides who eagerly pointed out where the great events of Homer's *Iliad* were supposed to have taken place. Ephesus and Smyrna were both popular but it was Egypt that drew Romans in their thousands, attracted by the unimaginable age of the ancient civilisation, by the great River Nile, by the worship of animals and by the variety of wildlife. Alexandria was a vast, busy, trading port. It was the gateway to the east and it controlled the corn supply to Rome. The population was arrogant and light-hearted and there were constant riots among the cross-section of nationalities that worked in the harbour.

Among other attractions, there were the pyramids, which the Romans were still lucky enough to see with their smooth surface covered in hieroglyphics. This surface was more or less worn away by the end of the Middle Ages and we can see only the steps that lay beneath. There were, also, the luxury resort of Canobus, the ancient monuments of Memphis and the ruins of Thebes. The Pyramids were only one of the Seven Wonders of the World, a list that was drawn up by Antipater of Sidon in the second century BC. (The others were the Colossus of Rhodes, the Zeus of Phidias at Olympia, the Mausoleum at Halicarnassus, the temple of Artemis at Ephesus, the hanging gardens of Babylon, and the lighthouse of Pharos.) But it is unlikely that there were any round trips to take them all in.

Ignoring Seneca, people travelled, if not to learn, then to escape some scandal at Rome. They preferred history to culture for they were always interested in their past. They felt a duty to visit the birthplaces of their emperors, to follow in the footsteps of Alexander the Great, to gaze on the ancient Persian battlefields. Temples often contained curious treasures donated by famous historical or mythological figures – the sword of Julius Caesar, one of Leda's eggs, the ship of Aeneas, the cloak and armour of Odysseus, cups consecrated to the Argonauts, the clay from which Prometheus fashioned men. There were natural treasures, too – vast elephant tusks, enormously long snakes. Temples were like museums and there were always guides ready to show the tourist round and relieve him of an offering. The enthusiasm which people showed for these relics – and their questionable authenticity – can only have been equalled by the scandalous popularity of relics in the later Middle Ages that led Martin Luther into his quarrel with the Pope.

Art was, in fact, less important than nature as a tourist attraction, although Greek art and sculpture was always revered. Love of Nature was deeply ingrained in the Roman character – a Nature gentle, mysterious and lush. People went far to see the rare or sacred: grottoes, giant trees or poetical streams. Seneca described the religious aspect of this interest:

> 'You see a grove. The ancient trees are thickly clustered together; their height and their interlacing foliage shut out the sky, a huge darkness in the open fields. And a bewilderment seizes you, teaches you the presence of a god. Or some deep grotto has been hollowed out by Nature alone,

*Hay: 'Let your rustling mattress swell with thefts from your mule: pale Care comes not to hard couches.'*

*(Gift tag)*

*'I strolled through the paths of my garden to seek the freshness of a day newly born. I saw the grass bent down by hoar frost which touched the sweet leaves of the kitchen garden. The cabbage heads sparkled with bright drops.'*

and has eaten its way far into the solid rock; the soul feels a something higher: and it is meet to place altars and reverence the well-heads of great streams, the spot where a torrent bursts forth from the dark earth, where hot springs bubble up, or lakes unfathomable or mysteriously sombre.'

Romans did not appreciate rugged scenery or mountains or harsh landscapes. Seneca regarded Corsica as a bare rock. Etna was climbed only for scientific reasons. The Alps were regarded as a dangerous and awkward barrier. This inability to appreciate the arousal of any emotion other than fear and awe by such places was universal among the Romans; it continued through the Middle Ages and the Renaissance and even into the late eighteenth century. Dürer's watercolours of the Alps are among the very earliest insights into their beauty. When we find how like ourselves the Romans were in many ways, it is worthwhile remembering those of their attitudes which were markedly different from ours.

It was a more domestic Nature that the Romans liked – Lake Como lined with villas; the sea-shore where Catullus saw the early morning wind stirring the calm water and heard the waves lapping against the beach; or, best of all, to return home to the quiet country kindliness of the Italian villa of Martial's friend Faustinus:

*Damascene plums: 'Take plums wrinkled by shrivelling old age abroad: they are used to lighten the load of an obstinate stomach.'*

*(Gift tag)*

'The Baian villa, Bassus, of our friend Faustinus keeps unfruitful no spaces of wide field laid out in idle myrtle beds, and with widowed planes and clipped clumps of box, but rejoices in a farm, honest and artless. Here in every corner corn is tightly packed, and many a crock is fragrant of ancient autumns. Here, when November is past, and winter is now at hand, the unkempt pruner brings home late grapes. Fiercely in the deep valley roar bulls, and the steer with brow unhorned itches for the fray. All the crowd of the untidy poultry yard wanders here and there, the shrill-cackling goose, and the spangled peacocks, and the bird that owes its name to its flaming plumes (the flamingo), and the painted partridge, and speckled guinea fowls, and the impious Colchians' pheasant. Proud cocks tread their Rhodian dames, and cotes are loud with pigeons' croon; on this side moans the ringdove, on that the glossy turtle. Greedily pigs follow the apron of the bailiff's wife, and the tender lamb waits for its dam's full udder. Infant home-born slaves ring the clear-burning hearth, and thickly-piled billets gleam before the household gods on holidays. The wine seller does not idly sicken with pale-faced ease, nor the anointed wrestling master make waste of oil, but he stretches a crafty net for greedy fieldfares, or with tremulous line draws up the captured fish, or brings home the doe entangled in his nets. The kindly garden keeps the town slaves cheerfully busy and, without the overseer's order, even the wanton long-curled pages gladly obey the bailiff; even the delicate eunuch delights in work. Nor does the country visitor come empty-handed: that one brings pale honey in its comb, and a pyramid of cheese from Sassina's woodland; that one offers sleepy dormice; this one the bleating offspring of a shaggy mother; another capons debarred from love. And the strapping daughters of honest farmers offer in a wicker basket their mothers' gifts. When work is done a cheerful neighbour is asked to dine; no niggard table reserves a feast for the morrow; all take the meal, and the full attendant need not envy the well-drunken guest . . .'

*'Young ladies, gather rosebuds while both the rose and you are young, for life too soon ends.'*

These were simple country pleasures but many people, after their business and their travelling, looked forward to the racier pleasures of the town. So let us join them at the races and the gladiatorial shows.

# VIII

# Entertainment

The remains of the theatre of Djemila in North Africa. The Romans did a great deal of building in North Africa. Here we see the 'scaenae frons' or main 'backcloth' of the theatre.

Romans enjoyed their leisure and made plenty of time for it. Their amusements were similar wherever they built their baths, their amphitheatres, their circuses, their theatres, their stadia and other arenas. But there was nowhere to dazzle the eye so much as in Rome itself, where the greatest of all spectacles were held by emperors and senators anxious to curry favour with the people or pacify the idle mob. Juvenal used a famous phrase for this practice:

'Now that no-one buys our votes, the public has long since cast off its cares; the people that once bestowed commands, consulships, legions and all else, now meddles no more and longs eagerly for just two things – bread and circuses.'

The phrase was also used by Fronto, in the time of Trajan:

'He knew that the Roman people loved most of all two things, bread and games: that the goodness of government is shown both in its earnest aspects and its amusements: and that whilst neglect of serious business was harmful, neglect of amusements caused discontent; even distributions of money were less desired than games; further, largesses of corn and money pacified only a few or even individuals only, but games the whole people.'

Augustus recorded with pride that, during his reign, he gave three gladiatorial shows in his own name and five more in the names of his sons and grandsons. Ten thousand men fought in these shows. He gave an exhibition of athletes twice in his own name and once in the name of his grandson. He gave games twice in his own name and twenty-three times in the names of various other magistrates. Best of all, he recorded that on twenty-six occasions he provided hunts of wild animals in the Circus, the Forum or the Amphitheatre. Something like 3500 creatures were slain in these hunts. He also provided a spectacular naval battle on the Tiber.

The Romans had no weekend for their leisure but there was a whole succession of festivals during the year that amply compensated them. Under the early empire there were something like seventy days of games, paid for out of public or imperial funds, either in honour of a god or to commemorate the emperor's victories. By the time of Claudius, in mid-century, there were nearly 160 days of holiday, of which nearly 100 were devoted to games of one sort or another. The modern five-day week provides 104 days of weekends and another three or four weeks of holiday, so the Romans benefited by about a month. The games in honour of Ceres, the god of grain, were in April; those in honour of Caesar's victories were in July; the Games of the Plebeians were in November. These were only a few of the festivals. There was also the great Saturnalia in December, when everything was turned upside down, slaves wore their masters' clothes and, according to Seneca:

'The whole city is in a sweat! Festivity at State expense is given unrestricted licence. Everywhere there echoes the noise of preparations on a massive scale. . . . The man who said that December used to be a month but is now a year was, in my opinion, not far wide of the mark.'

The spectacles were also a chance for the public to be with their emperor. They might covertly air their political opinions with demonstrations of cheering at his appearance or by silence if he was out of favour, without fear of being singled out for recrimination. It was, too, a time when the emperor was most likely to grant petitions presented to him, anxious to condescend to the mob. Gifts of food and presents were distributed freely to the audience. Nero dispensed prize tickets entitling the recipients to jewellery, gold, silver, tame beasts and even country estates.

There was also the opportunity for social meetings at the games or the theatre. Ovid described them as the perfect place to pick up a girl. Juvenal described the girl's viewpoint:

'Ogulnia's mad on the Games. To see them she'll hire dresses, attendants, a carriage, a baby-sitter, cushions, lady companions and a cute little blond to carry her messages.'

For propriety's sake and out of respect for himself, Augustus decreed that all citizens should turn out properly dressed in their togas.

The Circus was one of the most popular attractions and drew vast crowds, who pressed through the city streets in the early hours of the morning, eager to get the best available seats. The emperor Elagabalus was so irritated by the disturbance that he ordered snakes to be thrown into the crowd to disperse

*'Do not imagine that a woman is always sighing with feigned love when she clings to a man in a close embrace, body to body, and prolongs his kisses by the tension of moist lips. Often she is acting from the heart and in longing for a shared delight tempts him to run love's race to the end.'*

*Whips: 'Play, ye jovial slaves, but play only; I will keep these sealed up for five days.' (During the Saturnalia)*

*(Gift tag)*

them. The circus – the Circus Maximus in Rome – was the scene of the chariot races. The betting was fierce and the rivalry between the clubs – whites, greens, reds and blues – was intense. The rivalry spread outside the circus and affected people in their everyday lives, causing violence and vandalism and often giving rise to political rivalry as well.

Pliny was less enthusiastic:

'The races were on, a type of spectacle which has never had the slightest attraction for me. I can find nothing new or different in them: once seen is enough, so it surprises me even more that so many thousands of adult men should have such a childish passion for watching horses and drivers standing in chariots, over and over again. If they were attracted by the speed of the horses or the drivers' skill one could account for it but in fact it is the racing colours they really support and care about and if the colours were to be exchanged in mid-course during a race they would transfer their favour and enthusiasm and rapidly desert the famous drivers and horses whose names they shout as they recognise them from afar.'

Juvenal saw the other side of it:

'Now the spring races are on: the praetor's dropped his napkin and sits there in state (but those horses just about cost him the shirt off his back, one way and another); and if I may say so without offence to that countless mob, all Rome is in the Circus today. The roar that assails my eardrums means, I am pretty sure, that the Greens have won – otherwise you'd see such gloomy faces, such sheer astonishment as greeted the Cannae disaster, after our consuls had bitten the dust. The races are fine for young men: they can cheer their fancy and bet at long odds and sit with some smart little girl-friend.'

The Circus Maximus was 550 metres long and 180 metres wide and could hold up to 250,000 spectators – more than a quarter of the population of Rome. It was refurbished several times and was decorated with statues and marble veneer. There were two long sides and one rounded end where the spectators sat. The stables were at the squared-off end and that was where the race began. The central rib round which they ran was known as the 'spina' and there were three obelisks at either end. There might be up to twenty seven-lap races a day, each race covering about nine kilometres.

Horses were provided by stud farms. The charioteers themselves were usually slaves or freedmen, although one or two emperors, including Nero, tried their hand. The charioteer Diocles won more than 4000 races, mostly with two-horse chariots. Two- and four-horse chariots were the most common; occasionally there were as many as ten horses. The charioteers stood up, wearing only a short tunic, with bare arms and a helmet cap, which gave some protection if they fell off and were dragged along the ground. They held a whip and wore a knife with which to cut the reins attached to their waist when they crashed. There was also the risk that they would be run over or trampled on when they fell; so they rubbed themselves all over with boar's dung for protection and ingested some more for the same reason.

The chariots, in their racing colours, waited in their boxes for simultaneous release. The presiding magistrate held aloft his white cloth and threw it into the arena to signal the start of the race. The horses sprang forward, making for the inside place nearest the 'spina' as they went anti-clockwise round the course. The greatest danger was in rounding the ends of the 'spina', where the innermost ones grazed the corner posts and colliding wheels caused the worst crashes. Slaves rushed across the sand to drag bodies, chariots and horses free

This mosaic showing a wounded gladiator engaged in combat comes from Zliten, Tripolitania. Mosaics of excellent quality have been found in this area.

*'The Germans are not cunning or sophisticated enough to refrain from blurting out their inmost thoughts in the freedom of festive surroundings.'*

of the course before the chariots came round again. Other slaves stood ready with buckets of water to throw over the wheels of the chariots as friction increased the danger of fire. Markers went up to show the numbers of laps that had been run and, as the race neared its end, the crowd would be on its feet, 250,000 strong, screaming and cursing encouragement and despair. The popular winner was the hero of the city.

The amphitheatre provided the widest range of entertainment, although the best always ended in death. People came flocking from around Rome for a really big show and lodged in tents pitched along the road. Tacitus complained that children learnt about gladiators and races when they were still in the womb and talked about nothing else in the classroom. The violence was an outlet for the passions of the mob that would otherwise have been turned against the State.

Advertisements announced the coming attraction and usually emphasised who was paying for it, since the more gory it was the more popular the magistrate who footed the bill. These advertisements were painted on public buildings and often on tombstones alongside the road entering the city. Some tombstones even have inscriptions requesting that they should not be defamed in this way. The advertisements would include such inducements as the provision of an awning at the amphitheatre or the sprinkling of water half way through the performance to settle the dust. Occasionally there were pessimistic little footnotes: 'if the weather permits' or, instead of a specific date, 'as soon as possible'.

The gladiators were usually run by private contractors and were carefully trained in special schools. They were generally slaves, though many were criminals and some were even free men who paid for the 'privilege' because they were down on their luck and hoped to make a reputation for themselves. The amphitheatre was also a recognised way to get rid of large numbers of unwanted prisoners. There were three gladiators' schools in Rome and several more around the empire; the one in Alexandria was especially reputed for its high standards. The best schools had their own masseurs and doctors; in the worst, the quarters were cramped and foul and suicide was common. One gladiator was said to have thrown himself over the side of a cart and got his neck broken in the spokes of the wheel. They were bought and sold like ordinary slaves and, unless fighting or training, were not allowed weapons in

This richly modelled gladiator's helmet is now in the Naples Museum and was retrieved from the ashes of Pompeii.

The interior of the Colosseum in Rome as it is today, with the floor surface removed. The Colosseum contained everything necessary for the magnificent spectacles which kept the Roman masses contented. There were cages for animals and mechanical elevators for lifting them to the floor of the arena.
The Colosseum could hold some 50,000 spectators. Special seating areas were reserved for the Emperor, for other dignitaries and for the Vestal Virgins. The seats in these areas were cushioned.

case they rose in revolt, as Spartacus had in the first century BC.

The Colosseum in Rome held 50,000 spectators. There were seats all round rising to many tiers and an awning, or 'valarium', that could be spread over the seats for shade and protection from the rain. The building contained eating places, lavatories, storage rooms for animals, changing rooms for gladiators and an area in the centre of the arena that could be opened up to make a pool for naval battles. Great arches supported the exterior of the building and there were covered walk-ways beneath and behind the seats.

There was a free banquet for gladiators the night before the fight, an excuse for many of them to get very sensibly – or insensibly – drunk. The actual performance began with a parade and the sombre announcement recorded by Suetonius: 'Hail, Caesar, those about to die salute thee' (Ave Imperator, morituri te salutant). There were one or two religious rituals – recalling the religious origin of the festivals – which had to be done exactly right: if there were any errors in procedure during the performance, the whole thing had to start over again, which could be an exceedingly costly business for whoever was staging the show. Acrobats then did a turn or two and a mock-fight opened the proceedings. The sound of the tuba announced the first real fight.

First came the 'retiarii', or net men, wearing only a loin cloth and shin guards, armed with a dagger, a trident and a net with which they tried to entangle 'myrmillones' armed with sword and shield and protected by a helmet and visor. The lightness and quickness of the retiarius was offset by the strength and armour of the myrmillon and the fight could go either way. Once the myrmillon was caught in the net, he had little hope, with the trident at his throat. It was the emperor who raised or lowered his thumb to grant him life or condemn him to death but it was the crowd who made the decision for him by showing their preference with loud shouts of praise or boos. When the decision went against the myrmillon, slaves dressed as Mercury, the messenger and godly guide of the dead to hell, came out to drag away the body, and to rake sand over the blood.

Most fights offered contrasts in weapons and styles of fighting. Next came a battle between Samnites and Thracians. The Samnites were armed with huge shields that covered almost their whole body and they had short, straight swords. The Thracians had small round shields and curved swords. Trainers stood behind the fighters and urged them on; if they were reluctant to fight, slaves lashed them on with red-hot irons. Some gladiators fought on horseback, wearing chain-mail and helmets with no eye-holes so that they rushed blindly at each other with their long spears. Others fought in chariots, with one man driving and another to fight. The favourites of the crowd might well be displaced by a new hero within an afternoon. Petronius described a critical crowd:

> 'My old friend Titus has a big heart and a hot head . . . he does nothing by halves. He'll give us cold steel, no quarter and the slaughterhouse right in the middle where all the stands can see it . . . (but) what good has Norbanus done us. He put on some half-pint gladiators, so done in already that they'd have dropped if you blew at them. I've seen animal-killers fight better. As for the horsemen killed, he got them off a lamp – they ran round like cocks in a backyard. One was just a carthorse, the other couldn't stand up, and the reserve was just one corpse instead of another – he was practically hamstrung. One boy did have a bit of spirit – he was in Thracian armour, and even he didn't show any initiative. In fact, they were all flogged afterwards, there were so many shouts of "Give 'em what for!" from the crowd. Pure yellow, that's all.'

A very different type of helmet from the one on the opposite page. This one has protective facial covering and is of the type worn by the Greek hoplite or foot soldier. It, too, was found at Pompeii.

*'Daughters, in our own day, are frail and delicate creatures, fonder of brighter array, garments embroidered with gold, hair perfumed and set in every conceivable fashion, rings on their fingers, wrists dangling with bracelets and charms, necklaces and earrings heavy with jewels.'*

There were a few dissident voices. It is not surprising to find the voice of Seneca among them. His views were unusually humane and his Stoic philosophy profits enormously from that humanity:

'You ask me to say what you should consider it particularly important to avoid. My answer is this: a mass crowd . . . Nothing is more ruinous to the character as sitting away one's time at a show – for it is then, through the medium of entertainment, that vices creep into one with more than usual ease. What do you take me to mean? That I go home more selfish, more self-seeking and more self-indulgent? Yes, and what is more, a person crueller and less humane through having been in contact with human beings. I happened to go to one of these shows at the time of the lunch-hour interlude, expecting there to be some light and witty entertainment then, some respite for the purpose of affording people's eyes a rest from human blood. Far from it. All the earlier contests were charity in comparison. The nonsense is dispensed with now: what we have now is murder pure and simple. The combatants have nothing to protect them; their whole bodies are exposed to the blows; every thrust they launch gets home. A great many spectators prefer this to the ordinary matches and even to the special, popular demand ones. And quite naturally. There are no helmets and no shields repelling weapons. What is the point of armour? Or of skill? All that sort of thing just makes the death slower that is coming. In the morning men are thrown to the lions and the bears: but it is the spectators they are thrown to in the lunch hour. The spectators insist that each on killing his man shall be thrown against another to be killed in his turn; and the eventual victor is reserved by them for some other form of butchery; the only exit for the contestants is death. Fire and steel keep the slaughter going. And all this happens while the arena is virtually empty.

'"But he was a highway robber, he killed a man." And what of it? Granted that as a murderer he deserved this punishment, what have you done, you wretched fellow, to deserve to watch it? "Kill him! Flog him! Burn him! Why does he run at the other man's weapon in such a cowardly way? Why isn't he less half-hearted about killing? Why isn't he a bit more enthusiastic about dying? Whip him forward to get his wounds! Make them each offer the other a bare breast and trade blow for blow on them." And when there is an interval in the show: "Let's have some throats cut in the meantime, so that there's something happening!" Come now, I say, surely you people realise – if you realise nothing else – that bad examples have a way of recoiling on those who set them? Give thanks to the immortal gods that the men to whom you are giving this lesson in cruelty are not in a position to profit from it.'

Spectacles involving wild and tame animals were no less cruel. These were sometimes animal hunts, or 'venationes', sometimes battles between different kinds of animals, and sometimes massacres in which animals were let loose against unarmed Jews or criminals. There were also professional gladiators, known as 'bestiarii', who were especially trained to fight wild animals.

Animals were brought to Rome from distant countries that were never seen again in Europe until the nineteenth century. There were elephants, panthers, leopards, bears, hippopotami, hyaenas, ostriches, deer, bulls, crocodiles and lions. Pompey produced a rhinoceros, a lynx and an African ape. Julius Caesar produced a giraffe. Varro thought that tigers would be impossible to capture but they appeared in 11 BC. A tremendous amount of activity was involved in capturing and transporting these creatures for the

*'Name an imperial favourite and you will soon enough blaze like those human torches, half choked, half grilled to death, those cakined corpses they drag with hooks from the arena, and leave a broad black trail behind them in the sand.'*

*'Shame on the soul, to falter on the road of life while the body still perseveres.'*

108

The gallery beneath the great amphitheatre at Arles. It is still in a remarkably good state of preservation and, along with the Roman remains at Nîmes, Lepcis Magna and Verona, is one of the most remarkable structures to come down to us from antiquity.

It is built of concrete and ashlar and provides a fine example of Roman engineering and architectural skill. The building has vaulted sub-structures.

The Arch of Constantine was built after Constantine's victory over Maxentius in AD 312. The arch's inscription refers to 'divine inspiration' as an attribute in securing the great victory and this has helped to promote a legend.

amphitheatres. There was no restriction in hunting wild animals – except elephants, which were reserved for the emperor. Nets were used to close off areas. Trained dogs, horsemen, beaters with long sticks capped by red feathers and slaves with flaming torches drove the terrified animals into the nets, to be packed into crates.

Vast numbers of animals were killed in Rome alone. One hundred lions were slaughtered at Pompey's games, 400 at Caesar's games; nearly 11,000 animals were killed during the four months of Trajan's games in AD 107. Inevitably some animals became virtually extinct in certain areas. The hippopotamus vanished from Nubia, the lion disappeared from Mesopotamia, the elephant died out in North Africa. As governor of Cilicia, Cicero complained that his hunters were having a hard time meeting the demand for panthers.

For a single spectacle, elephants came from India, boars from the Rhine, lions from the Atlas mountains. Once again, it was the contrasts of contestants that gave the greatest pleasure. Rhinoceroses were set against elephants with specially sharpened tusks and metal tips; bears and bulls were chained together to fight each other; hunting dogs were trained to pursue almost any beast.

Animals were also tamed to perform extraordinary feats. There were elephants trained to hold torches and lions trained to draw chariots. The emperor Domitian put on a display of lions that were trained to catch hares and bring them back to their master without harming them. Four elephants were trained to carry a fifth in a litter and to bang cymbals while one of their fellows danced. Sea-lions barked in answer to their names and apes were trained to act plays and to drive chariots. Lions, panthers, bears, boars and wolves roamed around the emperor's court.

But the crowd soon tired of this. Their final thrill was to watch people, tied to stakes or unarmed, being mauled and devoured by the animals. Ingenious mechanical traps in the ground might open up to swallow men and drop them in to pits of animals below. Their screams were drowned by the shouting of the crowd. Some criminals were tarred and resined and set alight. They sometimes wore a special tunic, the 'tunica molesta', which was treated so that it burst suddenly into flame. Juvenal watched this torture and wrote:

> 'If Mucius, whom of late you saw one morning in the arena, when he laid his hand upon the fire, seems to you enduring and unflinching and strong, you have the intelligence of Abdera's rabble (notorious for their stupidity). For when it is said to you, while the torturing tunic is by you, "Burn your hand", it is the bolder thing to say, "I refuse".'

Finally, the amphitheatre might be flooded for a naval battle, a 'naumachiae'. The struggle between Athenians and Persians was a popular theme. Special lakes were dug. In 46 BC, Caesar celebrated his victories by digging a lake on the Campus Martius and setting an Egyptian against a Tyrian fleet. One thousand marines and 2000 oarsmen took part in a selection of biremes, triremes and quadriremes. In 2 BC, Augustus had a lake dug that was 550 metres long and 370 metres broad and contained thirty triremes and biremes. Claudius involved 19,000 warriors in a fight between Sicilians and men from Rhodes, in AD 52. Nearly thirty years later, Titus boarded over the entire lake for the first two days and held a gladiatorial and chariot-racing spectacle before taking the boards away and setting Athenians against men from Syracuse.

Most Romans did not moralise about the cruelty involved in these various spectacles and it would distort their view of life to analyse their attitude now.

A sectional view of a typical Roman amphitheatre. This impression is based largely on the evidence provided by the amphitheatre at Nimes. Note, particularly, the skilful arrangements for the canopy. This could be drawn across the entire open area in bad weather.

As with the other reconstructions in this book our artist worked out detailed elevations before proceeding to the final impression. Below we show two of the details used in the creation of this impression – the side elevation of the interior structure and of the façade.

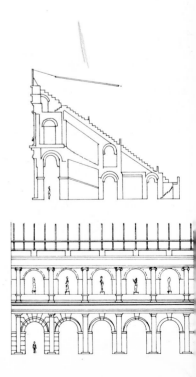

The force of habit, the expectation and the sheer splendour of the occasion had an intoxicating effect. St Augustine told a story about his young Christian friend, Alypius, who went to Rome for a while to study law. He was asked along to a gladiatorial show and, when pressed to join his comrades, protested that he would do so only if he could keep his eyes shut and pretend that he wasn't there. This was all right until he heard a particularly piercing cry in the arena which made him look up sharply out of curiosity. To his horror, he found himself aroused by what he saw. His soul, said Augustine, received a more severe wound than the body of the man who cried out. He gazed in fascination, found himself lusting for blood and screaming with the others for more. He went again to the amphitheatre at the very next opportunity.

With the example of the gladiators before them, Romans were never as keen as the Greeks on participation in sport and athletics. They were essentially spectators. They very sensibly disdained the cruel form of boxing with the 'caestus', a special glove weighted with iron and armed with metal spikes on the knuckles. And although they might enjoy a work-out at the gymnasium in the baths, they left foot races in the stadium to the Greeks. Nero was one of the few emperors who was at all keen on athletics. Most Romans considered them ignoble and Augustus tried to ban women from the stadium.

Many of the athletes were itinerants who formed their own guilds. Seneca regarded them as stupid and said that their whole life revolved around drinking, sweating and talking about their diet. They had nothing in their brains at all, he said. Galen, the physician, was even more rude. Perhaps they

The gladiatorial barracks at Pompeii. These were situated next to the Large Theatre. The famous architect Vitruvius suggested that these quarters, with their square colonnade, should form an annexe to the theatre so that the audiences might take shelter from the rain and also so that preparations could be more easily and conveniently made for the performances.

offended his professional pride by daring to put themselves up as experts on diet. They lived like pigs, he said, and did nothing but eat, sleep, excrete and wallow in dust and mud; they became physically grotesque by overdeveloping their muscles and in consequence were less fit and healthy in other ways. His final condemnation was that their lifestyle did not even profit them financially.

Juvenal agreed with Augustus that women athletes should be banned:

> 'And what about female athletes, with their purple track-suits, and wrestling in mud? Not to mention our lady fencers – we've all seen them, stabbing the stump with a foil, shield well advanced, going through the proper motions . . . Hark how she snorts at each practice thrust, bowed down by the weight of her helmet; see the big, coarse puttees wrapped around her ample hams – then wait for the laugh when she lays her weapons aside and squats on the potty!'

There was one place, at least, where everyone agreed to find harmless relaxation and pleasure – at the baths. They were as much a meeting place as a washing place. In the larger baths, men and women had separate facilities; in the smaller ones they bathed at separate times. Mixed bathing was generally disapproved of but not unknown. If Martial is anything to go by, men were more interested in boys than girls at the baths. Men usually bathed after the morning's work and before the main meal of the day. The cost was minimal and often the baths were free for several days on end, paid for by some rich patron who wanted to become popular.

In the large baths, there was a general entrance hall or waiting room. Then you would go into the changing room, where there were shelves for your clothes and your towels. One character in *The Golden Ass* took his own towel:

> '(He) fetched a towel from the cupboard and a little flask of toilet water and went along to the public baths.'

Men sometimes wore leather trunks but more often bathed naked. Women wore drawers or an even larger, voluminous costume. Women also had beauty parlours in the baths and could be attended by male slaves and given massages by slaves. But for this they had to pay double the amount that men paid for the baths. After changing, you went into the 'tepidarium', the warm room. You progressed from there to the hot room, the 'caldarium', which was nearest the boiler. This was usually quite small and you probably would not stay in it for long. After this you were rubbed with olive oil and scraped down with a knife, or 'strigil'. If you were hardy, you then plunged straight in to the cold bath in the 'frigidarium', but it was quite in order to take things steadily and go by way of the 'tepidarium' again. You might even have another quick dip in the hot plunge bath in the 'caldarium', to warm yourself up on a cold day. Trimalchio and his friends did things a little differently:

> 'We did not take our clothes off but began wandering around or rather exchanging jokes while circulating among the little groups . . . We entered the baths where we began sweating at once and we went immediately into the cold water. Trimalchio had been smothered in perfume and was already being rubbed down, not with linen towels but with bath robes of the finest wool.'

But another character in the *Satyricon* wasn't quite so sure of the merit of too many baths:

> 'I don't have a bath every day. It's like getting rubbed with fuller's earth, having a bath. The water bites into you, and as the days go by, your heart turns to water.'

Citizens took great pride in their public baths and were quite prepared to

'*You must inevitably either hate or imitate the world. But the right thing is to shun both courses: you should neither become like the bad because they are many, nor be an enemy of the many because they are unlike you.*'

'*Associating with people in large numbers is actually harmful: there is not one of them that will not make some vice or other attractive to us, or leave us to carry the imprint of it or be daubed with it all unawares.*'

save up money to finance a building that would do them credit. Pliny wrote to Trajan:

'The public bath at Prusa, Sir, is old and dilapidated, and the people are very anxious for it to be rebuilt. My own opinion is that you could suitably grant their petition. There will be money available for building it, first from the sums I have begun to call in from private individuals, and secondly because the people are prepared to apply to building the bath the grants they usually make towards financing the distribution of olive oil. This is, moreover, a scheme which is worthy of the town's prestige and the splendour of your reign.'

The great baths of Diocletian and Caracalla were particularly splendid, so were Hadrian's baths at Lepcis Magna in North Africa, with high cross-vaulted ceilings painted with motifs of people and animals, and with marble panels on the walls and marble floors. These great public buildings could not fail to impress the average citizen that he belonged to a rich and mighty civilisation. But we have come to learn that Seneca was not average. He compared modern luxury with the old simplicity:

'We think ourselves poorly off, living like paupers, if the walls are not ablaze with large and costly mirrors, if our Alexandrian marbles are not decorated with panels of Numidian marble, if the whole of their surface has not been given a decorative overlay of elaborate patterns having all the variety of fresco murals, unless the ceiling cannot be seen for glass . . . There was a time when bath-houses were few and far between and never in the least luxuriously appointed – and why should they have been, considering that they were designed for use, not for diversion, and that admission only cost you a copper? There were no showers in those days and the water did not come in a continuous gush as if from a hot spring . . . Heavens what a pleasure it is to get into one of those half-lit bath-houses with their ordinary plastered ceilings . . . Writers who have left us a record of life in ancient Rome tell us that it was just their arms and legs, which of course they dirtied working, that people washed every day, bathing all over only once a week on market day.'

But people did not go to the baths just to bathe – or just to socialise. There was usually a gymnasium, as well. They played a form of tennis, not with a racquet but with the hand. They also played a variety of ball games. There was 'trigon' in which they threw a small handball between three people standing in a triangle. 'Harpastum' used a similar ball which was scrambled for by two sets of players. The ball for 'follis' was much larger and was filled with air and struck with the hand. There was also hoop-rolling and wrestling. Altogether there was plenty going on and plenty of noise, as Seneca found out when he lived above some baths:

'Imagine what a variety of noises reverberates about my ears! . . . When your strenuous gentleman, for example, is exercising himself by flourishing leaden weights; when he is working hard, or else pretends to be working hard, I can hear him grunt . . . Or perhaps I notice some lazy fellow, content with a cheap rub-down, and hear the crack of a pummelling hand on his shoulder, varying in sound according as the hand is laid on flat or hollow . . . Add to this the arresting of an occasional roisterer or pickpocket, the racket of the man who always likes to hear his own voice in the bathroom, or the enthusiast who plunges into the swimming tank with unconscionable noise and splashing . . . then the cake-seller with his varied cries, the sausage man, the confectioner and all the vendors of food hawking their wares, each with his own

*'What do the baths bring to your mind? Oil, sweat, dirt, greasy water, and everything that is disgusting. Such, then, is life in all its parts, and such is every material thing in it.'*

*A wrestler: 'I do not like him because he wins, but because he knows how to yield, and has learned the better art of recovering himself.'*

*(Gift tag)*

The beautiful Roman bath in the British spa of that name. Even in Roman times Bath had a reputation for its healing waters. Most of the buildings were erected about AD 100 but they were subsequently altered and added to. They originally contained three deep plunge baths. In the middle of the north side of the great bath a fountain of cold, therapeutic, water was provided for the bathers. The Great Bath was supplied from natural hot springs and some of the water channels are still in use. The Bath was completely covered by a great vaulted roof with circular openings at each end to allow steam to escape. Small fragments of the mosaic floors are still visible.

distinctive intonation . . . Among the things which create a racket all around me . . . I include the carriages in the street, the carpenter who works in the same block and the man in the neighbourhood who saws and this fellow tuning horns and flutes at the Trickling Fountain and emitting blasts instead of music.'

True to his Stoicism, Seneca claimed that he was not in the least disturbed by all these noises: he was far too busy concentrating on his writing. He merely records them out of interest!

But Seneca, despite his writing, found time, like many people, to go to the theatre. There he recorded the gestures used by actors to portray embarrassment, sadness or fear: the head hung down, the voice was lowered, the eyes were fixed on the ground. The semi-circular or horseshoe-shaped theatres were never as popular as the amphitheatres or the circus but they were large by modern standards. Pompey's Theatre held 27,000 people. The orchestra in front of the stage was reserved for senators and high-ranking magistrates. Knights sat in the front rows of the auditorium and the rest of the noisy spectators crowded on to the seats rising up behind. With so many people and so much noise, the plots had to be simple and clear and the gestures of the actors had to be immediately recognisable.

Being an open theatre, the season was from about April to November. The curtain was not lowered in the interval, as there was no roof; instead it was raised from a pit below the stage by a pulley. The stage itself was long and narrow: it could be anything up to fifty metres long. This helped to make asides more realistic; actors could catch sight of each other from a distance or miss each other completely; and there was plenty of space for all kinds of stage 'business'. The regulation backdrop consisted of the front of two houses with an alley between.

Tragedies and comedies were largely based on the Greek theatre, although Rome had its own well-known comic writers such as Naevius, Plautus and Terence. Naevius wrote in the third century BC and his plays are full of social digs and coarse plots, with titles like 'Testicularia' and 'Triphallus'. He described a coquette in the 'Girl from Tarentum':

'As if she was playing ball in a ring, she runs from one to another, being everything to everybody, she nods and winks, she touches and embraces, she squeezes a hand here, presses with her foot there, flashes her ring, makes as if to kiss, sings a few notes and offers suggestive signs.'

Plautus, who was himself an actor and trader, portrayed a miser to rival Molière, Shakespeare or Ben Jonson. Euclio was so mean that he tied a bag in front of his face during the night in case he wasted his breath, he wouldn't give you his washing water or even hunger, if you asked for it, and he stored away his nail parings.

Even this material found it hard to compete with the attractions of gladiators and chariot-racing. Plays went out of fashion and dance and mime became increasingly popular. In the plays, all actors had been male, trained by professional producers, but in the mimes there were both male and female performers – slaves and freedmen – and actresses were even allowed to perform naked during the festival of Floralia. Sensationalism became the only way to bring in a full house. Scenes of sensuality under the guise of classical mythology – with singers, music and dance – were received with great enthusiasm. Above all, the audiences loved the pantomime, which mimicked everyday life: there were topical jokes, farce, dancing girls, acrobats, jugglers and even tightrope walkers. The writer Quintilian described some of the more

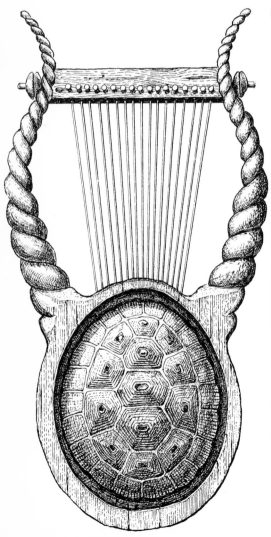

Below right: A wall painting from Herculaneum showing a music lesson.

Below: A beautiful example of a Roman lyre. The sound box is made from the shell of a tortoise. The strings were looped round bone pegs and these could be turned to tune the strings. A plectrum for plucking the strings was also used.

skilful arts of the pantomime. He was clearly full of admiration:

'Their hands demand and promise, they summon and dismiss; they translate horror, fear, joy, sorrow, hesitation, confession, repentance, restraint, abandonment, time and number. They excite and they calm. They implore and they approve. They possess a power of imitation which replaces words. To suggest illness, they imitate the doctor feeling the patient's pulse; to indicate music they spread their fingers in the fashion of a lyre.'

Praetors who paid for and presented the show often paid best for the lewdest scenes. Both Ovid and Martial complained that their poems could hardly be thought indecent compared to what happened on the stage. Women loved the theatre and the colour and sensuousness of the mime. A famous actor or a beautiful boy dancer could win their hearts and much else besides, as Juvenal could tell:

'Check every tier of seats at all the theatres in the town: will they yield one single candidate you could love without a qualm? When pansy Bathyllus dances Leda, all fouettes and entrechats, just watch the women. One can't control her bladder, another moans in drawn-out ecstasy as though she was coming. Your country girl's all rapt attention, she's learning fast.'

In general, actors were scorned by men, although Nero himself took to the stage much to everyone's embarrassment. Emperors who went to watch the theatre had often to watch mimed jibes at some recent action of theirs, while the audience howled with delight.

Despite a decree in AD 15 that pantomimes and the dancing that accompanied them might only be seen in public, good dancing soon became an essential attribute for anyone who wanted to make their way in society. All wealthy houses included their dancing masters and their pantomime actors. Ovid advises a man who wants to please his lady to flex his arms and dance with her at the feast.

To sing and play music were also social accomplishments. The lyre was still in use but the cithara was more popular, with its broad, wooden soundbox and anything up to eleven strings. The pegs for tuning were made of bone and the instrument was played with a bone plectrum. There were several sizes – some, said Seneca, as large as litters! Wood and ivory aulos were the main wind instruments; these used reeds and were roughly equivalent to the clarinet or the oboe. There was a great variety of types and sizes. Sometimes they were played in pairs simultaneously. Whistles and pan pipes were common and there was the usual percussion accompaniment of cymbals, drums and tambourines, also military tubas and cornu. There was a water organ, or 'hydraulis'. Air was pumped into a chamber in which there was an inverted bowl sunk in water. Surplus air in the chamber was forced by compression into the pipes and provided an even flow of air through the instrument. Music was particularly important in religious processions but there were rarely any concerts of large numbers of instruments playing set pieces to large numbers of people.

In private houses, Greek slaves played for the guests, who might occasionally join in. There would also be slaves to dance for the guests – a more usual form of entertainment than to follow Ovid's advice and take the floor themselves. Cicero was firmly convinced that no one danced unless they were either drunk or insane and no Roman could possibly have danced gracefully in a toga: it became a catch-phrase that anything absurd was 'like dancing in a toga'.

*Cut leeks: 'As often as you have eaten the strong-smelling shoots of Tarentine leeks, give kisses with shut mouth.'*

*(Gift tag)*

*Wood-pigeons: 'Ringdoves check and blunt the manly powers: let not him eat this bird who wishes to be lickerish.'*

*(Gift tag)*

## A Dinner Party

*After their visit to the baths, Martial invites six friends to share a meal with him on his crescent couch, which holds seven in all, himself included:*

'My bailiff's wife has brought me mallows that will unload the stomach, and the various wealth the garden bears; amongst which is squat lettuce and clipped leek, and flatulent mint is not wanting for the salacious herb; sliced eggs shall garnish lizard flesh served with rue, and there shall be a paunch dripping from the tunny's brine. Herein is your whet: the modest dinner shall be served in a single course – a kid rescued from the jaws of a savage wolf, and meat balls to requite no carver's knife, and beans, the food of artisans, and tender young sprouts; to these a chicken, and a ham that has already survived three dinners, shall be added. When you have had your fill I will give you ripe apples, wine without lees from a Nomentan flagon, which was three years old in Frontinus' second consulship. To crown these shall be jests without gall, and a freedom not to be dreaded the next morning, and no word you would wish unsaid; let my guests converse of the Green and the Blue; my cups do not make any man a defendant.'

*(Martial)*

---

This is a recreation of a particular room in the House of Neptune and Amphitrite at Herculaneum – as it might have appeared when it was used for a dinner party. The master of the house, a wealthy Roman, reclines in his toga. The other younger men are relaxing in a casual tunic known as a 'synthesis'. These were usually brightly coloured. The couches are made of wood and are comfortably cushioned and elegantly draped.

The food they are being served is highly spiced – the Romans had a fondness for rich foods. A slave boy is filling the master's cup. Soft music accompanies this banquet – music that to our ears would have a distinctly Greek feel about it. The alcove has a chest in it in which valuables were kept. The floor is a black and white mosaic and the centre fountain cools the warm Roman evening.

To a modern eye the walls may seem somewhat over decorated and yet to a Roman this room would have seemed the height of elegance and opulence.

---

Dancing, music and mime were all ingredients for one of the wealthy Roman's most enjoyable activities – the dinner party. Poetry was another ingredient and Martial, who made his living out of his poems, was not quite sure whether he had been invited for the dinner or the poems:

'This, no other, is your reason for inviting me to dine, that you may recite your verses, Ligurinus. I have put off my shoes; at once a huge volume is brought along with the lettuce and the fish sauce. A second is read through while the first course stands waiting; there is a third, and the dessert does not yet appear; and you recite a fourth, and finally a fifth book. Sickening is a boar if you serve it to me so often. If you don't consign your accursed poems to the mackerel, you shall dine at home alone.'

Story-telling at dinner parties was also common. A character in *The Golden Ass* prepared to capture the interest of his listeners:

'He made a little heap of the coverings of his couch and propped himself up on it with his left elbow: then with his right hand he signalled for attention in the oratorical style, protruding the forefinger and middle finger, pointing the thumb upward and folding down to the two remaining fingers for good luck.'

Pliny tantalised a guest with the sort of entertainment he *would* have had if he had bothered to turn up:

'Who are you, to accept my invitation to dinner and never come? Here's your sentence and you shall pay my costs in full, no small sum either. It was all laid out, one lettuce each, three snails, two eggs, barley-cake and wine with honey chilled with snow (you will reckon this too please, and as an expensive item, seeing that it disappears in the dish), besides olives, beetroots, gherkins, onions and any number of similar delicacies. You would have heard a comic play, a reader or singer, or all three if I felt generous.'

What Pliny offered in the way of food was nothing, however, compared

*Mushrooms: 'Silver and gold, and a mantle, and a toga it is easy to send; to send mushrooms is difficult.'*

*(Gift tag)*

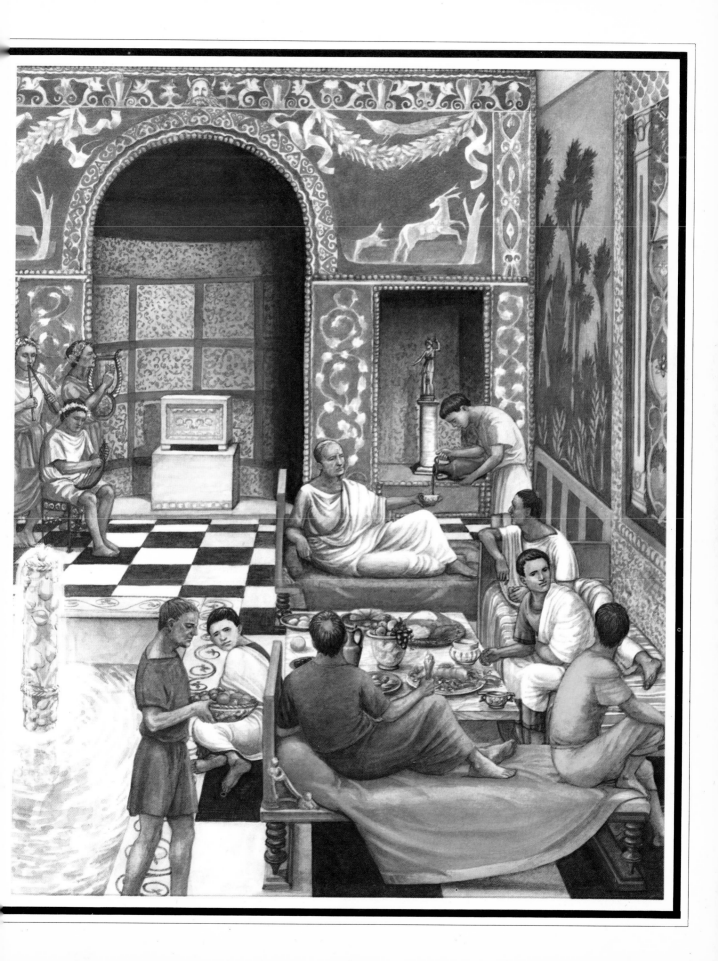

with a really good feast at which the quantities of food and drink consumed and the elaborate nature of their presentation were outstanding. Trimalchio's feast in the *Satyricon* was an epic of its kind:

'There were some small iron frames shaped like bridges supporting dormice sprinkled with honey and poppy seed. There were steaming hot sausages, too, on a silver gridiron with damsons and pomegranate seeds underneath.'

At one point in the dinner party:

'Four dancers hurtled forward in time to the music and removed the upper part of the great dish, revealing underneath plump fowls, sow's udders and a hare with wings fixed to his middle to look like Pegasus . . . quite exquisite things.'

It was customary to have a feast several days after a funeral and one of these, in the *Satyricon*, went something like this:

'For the first course we had a pig crowned with sausages and served with blood puddings and very nicely done giblets, and of course beetroot and pure wholemeal bread . . . The next course was cold tart and a concoction of first-class Spanish wine poured over hot honey. Scattered round were chickpeas, lupines, a choice of nuts and an apple a piece . . . To finish up with, we had some cheese basted with new wine, snails all round, chitterlings, plates of liver, eggs in pastry hoods, turnips, mustard . . . There were pickled cumin seeds, too, passed round in a bowl, and some people were that bad-mannered they took three handfuls.'

Bad manners were encouraged by the custom of clients fishing for invitations from their patrons and then trying to grab enough food to last them until the next invitation. Martial knew the habit well:

'Whatever is served you sweep off from this or that part of the table: the teats of a sow's udder and a rib of pork, and a heathcock meant for two, half a mullet, and a bass whole, and the side of a murry, and the leg of a fowl, and a pigeon dripping with its white sauce. These dainties, when they have been hidden in your sodden napkin, are handed over to your boy to carry home: we recline at table, an idle crowd. If you have any decency, restore our dinner; I did not invite you, Caecilianus, to a meal tomorrow.'

But by the next day, Caecilianus will have sold most of the food for ready cash.

The reason for much of the extravagance at dinner parties was to show off the wealth of the host. To become a topic of conversation in society, it was imperative that he achieved a certain notoriety for excess. Moderation got you nowhere. Martial said of one acquaintance that he was not content with being a glutton but he wanted to be known as one. It was not uncommon to take an emetic after a heavy meal. Seneca rounded on those who 'eat to vomit and vomit to eat', whose food came from every corner of the world yet was never even digested. He also criticised the latest habit in luxury living: the kitchen was brought to the table so that the food would remain scalding hot.

Laws were passed unavailingly to try to limit extravagance. Even in the second century BC, a limit of five guests besides the family was put on feast-day dinners and no more than three guests were allowed on other days. Prices of luxury foods were frequently fixed. But the limits on expense rose steadily with inflation and by the time of Tiberius all serious efforts to restrain the rich had been dropped.

Martial's experiences, however, were not always of extravagant generosity at dinner parties:

*It was a customary politeness at dinner to say: 'Your drinking will be sufficient to recommend the wine.'*

*'Just a few words in your ear, brief and straight to the point. Yesterday afternoon, near the portico of Apollo on the Palatine Hill, I saw her taking a stroll – saw her, wanted her, wrote her, sent the letter and asked her. Back, in a shaky hand, came the answer: "I can't." You were the reason, my friend – you and your vigilant guard.'*

*Gold-inlaid dishes: 'Do not insult large gold-inlaid dishes with a small mullet: at the least it ought to weigh two pounds.'*

*(Gift tag)*

'Twice thirty were we, Mancinus, your invited guests, and nothing was served us last night but a boar. There were no grapes such as are left to hang late upon the vine, nor honey apples that vie with luscious combs; nor pears that hang tied with the pliant broom; nor pomegranates that copy the transient roses. Rural Sassina sent no cones of cheese; there came no olive from Picenian jars. A boar, and nothing else! and this too a tiny one, and such as could be slaughtered by an unarmed dwarf.'

Martial himself gave many little dinner parties and was proud that his guests could say what they wanted and need not fear that they would be reported by an informer for some unfortunately fatal slip of the tongue. Great care had normally to be taken not to say anything that could be misinterpreted by the emperor or his friends. In the time of Tiberius and Caligula, informers were richly rewarded. Soldiers dressed in civilian clothes and encouraged their dinner companions to talk treasonably, whereupon

The House of Neptune and Amphitrite – see also the caption to our artist's reconstruction on Page 119.

*'Intent on stuffing themselves, they follow their noses and the shrieking women's voices to the kitchen and, like a flock of starving and screeching peacocks, they stand on the tips of their toes biting their finger nails and waiting for the food to cool.'*

they clamped them in chains. So conversation was limited to harmless news at most dinner parties and Martial was so exasperated that he invited one man to dinner on the strict condition that he mentioned no news at all.

A painting of a rather brazen young girl. These funerary paintings have a curiously realistic and haunting quality. This is a particularly fine specimen.

---

## A Little Dinner

*'If you are troubled by the prospect of a cheerless dinner at home, Toraniua, you may fare modestly with me. You will not lack, if you are accustomed to an appetiser, cheap Cappadocian lettuces and strong-smelling leeks; a piece of tunny will lie hid in sliced eggs. There will be served – to be handled with scorched fingers – on a black-ware dish light green broccoli, which has just left the cool garden, and a sausage lying on white pease-pudding, and pale beans with ruddy bacon. If you wish for what a dessert can give, grapes past their prime shall be offered you, and pears that bear the name of Syrian, and chestnuts which learned Neapolis has grown, roasted in a slow heat; the wine you will make good by drinking it. After all this spread, if – as may be – Bacchus rouses a usual appetite, choice olives which Picenian branches have but lately borne will relieve you, and hot chick-peas and warm lupines. My poor dinner is a small one – who can deny it? – but you will say no word insincere nor hear one, and, wearing your natural face, will recline at ease; nor will your host read a bulky volume, nor will girls from wanton Gades with endless prurience swing lascivious loins in practised writhings; but the pipe of little Condylus shall play something not too solemn nor unlively.'*

*(Martial)*

---

Conversation ran also on the latest ailments and the latest cures, why corpses decayed faster in moonlight than in sunlight or whether touching dew-drenched trees gave you leprosy. There were plenty of lewd jokes for the Romans were admirably open about sex. The talk would soon turn to the mischievious Priapus, the fertility god, who also watched over the garden, terrifying the birds with his great red member. Martial had a story on the subject:

'A thief of too notorious rapacity, a Cilician, was minded to plunder a garden; but in the immense garden was nothing . . . but a marble Priapus. Being loath to return with empty hands, the Cilician carried off Priapus himself!'

There was also all the scandal of the town: who was going to leave how much money to whom; who had given the greatest banquet or the best games; who was whose lover? The gossips loved it and Martial, himself a gossip, loathed the gossips:

'You are a good fellow, Cotilus. So they all say. But what is a good fellow? One who has his hair nicely curled and smells of balsam and cinnamon; who can hum the tunes of Alexandrian and Spanish dances, and sits all day long between the ladies, whispering, writing and reading billets doux; who also hates being jogged by his neighbour and knows also everyone's lady-love; one who runs from one party to another, and knows the pedigree of the best racehorse by heart. Is this right, Cotilus? Then it is no easy matter to be a good fellow.'

Worse still was the woman who always wanted music when you wanted conversation, who thrust herself on dinner parties uninvited and became a literary bore. This time it was Juvenal's turn to let fly:

*'The Germans believe that there resides in women an element of holiness and a gift of prophecy and so they do not scorn to ask their advice.'*

The remains of what are possibly the guest apartments in Hadrian's great villa at Tivoli. The villa was one of the most lavish in the Roman world.

'If your wife has musical tastes, she'll make the professional singers come when she wants . . . yet a musical wife's not so bad as some presumptuous flat-chested busybody who rushes around the town gate-crashing all-male gatherings, talking back straight-faced to a uniformed general *and* in her husband's presence. She knows all the news of the world . . . Worse still is the well-read menace, who's hardly settled for dinner before she starts praising Virgil . . . I hate these authority citers, the sort who are always thumbing some standard grammatical treatise, whose every utterance observes all the laws of syntax, who with antiquarian zeal quotes poets I've never heard of. Such matters are men's concern.'

As for the flirtatious, who seized on dinner parties and social gatherings to make their conquests, it was Ovid who had all the most sensible advice for the young. Cleanliness, said Ovid, was of paramount importance. The man should wear a clean toga, not too extravagant, clean sandals with buckles that were not rusty and should not address the girl as if she were a public meeting. On her part the girl should never let it be known that she was taking endless pains to titivate herself: she should just announce that she was resting in bed and would be up shortly. Ovid had more detailed advice on the actual seduction and Rome loved it but the emperor decided it was counter to his policy of cleaning up the city and Ovid was banished to the Black Sea.

Horace thought there were better things to do than to chase married women:

'You may well find the pain and hardship far outweigh any real pleasure. She may be decked out in emeralds and snowy pearls, but that doesn't give her a straighter leg or a softer thigh than Cerinthus boasts. And often the girl with the cloak is better still. Also she carries her wares without disguise, showing what she has for sale quite openly; if she possesses a good feature she doesn't parade it and flaunt it while trying to hide her blemishes. Sheiks have an interesting habit: when buying horses they cover them before inspection, for fear a handsome shape with (as often) a tender hoof underneath may take in the buyer as he gapes at the lovely haunches, the small head and the high neck. And they're very wise . . . With a married lady you can't see anything except her face. The rest is covered by her long dress.'

A daily scene in the life of the citizens of Pompeii. This fresco was uncovered in the back room of a Pompeian tavern and shows a group drinking in the tavern.

The 'girl with the cloak' was a prostitute. There were a great many in Rome and other cities and towns throughout the empire. Pompeii was renowned for its brothels, which were covered inside with suggestive paintings. Prostitutes were usually slaves. Greeks were common and Syrians were appreciated for their appetising dancing. The mark of a prostitute in the street was often a brightly-coloured toga, which any other woman would never have worn. They were permitted to walk the streets and have their own brothels if they registered with the police. The price of a prostitute might be between two and twelve asses at a time when the cost of the baths was about half an as. Freedmen and slaves frequented them most and the young free-born citizen would probably be encouraged to go along to get some experience.

Courtesans were a class above prostitutes. They lived with their mothers or with their procurers ('lena'). They could usually sing and play a musical instrument and might even have a smattering of literature so that they could make intelligent conversation. Apart from these outlets for physical satisfaction, mistresses were common among married men and household slaves were always available.

There were less strenuous forms of entertainment. The emperor Claudius greatly enjoyed dice. There was a form of backgammon, known as 'duodecim scripta', a little different from the modern game. Another popular board game was 'little robbers', or 'latrunculi'. Women had pet animals – birds were popular – and whiled away their day visiting, talking, reading, listening to music or writing poetry or letters.

For those who wanted to get out of the city into the fresh air of the countryside, there was hunting and fishing. Pliny wrote to a friend:

'Are you reading, fishing or hunting or doing all three? You can do all together on the shores of Como, for there is plenty of fish in the lake, game to hunt in the woods around and every opportunity to study in the depths of your retreat.'

Another writer, Ausonius, had a friend who was equally torn between work and pleasure. Ausonius wrote to him to encourage him to write some poetry but strongly suspected that his friend was either being extremely active in pursuing thieves and cattle raiders (or doing some raiding himself), or that he was thoroughly enjoying himself after a good day's fishing, having caught plenty of sturgeon, tunnyfish and plaice.

Martial, on the other hand, was concerned for a friend of his who had gone off hunting:

'Use more sparingly, I warn you, Priscus, your tearing hunter, nor rush so violently after hares . . . Snares even a plain has: though there be no ditch, nor mound, nor stones, level ground can oft deceive . . . If perilous hardihood delight you, let us then – safer is such courage – lay snares for Tuscan boars. Why does rash riding please you? More often its issue, Priscus, is to break up the rider rather than the hare.'

---

## The Mimic

'You mimic well, I'm bound to say,
A puppy's yap and horse's neigh,
Your imitation of the bleat
Of sheep or goats is very neat,
And if you cry "Hee-haw" for
                              choice
We'd say it was a donkey's voice.

The raven's croak, the farm cock's
                              crow,
All cries of birds and beasts we
                              know
You copy to the life – but can
You reproduce the voice of man?'

(Ausonius)

---

From all this, it would appear that the Romans had plenty of leisure time and a full round of entertainments. But they were severely restricted by the availability of light and had to arrange their working day to give themselves time to relax and enjoy themselves in the afternoon. There were no theatres or concerts in the evening. Most people went to bed at nightfall. Only the odd tavern, the brothel, a late dinner party or the occasional festival offered entertainment after dark.

There were many complaints that loose morals and adult pleasures had a bad influence on the young. Tacitus was not the only one to notice that children were more interested in the races than in their schoolwork. Some people put it down to the influence of Greek slaves in the home, who were always being suspected of lowering the moral tone of respectable establishments. It is time to take a closer look at the upbringing of those children and to see how well educated their parents were, as well.

*Raisin wine: 'The vintage of Cnossos in Minoan Crete brought forth for you this, which is wont to be the poor man's mead.'*

*(Gift tag)*

*Vinegar: 'Let not a jar of Egyptian vinegar be mean in your eyes. When it was wine it was more mean.'*

*(Gift tag)*

# IX

# Schools and writers

'Thank heaven for education; it made me what you see me now,' said an ex-slave in the *Satyricon* but the opportunities for slaves and the poor to get an education were small compared to the children of the rich. In the early days of the Republic, children were looked after by their mothers until they were seven; then their father took the boys in hand until they were sixteen. They would accompany him on his official rounds and were then apprenticed to another citizen to acquire a skill. Subsequent military service led to a public career. But in time the early upbringing was given over to a nurse and a tutor, or 'paedagogus', who was invariably a figure of fun.

When more formal education was introduced, the girls only joined in the first part, then they stayed at home and learnt the skills of a wife and mother. For the boys, there were the elementary school, the grammar school and the

A Roman ink well and pen. Ink in Roman times was very different from our own. It was made from a mixture of soot, resin, wine dregs and cuttlefish. This curious mixture seems to have been quite legible and enduring on papyrus.

'A man who does nothing
but oppose his son and
insists on having his own
way is wasting his time –
asking for trouble and
laying up a hard winter for
his old age.'

A Roman scroll. Roman books
were written on papyrus and the
papyrus was then mounted on
rollers such as those shown here.
These rollers had projecting
knobs which were sometimes
made from ivory or ebony. Their
covers were of vellum and they
were tied with scarlet ribbons,
labelled and stored either in
round boxes or in shelves divided
up into pigeon-holes.

Public libraries came into being
in Rome in the first century BC.
Augustus founded one library on
the Palatine and another in the
Campus Martius. These libraries
had separate rooms for Greek and
Latin texts and, of course, a
reading room.

school of rhetoric. They learnt reading, writing and simple arithmetic at the
elementary school, from the age of seven to twelve. The schoolroom might be
a bare room with a chair for the master and benches for the boys or it might be
just an awning outside a shop. The master had chalk and a blackboard. The
boys had a stylus and wax tablet. The stylus had one sharp end with which to
write on the tablet and one blunt end with which to wipe out the scratched
mark. At this stage the child would not yet use a pen and ink: when he did, the
pen was made from reed or bronze and the ink was made from cuttlefish or
some artificial compound mixed with water; parchment would be used to
write on. Arithmetic was learnt with the help of an abacus or a counting
board and was mainly used to help with everyday trade and commerce.
Children were taught simple proverbs by heart to help them learn to read and
write: 'Man's life is not a gift but a loan'. They were also taught to respect
their teacher and their parents. But Horace begged for a little light relief:

'What harm can there be in presenting the truth with a laugh, as teachers
sometimes give their children biscuits to coax them to learn their ABC.'

Having washed his teeth and dressed in the early morning, the schoolboy
would go and say good morning to his parents and set off for the classroom
together with his 'paedagogus' and a slave to carry his case with the wax
tablet inside. The teacher would kiss him on arrival and the boy would
squeeze up on the bench with his fellow. He would go home for a lunch of
bread, olives, cheese, dried figs, some nuts and a drink of water and return to
the classroom for the afternoon. Then he would be off to the baths, still
accompanied by his slave.

Discipline was strict and flogging not uncommon, although Quintilian,
who wrote at length about education, thought that it was degrading to the
flogger and provoking to the flogged. But he also believed that flogging was
bad even for a slave, an attitude which many Romans would regard as
thoroughly eccentric. Most people believed that flogging was an integral part
of a boy's education, however, even if the use of a leather whip was
occasionally taking the punishment too far.

At the grammar school, the 'grammaticus', the emphasis was on literature.
Children were also taught to read and to recite passages that they learnt by
heart. All reading was done aloud – by children and adults alike. (Much later,
St Augustine was regarded as very odd because he read without even moving
his lips.) Homer, in translation, was the most popular author with teachers
but Virgil joined him and even Horace, who had been thoroughly beaten by
his own teacher during his childhood studies of the *Odyssey*, came to be
regarded as a poet worth reading. One aspect of this part of a boy's studies was
the comparison and criticism of different texts. Comparison was difficult:
when every copy was written out by hand, there were invariably differences
between each copy. But many schools would, anyway, only have one copy of
the relevant book.

Reading aloud prepared the boys for the next stage – rhetoric and oratory.
No one got on well in public life unless they were good public speakers. The
subtle skills of the Greeks were at first highly suspect but their style of rhetoric
soon gained a strong foothold. The main feature of the rhetorical education
was to make speeches of various types on set subjects: whether a man should
marry or not; whether a certain historical figure should have acted as he did in
a particular situation; or to persuade a god or goddess not to take revenge on a
hero who had acted wrongly. The method of delivery was important: the
speaker should be aware of the right things to say, should set them out
logically and persuasively, should appeal to the vested interests of his listeners

> ## Schoolmasters
>
> *'What have you to do with us, accursed pedagogue, a fellow odious to boys and girls? Not yet have crested cocks broken the hush of night, already with menacing voice and with thwacks you raise an uproar . . . We neighbours don't ask for sleep all the night; for some wakefulness is a trifle, to wake all night is no joke. Dismiss your pupils. Are you willing, you blatant fellow, to accept for holding your tongue as much as you accept for bawling?'*
>
> *( Martial )*

and should unashamedly use gesture and inflection to get them on his side. All this was excellent practice for the lawyer, as well.

Juvenal thought the whole system ridiculous:

'Do you teach declamation? You must possess iron nerves to sit through a whole large class's attack on "The Tyrant". Each boy stands up in turn and delivers by rote what he's just learnt at his desk; all gabble off the same stale old couplets and catchphrases – bubble and squeak rehashed without end, sheer death for the poor master . . . What wouldn't I give – just name your figure, I'll pay it, cash on the nail – for any boy's father to hear him as often as I do!'

Tacitus agreed wholeheartedly with Juvenal. He found it difficult to tell what caused the most harm to the pupils in the schools of rhetoric – the school itself, their fellow pupils, or what they studied – and he regarded the 'persuasive' and 'controversial' subjects which they were supposed to argue as idiotic, unrealistic and pompous. He referred to such subjects for debate as 'The Tyrannicide's Reward', the 'Choices of the Raped', and 'The Incestuous Mothers', which were spoken about daily in the schools but never discussed with noble phrases in public.

Petronius joined the attack:

'I'm sure the reason such young nitwits are produced in our schools is because they have no contact with anything of any use in everyday life. All they get is pirates standing on the beach, dangling manacles, tyrants writing orders for sons to cut off their father's heads, oracles advising the sacrifice of three or more virgins during a plague – a mass of sickly sentiments . . . People fed on this sort of thing have as much chance of learning sense as dishwashers have of smelling clean.'

Seneca quoted the following popular subject for debate: There was a young man who was captured by pirates. He sent a message to his father asking to be ransomed. His father could not or would not come up with the money. But the daughter of the pirate chief promised to help the young man escape if he, in turn, swore to marry her. They returned to the young man's father, who promptly ordered his son to divorce the pirate chief's daughter and marry the young heiress that he had lined up. The young man refused and his father disinherited him. The question was, bearing in mind the father's right of authority over his family but also bearing in mind his refusal to come up with the ransom, should he have acted as he did? Rows of boys bent to their desks to prepare their notes for their deathless speech.

If that sounds like something out of a modern Gilbert and Sullivan opera, then the alternatives were not much better. The subjects included young men reduced to fight in the gladiator schools to pay for their father's funerals, a poor man whose bees collect pollen in a rich neighbour's garden and are killed

**'A man does not sin by commission only but often by omission!'**

Wax tablets joined together and a stylus used for writing on the wax. The holding end of the stylus could be used for erasing mistakes and smoothing out the corrected area of the wax.

Perhaps one of the most famous of all the pictures recovered from Pompeii. This young lawyer and his wife have an astonishingly modern and life-like appearance. We know his name, Terentius Neo. Like most of their friends and neighbours they died in the great eruption of Vesuvius.

when the rich man poisons the flowers, noble maidens sold to brothels, more noble maidens who have been dishonoured and are allowed to choose between marriage with or punishment of their dishonourer, and wicked stepmothers. In one relatively simple plot, several young men on their way from Rome to Ostia saw some fishermen about to haul in their nets. They took a youthful gamble and bought the catch in advance for ready money. But when the nets were pulled in they contained no fish – only a basket of gold. Needless to say, both sides claimed the treasure. What happened next?

Unfortunately there were enough proud fathers only too keen to push their sons through school. Some, like the father of Horace, made great sacrifices to give their sons the very best education. Others were less discriminating but no less ambitious, as Juvenal points out:

> 'Nowadays, when autumn is ending, a father will rouse his drowsy son soon after midnight. "Wake up, boy!" he'll bawl, "Get out your notebooks! Scribble away, son, mug up your cases, study those red-letter legal tomes! If the army's your choice, put in for the vinestaff at once (the centurion's badge of office), make sure your commander-in-chief takes note of your crewcut, your hairy nostrils, those broad shoulders; destroy some Moroccan encampments or forts on the Scottish border . . .'

If the lad was too nervous for the army, then trade was the answer. Petronius portrayed another father who saw a straight choice between law and trade:

> 'I've just bought the boy some law books as I want him to pick up some legal training for home use. There's a living in that sort of thing. If he objects, I've decided that he'll learn a trade – barber, auctioneer, or at least a barrister – something he can't lose till he dies. Well, yesterday I gave it to him straight. "Believe me, my lad, any studying you do will be for your own good . . . An education is an investment and a proper profession never goes dead on you."'

Below: Cicero was a statesman, a scholar, a lawyer and a writer who did his best to defend Republican principles. Perhaps the greatest tribute paid to Cicero came from Julius Caesar who said of him: 'It is better to have extended the frontiers of the mind than to have pushed back the boundaries of Empire.' An apt compliment from Caesar.

A relief from a sarcophagus which shows various stages in the upbringing of a child. The section of the relief we show here illustrates the Roman acceptance of paternity by the father – only when the father had seen the baby and lifted it in his arms was the child accepted into the family.

This section also shows a later stage – training in the handling of a chariot.

Quintilian had plenty of encouragement for the ambitious father – educationalists always do! He believed that every boy was capable of intelligent work but that it was important for the child's nurse to speak correctly and have a good character – for the impression she made on the boy would be as indelible as a wool dye. It was equally important that both parents should be well-educated so that they could help their son in his studies. As for teachers, they should push the lazy, encourage honest imitation and put a brake on the precocious. Holidays helped the young to keep lively and freshened their minds.

According to Juvenal, the teachers themselves lived a hard and unrewarding life:

> 'What schoolmaster, even the most successful, commands a proper return for his labours? Yet even this little, however trifling . . . is further whittled away when the pupil's unfeeling attendant, and the cashier, have each taken their cut. Better give in, then: bargain, be beaten down for a lower fee, like a hawker peddling blankets and winter rugs – so long as you get *some* recompense for presiding, before it's light, in a hell-hole any blacksmith or wool-carder would refuse to train apprentices in; so long as you get *some* return for enduring the stink of all those guttering lanterns – one to each pupil, so that every Virgil and Horace is grimed with lampblack from cover to cover . . . and when the school year's ended, you'll get as much as a jockey makes from a single race.'

(That put the teacher, the lawyer and the poet all in the same boat; none of them earned in a year as much as a charioteer earned in one race! No doubt they met together at times and bewailed their fate.)

Apart from tax relief for teachers, the State did give a certain amount of encouragement to education. Caesar gave Roman citizenship to Greek teachers and Vespasian gave salaries to teachers of rhetoric in Rome. Trajan provided free education for many of the poorer citizens of Rome and Pliny, in his capacity as a private citizen, offered to put up money to help parents found a local school when he was a provincial governor. There were undoubtedly many more such private and public philanthropists.

Centres of higher education grew up round individual professors rather than definite universities. Various emperors gave encouragement to centres at Rome, Athens, Alexandria, Carthage, Antioch, Ephesus, Beirut, Trier, Lyons, Rheims, Vienna and Besancon, to name a few. In Athens, competition between professors led to gangs of their students seizing on new arrivals as soon as they landed and virtually forcing them to attend their own lectures! Most of these professors were concerned with the liberal arts; those who attempted to teach such technical subjects as music, medicine or architecture had always to vouch that they involved a wide knowledge of liberal studies as well. The effect of this wide spread of learning was, as Juvenal put it, that:

> 'Today the whole world has its Graeco-Roman culture. Smart Gaulish professors are training the lawyers of Britain. Even in the furthest north there's talk of setting up a Rhetorical Faculty.'

*'Parents demand quite impossible standards from any master: his grammar must be above cavil; history, literature, he must have all the authorities pat at his fingertips. They'll waylay him en route for the public baths and expect him to answer their questions straight off the cuff.'*

Clearly it was important for the students to have books – Greek texts and Latin poets. Books were in two forms. The earlier form was on a papyrus roll. The pith of the papyrus was cut into strips and two layers of these strips were laid across each other at right angles and glued together to form a sheet of 'paper'. Several sheets were then glued together to form a roll. This was wound round a stick, which was often ornamented with metal bosses at either end. This 'volumen' gives us our word 'volume'. The writing was usually at right angles to the length of the roll and the punctuation was minimal; often

'Wisdom does not lie in books. Wisdom publishes not words but truths. . . . There is nothing small or cramped about wisdom.'

## Local Education

*'I was visiting my native town a short time ago when the young son of a fellow citizen came to pay his respects to me. "Do you go to school?" I asked. "Yes," he replied. "Where?" "In Mediolanum (Milan)." "Why not here?" To this the boy's father (who had brought him and was standing by) replied: "Because we have no teachers here." "Why not? Surely it is a matter of great importance to you fathers (and luckily there were several fathers listening) that your children should study here on the spot? Where can they live more happily than in their native place? Where can they be brought up more strictly than under their parent's eye or with what less expense than at home? If you put your money together, what would it cost you to engage teachers? And you could add to their salaries what you now spend on lodgings, travelling expenses and all the things which cost money away from home – and that means everything. Now, as I have not yet any children of my own, I am prepared to contribute a third of whatever sum you decide to collect, as a present for our town such as I might give to a daughter or my mother . . . I hope that you will introduce teachers of repute so that nearby towns will seek education here, and, instead of sending your children elsewhere as you do today, you will see other children flocking here to you.'*

*(Pliny)*

there was virtually no space between the words, only the occasional dot to help the reader. These rolls were stored on shelves, with one embossed end sticking out, ready to be taken down.

The volumen were hard to read, as you had to unroll them to the right point to find your place. The form of book that became increasingly popular was much more like our modern book. This was written on vellum or parchment and was known as a 'codex'. In the making of vellum, the skins were thoroughly washed and then rubbed with pumice and chalk and sewn together in folded sheets; they were usually given a cover of parchment. The remarkably permanent ink was made of soot and glue.

For reproduction, the books were copied by slaves from dictation or direct from another copy. Publishers generally paid a set fee for a book of letters or poems or a speech and then sold copies in their own shop. The author received no subsequent royalty and, unless he had a rich patron prepared to pay a high sum for the reproduction of his work, he probably got very little money at all. Cicero's friend Atticus, to whom he wrote a great many letters, was also his publisher. Many young authors never had a publisher but got their own slaves to make copies of their work and sold the copies directly to friends – if they could. In the shops, books were very often sold hanging from pillars.

'A white-haired old man entered the gallery. His face was lined and seemed to have in it a promise of something impressive. But his clothes were shabby and this made it clear that he belonged to the class of intellectuals so hated generally by the rich.'

Books were precious possessions and libraries were slowly built up. There was also a good trade in second-hand books, because of the rarity of new ones. There were some public libraries, with shelves and readers' tables, which were sometimes built out of city funds but were often the gift of a wealthy man or even the emperor himself. Stealing books from public libraries was a common problem. Private owners were equally worried about losing the books they lent. One nice touch in the public libraries was to have statues of literary figures with boxes of their books at their feet. Because of the cheapness of slave labour books were not, in fact, prohibitively expensive: Martial's first book of epigrams cost about eight sesterces in a cheap edition and about two or three times that amount in a more elegant edition. There were special praefects in charge of the libraries to censor the books.

Books of poetry were among the most popular. Poetry was important to the study and appreciation of eloquence and the amount of poetry read by students probably had a considerable effect on their patterns of speech and their style of oratory. Sometimes the teachers themselves might be poets. Many of the poets began young. Catullus and Ovid were both writing poetry before they received their 'toga virilis'. Lucan and Propertius began only shortly afterwards. Martial later discovered that some of his schoolboy poems were being sold in the shops. Augustus, Tiberius and Nero were all keen on poetry (Nero mostly on his own poetry) and the Augustan period became known as the Silver Age of poetry. Both Virgil and Horace benefited from the patronage of Augustus' confidant and adviser, Maecenas, and Martial, much later, constantly bewailed the fact that he had not got a Maecenas to befriend him.

But the lively interest of the intelligent citizen was not satisfied merely by books. Poetry – and many other forms of writing – were considered, quite rightly, to be at their best at public readings. Unfortunately, the average Roman's training led him into some deplorable histrionics. Readings in the street must have been generally disastrous. There was always a crowd to encourage any kind of distraction and the most melodramatic styles of declamation were probably the most applauded. The better-off hired 'auditoria' for public readings and Hadrian built the Athenaeum specifically for recitations.

Horace described the usual method of delivery:

'He rages like a bear, who managed to break the bars of his cage; the savage reciter puts the learned and unlearned to flight; when he has caught a man, he holds him fast and puts him to death with his reading, like a leech which will not let go the skin until it has sucked its fill of blood.'

Seneca suffered the reciter at a private gathering:

'He brings an enormous historical work, written very small, tightly folded

*A circular bookcase: 'Unless you provide me with choice books I will let in moths and savage bookworms.'*

*(Gift tag)*

An eighteenth-century artist's impression of the Colosseum in Rome. The artist, Giambattista Piranesi, was an Italian draughtsman and etcher whose prints of the buildings of classical Rome did a great deal to further the growth of interest in archaeology. Piranesi was noted for the accuracy of his interpretations of the famous Roman buildings.

A penny for your thoughts! But in Roman times there was no charge. These public lavatories clearly provide an excellent meeting place for the exchange of gossip and ideas among citizens and writers. Although we may not fully appreciate the companionship of such a place, Roman cities did at least have good sewage systems.

together; after he has read a considerable part of it, he says, "I will stop now, if you like." Immediately there is a shout of "Read! read!" from his hearers, who would really like to see him struck dumb on the spot.'

But Pliny was delighted by the fine crop of young poets that the new year had produced and clearly enjoyed listening to almost any recitation, although he had his own problems when listening to friends in private:

'I don't know what I am to do myself while he is reading, whether I am to sit still and silent like a mere spectator or do as some people and accompany his words with lips, eye and gesture.'

But Pliny's greatest problem was when his slave reader Encolpius got a sore throat from the dust and began spitting blood. Since his ability to read to Pliny was apparently his only recommendation, it was clearly a very serious situation both for Pliny and for Encolpius! The elder Pliny – the uncle of the letter writer – enjoyed being read to in his bath. Others gave readings in the public baths, as Horace reports:

'There are numerous people who read their work in the public square, or in the baths (a lovely resonance is obtained from the enclosed space).'

---

## Friendship

'Certainly you should discuss everything with a friend; but, before you do so, discuss in your mind the man himself. After friendship is formed you must trust, but before that you must judge. Those people who, contrary to Theophrastus' advice, judge a man after they have made him their friend instead of the other way around, certainly put the cart before the horse. Think for a long time whether or not you should admit a given person to your friendship. But when you have decided to do so, welcome him heart and soul, and speak as unreservedly with him as you would with yourself.'

(Seneca)

---

'Young men of Rome, I advise you to learn the arts of the pleader not so much for the sake of some poor wretch at the bar but because women are conquered as much as the people of the Senate by eloquent words.'

Besides public readings – given, it would seem, more for the benefit of the reader than the public – there were also poetry competitions. Nero started these primarily to give himself a platform for public recognition of his work. It was necessary that he emerged the victor in those competitions in which he participated. In other competitions, members of the audience were quite openly paid – with a decent meal, if not money – to shout enthusiastically and applaud their patron, just as they were paid to do so at public recitations in the street. The competition that Domitian initiated in AD 86 was known as the Capitoline 'agon' and occurred every four years.

Some poets made a considerable amount of money. Augustus was a generous patron and we know that Virgil was well-paid for the *Aeneid*. One way to win a reward for a poem was to dedicate it to the emperor. But the emperor could get tired of this after a while. There was a Greek, called Macrobius, who repeatedly tried to thrust flattering lines into Augustus' hands without receiving the reward for which he was hoping. One day, Augustus anticipated the Greek's offering and himself wrote down a few lines of verse which he gave to the poet. Macrobius read them over with great admiration and at once handed the emperor a few denarii, protesting that it was all he could afford. His quick response won him a gift of 100,000 sesterces from Augustus!

Juvenal was less impressed by the generosity of patrons:

'Your private patron, for whom you forsook the book-lined haunts of Apollo and the Muses, knows every dodge to avoid shelling out on you. Why, he's a poet himself, remember, and in a thousand years – *he* thinks – there's been no-one but Homer to touch him. If the sweet itch for renown stirs *you* to give a recital, he'll fix you up with some peeling dump of a hall in the suburbs, its doors all barred and bolted like the gates of a city under siege. He'll lend you a claque of freedmen and other hangers-on to sit at the end of each row, distribute the applause; but none of these noble patrons will underwrite the outlay on hiring seats and benches, the upper tiers and the framework of beams that supports them, the cushioned front-row chairs that have to be returned, double-quick, when the performance is over.'

Martial had a whole range of patrons, as we can tell from the variety of dedications for his poems, but he had a rival in the form of Statius, a poet with much more dignity but who nonetheless required patrons to pay his way. The two poets may well have attended the same dinner parties and vied for favour with their works. Martial was not always grateful for largesse. When Lupus gave him a suburban farm, Martial complained that it was too small: a cucumber could not lie straight in it, an ant could eat it in a single day, a mole could easily plough it up, the entire crop could fit into a swallow's nest – and Priapus, even without his member, could not find space to stand!

But even Martial had his moments of victory:

'A certain fellow, dearest Julius, is bursting with envy; because Rome reads me, he is bursting with envy. He is bursting with envy because in every throng I am always pointed out with the finger, he is bursting with envy. He is bursting with envy because each Caesar gave me the right of a father of three sons, he is bursting with envy. He is bursting with envy because I have a suburban farm and a small house in town, he is bursting with envy. He is bursting with envy because I am delightful to my friends, because I am often a guest, he is bursting with envy. He is bursting with envy because I am loved and my works approved. Let anyone, whoever he is, who is bursting with envy, burst!'

He could pride himself, also, on the knowledge that his reputation had spread abroad:

''Tis not city idleness alone that delights in my Muse, nor do I give these epigrams to vacant ears, but my book, amid Gettic frosts, beside martial standards, is thumbed by the hardy centurion, and Britain is said to hum my verses.'

But there were disadvantages to being well-known, both as a poet and as a man with a wealthy patron, as Horace found when out for a walk one morning:

'I happened to be strolling down Sacred Way, trying out some piece of nonsense as I often do and completely absorbed in it, when suddenly a fellow whom I knew only by name dashed up and seized me by the hand. "My dear chap," he said, "how are things?" "Quite nicely at the moment thanks," I said. "Well, all the best!" He remained in pursuit, so I nipped in quickly: "Was there something else?" "Yes," he said. "You should get to know me. I'm an intellectual." "Good for you!" I said.

The fellow admitted that he had nothing else to do and intended to accompany Horace wherever he went. It turned out that what he wanted was an introduction to the patron Maecenas. Horace invented every excuse to get away – a sick friend he had to visit at the other end of town – but it was no

*When asked which of the great speeches of the Greek orator Demosthenes he considered the best, Cicero replied: 'The longest one.'*

*'Be brief,' said Horace. 'More ought to be scratched out than left in.'*

*'He who is not glutted with the reading of a hundred epigrams is not glutted, Caecilianus, with any amount of badness.'*

The head of a young man. He exemplifies many of the idealized Roman virtues – firmness, a certain grave sobriety and that look of the man born to the disciplines of a great military empire. He is, at any rate, a Roman as Roman citizens might wish to be portrayed. Note the neatness of his hair-style and his carefully trimmed and curled beard.

*'Do not mate dogs when they are old for age brings disease and weakness to the litter.'*

good and Horace was far too mild-mannered to tell him to get lost. He was saved in the end only when some officials came to drag the fellow off to a court case he had missed in his determination to remain with Horace.

Martial had a similar problem:

'That no man willingly meets you, that, wherever you arrive, there is flight and vast solitude around you, Ligurinus, do you want to know what is the matter? You are too much of a poet. This is a fault passing dangerous. No tigress aroused by the robbery of her cubs, no viper scorched by tropic suns, nor deadly scorpion is so dreaded. For who, I ask you, would endure such trials? You read to me while I am standing, and read to me while I am sitting; while I am running you read to me, and read to me while I am shitting. I fly to the warm baths; you buzz in my ear; I make for the swimming baths: I am not allowed to swim; I haste to dinner: you detain me as I go; I reach the table: you rout me while I am eating. Wearied out I sleep: you rouse me as I lie. Do you want to appreciate the evil you cause? Though you are a man just, upright and harmless, you are a terror.'

But in the end, Martial at least had the wit to turn on his own work:

'He who is not glutted with the reading of a hundred epigrams is not glutted, Caecilianus, with any amount of badness.'

Roman society was delighted to see itself mirrored in the epigrams of Martial and in the satires of Horace and Juvenal. But they also read eagerly the lyric poetry of Catullus and the elegaic poems of Ovid, Propertius and Tibullus. Catullus did manage to inject some social criticism into his poems but he was best known for the poems he wrote about his love for Lesbia, whose unfaithfulness put him through hell:

'I hate, yet love: you ask how this may be.
Who knows? I feel its truth and agony.'

Another poem, that he wrote as a lament for the death of Lesbia's pet sparrow, was frequently imitated by other Roman poets. Catullus was not alone in his passionate or frustrated love. Gallus, who was born shortly after him, constantly complains at the fickleness of his mistress. Tibullus enjoyed

*'She is protected the best, whose inclinations are chaste. She who keeps pure since she must might just as well be impure.'*

A tavern in Pompeii. These taverns were often just rooms rented from large houses. They did not normally keep large stocks of wine on the premises but drew their supplies from the farms outside the town.

his passion for Delia and the countryside. Propertius preferred the town and Cynthia. Ovid had his Corinna, a composite figure of erotic womanhood.

Quintilian thought that Ovid was in love with his own genius, that Catullus was too bitter, that Tibullus was too smooth and that Julius Caesar should have concentrated on oratory rather than history. Quintilian himself was

The Romans were particularly partial to this type of mosaic flooring. The design motif consists of a fanciful array of sprigs, bowls and birds. The Romans liked a stylized portrayal of familiar everyday objects.

## Lesbia's Kisses

'My Lesbia, let us live and love
And not care tuppence for old men
Who sermonise and disapprove.
Suns when they sink can rise again,
But we, when our brief light has
                    shone,
Must sleep the long night on and
                    on.
Kiss me: a thousand kisses, then
A hundred more, and now a second

Thousand and hundred, and now
                    still
Hundreds and thousands more, until
The thousand thousands can't be
                    reckoned
And we've lost track of the amount
And nobody can work us ill
With the evil eye by keeping count.'

(Catullus)

widely read during Vespasian's reign. But history was always a popular subject – it appealed to the Roman sense of destiny. Caesar wrote some of the best, even though it reads suspiciously like propaganda. Sadly, much of his work has probably been lost. Most subsequent historians either had a point to make or were cramped by the fear of retribution. Livy won fame in his own day, writing during the reign of Augustus, but had to be careful about what he

## Lesbia's Sparrow

'O Venus and you Cupids, shed
A tear, and all in man that's moved
By beauty, mourn. Her sparrow's
                    dead,
My darling's darling, whom she
                    loved
More than she loves her own sweet
                    eyes,
Her honey of a bird. It knew
Its mistress as babes recognise
Their mothers, and it never flew
Out of her lap, but all day long,
Hopping and flitting to and fro,
Piped to her private ear its song.
Nevertheless, now it must go

Down the dark road from which they
                    say
No one returns. Curse you, you
                    spiteful
Swooping hawks of death who prey
On all things that make life
                    delightful! –
That was a pretty bird you took.
Bad deed! Poor little bird – by
                    dying
See what you've done! Her sweet
                    eyes look
All puffed and rosy-red with
                    crying.'

(Catullus)

*'Only the girls are fair game, cheat these little cheats, for most of them haven't a scruple.'*

said, in case he offended the emperor. Lucan began as Nero's protégé but made the mistake of writing a historical epic, the *Pharsalia*, about the struggle between Caesar and Pompey, in which he sided with Pompey as the champion of the Republic. He was ordered to cut open his own veins. Writing at the end of the century, Tacitus was able to get away with the complaint that Rome had fallen on bad times. He pulls no punches in his attack on Tiberius, long since safely dead. He also wrote a dazzling eulogy of his relative Agricola, the governor of Britain, and he wrote one of the rare original studies of a barbarian people in *Germania*. Suetonius was far enough removed from the events of the *First Twelve Caesars* to write up all the scandal of their private lives and his details make some of the best reading of all Roman history.

But Juvenal did not think there was much future in writing history:

'What about writers of history? Do all their labours bring them a bigger return, or merely consume more midnight oil? With unrestricted licence they pile up their thousand pages – and an enormous stationery bill: the vast extent of the theme, plus their professional conscience, makes this inevitable. But what will the harvest yield, what fruit will all your grubbing bring you? Does any historian pull down a news-reader's wage? Oh they're an idle lot, though, too fond of their shady deck chairs.'

The younger Pliny chose letter-writing instead and became well-known for the letters published in his lifetime on subjects as various as murder, floods, ghosts, volcanoes, illness, trials, education, public baths, books, friendship and his villas. His letters to Trajan were not published until after his death. Pliny was delighted at the popularity of his work, although he might have preferred to be known as a poet:

'I didn't think there were any booksellers in Lugdunum (Lyons), so I was all the more pleased to learn from your letter that my efforts are being sold.'

A more rare form of literary entertainment was the fable, as produced by Phaedrus in the time of Tiberius and Caligula. Horace had produced some fables but not as a separate book. Not surprisingly, since Phaedrus had begun life in Rome as a Thracian slave, his fables are full of the injustice of life and he daringly undermined the social and political order. In the tale of the jackdaw who dressed in peacock's feathers, he was even brave enough to attack Tiberius' favourite Sejanus and survived the ensuing lawsuit.

*'My verse is light and tender, as Catullus long ago,*
*'But what care I for poets past, when I my Pliny know?*
*'Outside the courts in mutual love and song he makes his name;*
*'You lovers and you statesmen, to Pliny yield your fame!'*

---

## The Caesars of Suetonius

*The historian Suetonius gave intimate details of the private lives of the first twelve 'Caesars', including Julius Caesar himself. He was born the year after Nero's suicide. This is how he described the first six of those Caesars, from Julius Caesar to Nero:*

*Julius Caesar:* Tall with black eyes and close-shaven; a womaniser but sensitive about his baldness.

*Augustus:* Handsome with curly yellow hair and a prominent Roman nose; he suffered from the cold and wore platform shoes.

*Tiberius:* Strongly built, with large eyes and long hair at the back of his neck; left-handed.

*Caligula:* Pale, hollow-eyed and ugly.

*Claudius:* Suffered from stammering, an uncontrollable nodding of the head and a strange guffaw; shaky on his legs but more dignified when sitting.

*Nero:* A thick neck and a paunch; blue-grey eyes and slender legs.

*A book of Cicero's works in parchment: 'If this parchment shall be your travelling companion, imagine you are taking a long journey with Cicero.'*

*(Gift tag)*

Dionysus and a panther from the House of Dionysus at Delos. Animals figured prominently in Roman poetry and literature. This is a particularly fine and dramatic representation of the wine god.

The wolf and the lion are the dominating predators and the ass gets used to repeated changes of ownership. The frogs complain about the lazy King Log and learn to leave well alone when they are given in his place the terrible King Water Snake. But Phaedrus felt that he was not appreciated: the barnyard fowl finds a pearl in a dung heap and declares that if only it had been found by someone who appreciated its beauty it would have been saved long ago but unfortunately it is only he that has found it and he prefers his food and so neither of them does the other any good. In the prologue to his book, Phaedrus acknowledges his debt to the master of fables:

'Matter which first old Aesop did rehearse
Hath Phaedrus polished in iambic verse.
Two boons my book hath: it can laughter raise
And give sage counsel in life's wildering maze.
Howbeit, should one think to criticise,
Since beasts, nay even trees, here sermonise,
Let him remember that in fables we
Divert ourselves with unreality.'

Prose fiction was rarer still. The two outstanding examples were the *Satyricon* of Petronius, written in the middle of the first century AD, and *The Golden Ass* of Apuleius, written in the middle of the second century AD. *The Golden Ass* tells the story of a young man who is turned into an ass and encounters some bizarre and often bawdy adventures. The style is swift and full of fun. The hero of the *Satyricon* has some equally odd experiences and one or two energetic sexual orgies. The story also contains Trimalchio's famous feast. But the events are broken up by bits of poetry and asides on a whole variety of subjects. Tacitus wrote a brief obituary on Petronius:

'He spent his days sleeping, his nights working and enjoying himself. Others achieve fame by energy, Petronius by laziness. Yet he was not, like others who waste their resources, regarded as dissipated or extravagant, but as a refined voluptuary . . .'

He became a favourite of Nero because of his apparently debauched tastes but was forced to commit suicide in AD 66 after being falsely charged by a jealous rival. He died in style. Having alternately opened and bandaged his veins to weaken himself slowly, he held a reception for his friends and finally dozed off into total oblivion in the middle of the dinner party, so that his death might appear accidental.

Scientific writing was various and unreliable but the encyclopaedists who gathered together volumes of assorted information were looked to as the prime source of general knowledge. We have already met some of the writers on medicine, farming, architecture and construction. Proper scientific studies were not much to the Roman taste but the elder Pliny was read for the variety of information his conscientious works contained. His observations are an odd mixture: he praises the nightingale's song, he discusses the favourite wines of the emperor Augustus, he describes the military officer who took thousands of pounds weight of silver plate with him on campaign against the barbarians, he explains that soap made from tallow and ashes was originally produced to redden hair and he concludes that the ostrich puts its head in the sand to hide.

He also discussed astronomy. Pliny believed there were about 1600 stars, made of fire and filled with air. Most people, on the other hand, believed that they were the souls of the departed. The moon and the constellations were thought to affect man's life and body; it was therefore thought to be a good idea to blood-let when the waxing moon had caused the blood to increase and the muscles to swell. Some Greeks had already hinted at a heliocentric view of the universe. (1500 years later, Copernicus caused an uproar when he published his theory based on ancient authority and his own observations.) Pliny himself spoke out confidently for a spherical rather than a flat earth. He quoted as proof the gradual appearance of a ship over the horizon. He added:

> 'Science and the opinion of the mob are in direct opposition. According to the former the whole sphere of the earth is inhabited by men whose feet point towards each other while all have the heavens above their heads. But the mob ask how men on the antipodes do not fall off; as though that did not present the opposite query, why they should not wonder at our not falling off. Usually, however, the crowd objects if one urges that water also tends to be spherical. Yet nothing is more obvious, since hanging drops always form little spheres.'

Another 'scientist' was Lucretius, who wrote in the first century BC. He had some very advanced views about the creation of the Universe, which he said had been achieved by the interaction of millions upon millions of tiny atoms. He also believed in the survival of the fittest: having described all manner of monsters and prodigies that died out because they could not feed or propagate, he concluded that:

> 'Whatever animals now feed on the breath of life, either craft or courage or speed has preserved their kind from the beginning of their being.'

The theories of Lucretius were based more on philosophy than on scientific study and philosophy was certainly more popular among the Romans than science. Although they believed themselves to be supremely fit, their survival, they knew, was also in the hands of the gods. Religion and philosophy combined to provide them with a moral attitude to life which was much more immediate to their particular problems than theoretical science.

*A book of Lucan's poems: 'Some are there that say I am no poet: but the bookseller that sells me thinks I am.'*

*(Gift tag)*

*A poem on the uses of cold water, which Martial thinks is only fit to be thrown away: 'These sheets, that speak to you of fountains and of the names of rivers, themselves will better swim in the waters they tell of.'*

*(Gift tag)*

# Gods and philosophers

A mosaic uncovered at Cirencester, known as Corinium in Roman times. The figure depicts Autumn with vine leaves in the hair. The Romans had many agricultural 'divinities' and these were frequently portrayed in mosaics.

**J**uvenal had little patience with religion:

'Can't you see how naive and comic a figure you cut these days, with your adamant belief that a man should stick to his word, that there's really something in all this religious guff, the temples, the mess of blood? That was how primitive man lived long ago.'

But even he could not shrug off the underlying Roman dependence on the goodwill of the gods:

'If you want my advice, let the gods themselves determine what's most appropriate for mankind and what best suits our various circumstances. They'll give us the things we need, not those we want; a man is dearer to them than he is to himself.'

Ovid took the practical line that since it was useful to believe that there were gods, people should continue to take incense and wine to their ancient shrines.

We have already met the family gods in the home – the influential spirits that represented unseen forces in everything around the Roman. There were the Lares, the spirits of the homeland, in the form of dancing boys; the Penates, who guarded the store-cupboard; and Vesta, who guarded the home fireplace. They stood together in the family shrine, the 'Lararium', at which prayers were said each day and small offerings were made. Proper respect for these spirits, or forces, and for the genius of their own ancestors ensured success for family ventures.

Major ventures required the co-operation of major gods. Some of these would also have a place in the home, in the form of little bronze figures. They also had their own temples, to which people went to offer up prayers and make sacrifices. Chief among these gods was Jupiter, who was the equivalent of the Greek Zeus. Juno was the senior goddess. There were Mars, the god of war and agriculture; Mercury, the messenger of the gods and the god of commerce; Neptune, the god of the sea; Bacchus, the god of wine; Apollo, the Greek sun-god, and many others. On the female side, there were Ceres, the goddess of corn; Venus, the goddess of love; Juno Lucino, the goddess of childbirth; Minerva, the goddess of wisdom; and Diana, the moon-goddess and goddess of hunting. There was also a State version of Vesta, who guarded the symbolic hearth of Rome and was attended by the Vestal Virgins.

There were innumerable temples to these and other gods throughout the towns and cities of the empire. Some were quite simple, many were richly decorated and stuffed with treasure presented by grateful citizens. Temples were built as thank offerings by the wealthy and as a service to the State or town by those who had received high public office. There were no regular services within the temples. They were places for the priests to carry out their official duties and sacrifices and for citizens to go quietly to pray. Sacrifices of bulls, pigs and sheep were usually made outside the temple. If a citizen wished to make a private sacrifice, he took his bull along to the priests who performed the task for him, selecting the best day and examining the entrails to make

*'Our whole universe is no more than a semblance of reality, perhaps a deceptive semblance, perhaps one without substance altogether.'*

A great deal can be discovered about Roman life from the coins that have survived in large quantities.

Here we have a temple representation and a triumphal arch.

sure that everything was favourable and that the sacrifice had been accepted.

There was clearly a certain amount of trial and error as to which god you adopted as your special protector. Although each god had his or her relevant field of interest, the tendency was to stick with the god who had a proven track record of success in your particular life. If things didn't seem to be turning out right, then you started making sacrifices to someone else. It was a highly practical attitude but nonetheless deeply felt.

Many positions in the priesthood were attached to public office and they could be held by a magistrate. The senior body of priests was the College of Pontiffs. There were sixteen at the time of Julius Caesar and their chief was the Pontifex Maximus. From the time of Augustus, the emperor was always Pontifex Maximus, a post which gave him considerable extra powers. Then there were 'flamens' and female 'flamens' to attend particular gods and goddesses. Best known were the Vestal Virgins, girls chosen between the ages of six and ten from the best families who were elected by the Pontifex Maximus and were allowed to retire at the age of forty. There were normally six Vestal Virgins and a new one was elected every five years. Scandals involving the loss of their virginity were quite frequent.

In theory, any magistrate or private citizen could perform a sacrifice but there were 'augurs' to help them in interpreting omens such as the flight of particular birds or the sound of thunder. There were also oracles, which could be appealed to for advice. The most famous of these, the Sybilline Oracles, were a collection of ancient cryptic writings which were only consulted in times of State emergency. It was said that when the Sybil had originally offered them to one of the early Etruscan kings there had been nine books. But the price she asked was too high and the king turned them down. She came back and offered him six books for the same price and again he turned her away. When she returned with only three books, still for the same price, he was so intrigued that he bought them but none of the three outlived the Romans. In one way or another they all disappeared.

When new towns were founded, one of the first important duties of the

*'Look round: You see a little supper room.*
*'But from my window, lo! great Caesar's tomb!*
*'And the great dead themselves, with jovial breath*
*'Bid you be merry and remember death.'*

More temples – a front view showing a sacrificial altar and a side view. Many of the reliefs on these coins are roughly executed – which seems something of a paradox when compared with the exquisitely detailed work on the various victory columns.

This figure represents the Lares, gods revered by the Romans as the spirits of their ancestors. Another category of household gods were the Penates, paternal gods, who ensured abundance.

This Roman bronze hand had a combined magical, religious and medical significance. The cult of Mithra is symbolised by the pine cone and the creatures were used in various potions.

citizens was to choose a protector for the town and erect a temple to him. Then they had to elect the priests. Priests from Rome or other major cities would travel all over the empire advising on duties and procedures in new temples. Their experience and their teaching were important elements in the Romanisation of distant provinces.

Festivals were an essential part of religious practice and many of the public games originated as religious celebrations and still began with processions of priests. The names that the games retained recalled their origins: there were, for example, the Ludi Ceriales, the games in honour of Ceres in April; there were the Ludi Florales in honour of Flora at the beginning of May; the Ludi Apollinares lasted several days in July; the Ludi Romani were held in honour of Jupiter. The Saturnalia and the Lupercalia were special festivals with their roots in primitive rites. The Lupercalia traditionally commemorated the she-wolf who had suckled Romulus and Remus: two half-naked youths ran round the perimeter of the original Palatine hill settlement carrying strips of goatskin with which they beat girls who came crowding round excitedly for punishment. Romulus was also honoured in the Quirinalia festival.

Although the festivals produced plenty of drama, most other facets of Roman religion offered very little spiritual – or sensual – uplift. Various cults, offering new gods, became increasingly popular. One of these cults was typically Roman and introduced no procedures outside the average Roman's experience. This was the imperial cult – the transformation of the emperor into a god. Eastern civilisations had commonly worshipped their kings as gods and the retention of this extra authority helped Roman emperors in their control of the Eastern provinces. But Augustus was careful. He allowed worship of his imperial 'genius' – the divine life-force within him, similar to the genius of family ancestors – outside Italy only, knowing full well that Romans with Republican sympathies would not stand for it in Rome itself. But Caligula declared himself to be a god in his own lifetime and soon it became common for temples to be raised to each emperor in turn. The unpretentious Vespasian was said to have died with the words:

'Oh dear, I think I'm becoming a god.'

Other cults also came from the east and brought with them colour, mystery and an intensity of experience that swept many Romans off their feet. Roman patricians were deeply resentful at first and tried to have the cults banned but they could not hold them down for long. The cult of the Asian fertility goddess, Cybele, was one of the more extreme: there were rumours of orgies, whippings and the use of knives to slash the bodies of the worshippers. The cult of Isis, the mother goddess of the Egyptians, also began in a flourish of sensuality and provided a convenient cover for prostitution in its initiation rites and the symbolic revival of Osiris, the husband of Isis. The cult remained extremely popular with Roman women and in time moderated some of its earlier excesses and became almost respectable. However, Isis was still the goddess of the earth and of corn and required fertility rites which gave plenty of opportunity for young men and women to meet in provocative circumstances. In any case, the rituals and the emotional drama gave many women much greater satisfaction than the increasingly 'like it or leave it' approach to their traditional gods.

Mithraism became even more widespread, particularly in the army, although it was on the decline by about AD 300 perhaps because of lack of support from the emperor. The cult of Mithra came from Persia and India. Life was seen as a struggle between good and evil. Mithra himself is usually portrayed slaying a bull: the blood from the sacrifice brought new life into the

# Gods and philosophers

world. Like Christianity, Mithraism offered immortality to the soul and a belief in heaven and the resurrection, and emphasised brotherly love, mutual help and humility. No women were allowed to join the cult. In certain other ways the general acceptance of Mithraism paved the way for Christianity.

The Romans were generally tolerant toward other religious beliefs provided the worshippers were also prepared to bow to the State gods and the emperor. The Christians refused and further angered the Romans by meeting together without permission. Pliny wrote a conscientious letter to Trajan asking how he should deal with the Christians in his province. He was confused because he had not yet come up against the problem:

> 'For the moment this is the line I have taken with all persons brought before me on the charge of being Christians. I have asked them in person if they are Christians and, if they admit it, I repeat the question a second and a third time, with a warning of the punishment awaiting them. If they persist, I order them to be led away to execution; for whatever the nature of their admission, I am convinced that their stubbornness and unshakeable obstinacy ought not to go unpunished.'

Trajan approved of the course Pliny had taken and agreed that Christians should not be hunted out; they should be punished only if the charge against them could be proved and should be let off if they repented, whatever their previous reputation. Pliny had also reported that anonymous pamphlets were being circulated containing names of supposed Christians. Trajan replied:

> 'Pamphlets circulated anonymously must play no part in any accusation. They create the worst sort of precedent and are quite out of keeping with the spirit of our age.'

Although followers of Mithra and Christ were confident of an afterlife, the average Roman was less precise on the subject: he believed that his spirit was reabsorbed into the universal life force. Outstanding personalities shone out as stars. Ordinary people feared the punishment of a dark underworld. There are many examples of tombs filled with materials on which the dead were supposed to sustain themselves – food, clothes and tools.

Burial followed an established ritual to appease the gods. There was a great deal of mourning so that the spirit of the dead person would be duly satisfied that he was missed. The body was then usually cremated, as an act of purification, and the ashes were put in an urn within the grave. Graves were not generally allowed in the city for reasons of health and space. They lined the roads on the way out of the city and they were also collected in special crematoria. Trimalchio felt very strongly about his monument:

> 'It's a big mistake to have nice houses just for when you're alive and not

Another representation of a Lar. Like the figure on the opposite page this household god was recovered from the Villa of Mysteries at Pompeii.

Another magical bronze hand, with symbols, each with a particular significance.

---

## Religious Processions

*'The fourth (priest) carried the model of a left hand with the fingers stretched out, which is an emblem of justice because the left hand, with its natural slowness and lack of craft or subtlety, seems more impartial than the right! . . . Next in the procession followed those deities that deigned to walk on human feet. Here was the frightening messenger of the gods of heaven, and of the gods of the dead: Anubis with a face black on one side, golden on the other, walking erect and holding his herald's wand in one hand, and in the other a green palm-branch. Behind danced a man carrying on his shoulders, seated upright, the statue of a cow, representing the goddess as the fruitful Mother of us all.'*

*(Apuleius)*

worry about the one we have to live in for much longer . . . I'll put one of my freedmen in charge of my tomb to look after it and not let people run up and shit on my monument. I'd like you to put some ships there, too, sailing under full canvas, and me sitting on a high platform in my robes of office, wearing five gold rings and pouring out a bagful of money for the people.'

For the mourners there was a feast and ritual purification to cleanse them of contamination by contact with the dead. A sow was often sacrificed to satisfy the earth goddess. Sacrifice was also made to the Lares and members of the household were sprinkled with water and had to step over fire. There followed a short period of mourning and then another feast. The birthday of the dead man was celebrated each year – the number of celebrations must have quickly added up.

Cicero and Seneca were both divided about the possibility of immortality but Pliny argued strongly against it:

'Every man's last hour brings exactly the same state of things that existed before his first hour. Souls and bodies no more have feelings and consciousness after death than they had before birth . . . All such ideas are only fit to pacify children, idle dreams of a state of mortality, which is anxious to last forever! What absurd folly to think that life can be renewed by death!'

Petronius expressed the same commonsense attitude towards fate in the *Satyricon*:

'A slave brought in a silver skeleton put together in such a way that its joints and backbone could be pulled out and twisted in all directions. After Trimalchio had flung it about on the table once or twice, its flexible joints falling into various postures, he recited:

"Man's life, alas, is but a span,

"So let us live it while we can,

"We'll be like this when dead!"'

Skeletons were common in mosaics as reminders of the shortness of Roman life, just as they were in the Middle Ages when the Black Death had taken hold of Europe. Thoughts about life and death were nothing to do with religion, however. It was philosophy that taught Romans to come to terms with life and to make the most of it. On the whole, Romans set greater store by life than Christians; they made the most of what they had, fully aware that they would die and have to face whatever came. In consequence, the two great philosophies – Epicureanism and Stoicism – were chiefly concerned with the conditions of the living.

Epicureanism has been popularly misinterpreted as a philosophy that recommends the total gratification of the senses and therefore gives unbridled licence to self-indulgence – a splendid justification for all lotus eaters. What Epicureus had said in the third century BC and what his disciple Lucretius re-affirmed in the first century BC was a little different. There was no reason to fear any god, for there was no divine plan to the accidental and haphazard arrangement of atoms that composed the world. Man was free to direct his own destiny and should rely on his own sensations for criteria of good and evil. But these sensations were not merely physical; they included the sensations of the mind and the spirit. No man, therefore, should commit any act that would cause discomfort or pain to the body or soul of someone else, for it would no longer be pleasurable. The wise man aimed at a tranquil life in a world that was, despite its faults, the best he had. Lucretius himself, who expressed lasting defiance of death, was said to have written between bouts of insanity.

**'For of old, in the belief that the souls of the dead are propitiated with human blood, they used at funerals to sacrifice captives or slaves of poor quality.'**

A reconstruction of a relief from the Ara Pietatis of Tiberius dating from the early part of the first century AD. This reconstruction shows the temple of Magna Mater. Note the Greek influence. Tiberius was particularly partial to the Hellenistic style. He was an energetic builder and the many superb monuments and villas he erected were quite distinct from those built by his predecessor Augustus. Tiberius's taste was both individual and highly distinctive.

# Gods and philosophers

Although a family could make a sacrifice in private to their household gods, it was more common for the priests to assist with the sacrifice and to help determine the omens.

Stoicism borrowed bits and pieces from many different philosophies, including its rival, Epicureanism. It began with the philosopher Zeno at the end of the fourth century BC and claimed that the universe was a single intelligible unity pervaded by reason. Man could rise above the apparent chaos of life (and the certain chaos of the Epicureans) by living in harmony with reason and by observing the stern ethics of universal order. Reason, God and Nature were all the same thing and man was a part of the universal cycle of life. This appealed to Romans very much. They liked the idea of order; they were brought up on stern ethics; and they felt more at home in the Universe when they believed that they were linked with it. Stoicism outstripped Epicureanism in popularity and was looked on benignly by the State, which became a sort of political manifestation of universal reason and order. In fact, Zeno had originally been greatly influenced by the achievements of Alexander the Great, who himself had wanted to establish a world state.

One of the most lucid and readable exponents of Stoicism was Seneca and many of his opinions expressed in this book are from his *Letters from a Stoic*. He is refreshing partly because he borrows quite openly from the best of Epicurean philosophy. In explaining to a friend how to write about the genius of a great historical figure, he gives a light simile to show the unity of the Stoic approach:

'Give up this hope of being able to get an idea of the genius of the greatest figures by so cursory an approach. You have to examine and consider it as a whole. There is a sequence about the creative process, and a work of genius is a synthesis of its individual features from which nothing can be subtracted without disaster. I have no objection to your inspecting the components individually provided you do so without detaching them from the personality they actually belong to; a woman is not beautiful when her ankle or arm wins compliments but when her total appearance diverts admiration from the individual parts of her body.'

The enemy of reason was superstition, which played a large part in Roman life. Popular as Stoicism became among thinking people, superstition was still more universal among the common people. There were a thousand little acts and beliefs carried out every day to ensure a trouble-free existence. Even Seneca succumbed to them:

'I read, wrote or spoke some sentence or other every New Year in order to ensure good luck in the coming year.'

But Juvenal mocked the superstitions of the Roman woman:

'When she wants to go out of town, a mile even, or less, she computes a propitious time for her tables. If she rubs one corner of her eye, and it itches, she must never put ointment on it without first consulting her horoscope . . . Women of lower rank and fortune learn their futures down at the race course, from phrenologist or palmist, with much smacking of lips against evil influence.'

There they would meet:

'Armenians and Syrians who'll pry out the steaming lungs of a pigeon, predict a young lover for the lady, or a good fat inheritance from some childless millionaire. They'll probe a chicken's bosom, unravel the guts of a puppy: sometimes they even slaughter a child . . .'

But they would listen to anything if the fortune-teller had a good enough reputation:

'Nothing boosts your diviner's credit so much as a lengthy spell in the glasshouse, with fetters jangling from either wrist: no one believes in his powers unless he's dodged execution by a hair's breadth, and contrived

149

to get himself deported to some Cycladic island like Seriphos, and to escape after lengthy privations . . .'

Astrology and dreams were both considered important in determining events. In time, even the emperor had his private astrologer and would do little without consulting him. Military commanders were particularly sensitive to dreams and the physician Galen found dreams very useful in determining the right treatment for his patients. There was widespread belief in the cure of diseases by means suggested in dreams. For the best results, the patient spent the night in the temple of Aesculapius – a deep and dreamless sleep was the last thing he wanted!

The spirits of the dead appeared often in dreams – and sometimes when men were awake. But there was no room for ghosts in the world of Juvenal:

'Today not even children – except those small enough to get a free public bath – believe all that stuff about ghosts or underground rivers or black frogs croaking in the waters of the Styx, or thousands of dead men ferried across by one small skiff.'

Pliny was not so sure. He wrote to a friend:

'I should like very much to know whether you think that ghosts exist and have a form of their own and some sort of supernatural power, or whether they lack substance and reality and take shape only from our fears. I personally am encouraged to believe in their existence.'

To support his belief, he told a ghost story:

'In Athens there was a large and spacious mansion with the bad reputation of being dangerous to its occupants. At dead of night the clanking of iron and, if you listened carefully, the rattle of chains could be heard, some way off at first, and then close at hand. Then there appeared the spectre of an old man, emaciated and filthy, with a long flowing beard and hair on end, wearing fetters on his legs and shaking the chains on his wrists . . .'

Those who stayed there did not sleep for fear. They had nightmares, they became ill, they died and the house was deserted until the philosopher Athenodorus decided to face up to the ghost. He sat up at night with his books and waited. Sure enough, the ghost began to rattle. The rattling came nearer. Athenodorus went on reading. The ghost shook his chains above the philosopher's head but Athenodorus went on reading. Still the ghost shook his chains and since he seemed to mean no harm the philosopher left his book and followed him to a courtyard where he suddenly vanished. Athenodorus marked the spot. The next day, he brought the magistrates along, dug up the spot and found the bones of a man twisted round with chains. The bones were given a public burial and the house was haunted no more.

It was all one with the auguries and the studies of entrails and the lucky and unlucky days which no sensible Roman would ever consider ignoring. And it was acceptable because the Universe itself was all one. But whatever it was that influenced men for good or bad – religion, superstition or moral philosophy – Seneca had the last word:

'Our forefathers complained, we complain, and our descendants will complain, that morals are corrupt, that wickedness holds sway, that men are sinking deeper and deeper in sinfulness, that the condition of mankind is going from bad to worse. But in reality they remain where they were, and will still remain so, save for trifling movements in one direction or another; like waves carried backwards and forwards by the ebb and flow . . . Vices belong to no particular age, but to all mankind. No age has been free from guilt.'

*'It's reason that sets us apart from dumb brutes . . . but today even snakes agree better than men.'*

*'Begin each day by telling yourself: Today I shall be meeting with interference, ingratitude, insolence, disloyalty, ill-will and selfishness – all of them due to the offenders' ignorance of what is good or evil.'*

# The Roman army

The power of Rome was based on its army, one of the most efficient military machines ever organised. In the first centuries of its growth, Rome was a nation in arms: citizens left their fields and their homes to take up their weapons in defence of their country. Then a professional army was created to extend the power of Rome throughout the Mediterranean and beyond. Once the empire was established, the army turned to garrison duty along the over-stretched frontiers, and as the empire declined it became increasingly an army of foreigners and mercenaries.

The Romans valued great deeds and nothing offered greater scope for glory than a military campaign. Pliny indicated the splendour of the theme when he congratulated a fellow writer on tackling the subject of the Dacian wars, better known to us as the campaign depicted on Trajan's famous column:

Part of a magnificent bronze parade helmet found on the face of a corpse in a tomb near Nola. This bronze helmet dates from the first century AD and is now in the British Museum.

'It is an excellent idea of yours to write about the Dacian war. There is no subject that offers such scope and such a wealth of original material, no subject so poetic and almost legendary although its facts are true. You will describe new rivers set flowing over the land, new bridges built across rivers, and camps clinging to sheer precipices; you will tell of a king driven from his capital and finally to death, but courageous to the end; you will record a double triumph, the first over a nation hitherto unconquered, the other a final victory.'

Servius Tullus was responsible for the earliest military organisation of Rome, in the sixth century BC. Property-owning citizens between the ages of seventeen and forty-six were called up only when needed – usually during the summer months – and disbanded in the autumn, at the end of the campaigning season. They were organised according to their wealth, since they had to provide their own equipment. Those between forty-seven and sixty were used for garrison duty in Rome itself.

The wealthiest were the cavalry. The horse was a costly item in the days when the ox was still the main draught animal. These were the original knights, whose title later became a purely civil distinction in the social hierarchy. Next came the heavy infantry, which formed the main body of the army. These were divided into 'hastati', 'principes' and 'triarii'. The first two were the younger, fitter soldiers, armed with two javelins (one light, one heavy), a sword, a large shield and either full body army or a breastplate. The 'triarii' formed the rear rank and were armed with a long spear. They were probably the older, more mature men, who would stand firm in a crisis. There

The Arch of Titus as it is today. This great arch was the entrance to the Roman forum on the via Sacra and was built to celebrate the triumph of Titus over Judaea, which fell to the Roman legions in 70 AD. It was actually built after the death of Titus, in the reign of Domitian (81–96 AD). The reliefs on the inside of the Arch show triumphal processions. One shows the Roman soldiers carrying loot from the Temple of Jerusalem, including the seven-branched candelabrum and the silver trumpets.

were also the light infantry, the 'velites', who could only afford a light javelin, a sword and a small, round shield; they had no armour.

Changes were made in the formation of the army in the fourth century BC, under Furius Camillus. He set the army on a longer-term footing and established the rigid discipline and excellent training that enabled the Romans to emerge victorious against Epirus, Macedon and, eventually, Carthage. Much of what we know about this army comes from Polybius, a Greek hostage taken after the defeat of the Macedonian army, who later wrote a history of the war between Greece and Rome.

A typical Roman army during this first period of overseas expansion consisted of four legions. Each legion was divided into sixty centuries, which were paired into maniples: there were therefore thirty maniples per legion, with anything between 4000 and 5000 citizens in each legion as well as 300 cavalry. A large number of variously armed allies were also attached to the legion. The legions were commanded by tribunes and the army itself was commanded by one or both consuls for the year. Citizens were organised into their military centuries for civil voting purposes, as well, and voted by centuries. The number of citizens within each century varied considerably and it is quite probable that the centuries of the wealthier patrician classes contained fewer men than other centuries (a century practically never contained exactly 100 men). This gave a voting advantage to the wealthier class, out of proportion to their true numbers.

In battle, the maniples of the 'hastati' formed the first line, with a space equivalent to one maniple between each maniple. Covering these spaces, in the second row, were the maniples of the 'principes' and, covering their spaces, the maniples of the 'triarii'. Thus the legion maintained an open, adaptable formation which could be closed up into the old-style phalanx simply by bringing the rear maniples forward into the gaps between the front maniples. Similarly, the soldiers themselves within each maniple were staggered so that they could fight openly or close ranks to make a tight wedge that could withstand almost any charge.

When Hannibal sent in his elephants at the battle of Zama, the second line of Roman maniples simply moved to one side, behind the first line, so that the elephants charged straight through the gap between all three lines of maniples and were killed in the rear of the legions. On other occasions the third line of maniples, the 'triarii', could be brought round from behind the first two lines to flank the enemy. On the dreadful occasion of Cannae, the wedge formation failed utterly. Hannibal waited for the Romans to advance and allowed his own line to bend in the centre to receive the attack. He then wrapped his army round the Romans, encircled them completely with his cavalry and gave the Roman army a lesson it never forgot. Between half and threequarters of the army was either killed or taken prisoner. One consul was killed, the other – Varro – was made the scapegoat. He was a typical example of the rash 'new man', said the senators; his father had been a merchant.

In attack, the soldiers threw their light javelins first and then their heavy ones as they advanced closer. The light javelin caught in the shield of their foe and could not be removed easily: it therefore unbalanced the man and made him lower his defences. The second javelin was intended to penetrate his armour or go straight to his body. Finally, the Romans drew out their short swords for close-combat stabbing. When the Romans came to grips with the Macedonian army that had once followed Alexander the Great to his victories in Persia, they pushed aside the long Macedonian spears and went to work mercilessly with their swords. Unable to retaliate effectively in the tight

*'You may break your heart but men will still go on as before.'*

*A British chieftain called the Romans: 'Pillagers of the world. . . . They are the only people on earth to whose covetousness both riches and poverty are equally tempting. To robbery, butchery and rapine, they give the lying name of "government"; they create a desolation and call it peace.'*

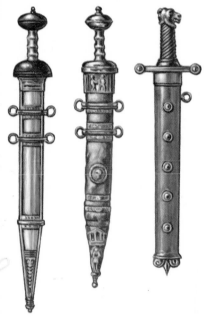

Three Roman swords. The one on the right is decorated with bronze. The senior centurion wore his sword on the opposite side to that of the legionary.

Left: Another view of the fortified Aurelian walls of Rome.

The Roman shield could withstand a great deal of punishment. This drawing shows how the shield was built up in layers.

mêlée, the Macedonians were routed and their power destroyed.

There were often as many allies fighting on the wings of the army as there were Roman citizens in the army itself. There were also ancillary troops, such as Balearic slingers, Numidian horsemen, Cretan archers and soldiers from Rhodes. These were treated as skirmishers or used in the opening phases of the battle before the legions made their main attack. During the second war with Carthage, at the end of the third century BC, the number of legions in the field increased considerably, as Rome drew on every available source of manpower to assert her authority.

More and more overseas campaigns – in Spain, Algeria and the East – required longer and longer military service. It was not surprising that the wealthier Roman citizens, with increasing business interests and larger farms to manage, started to resent the time they had to spend fighting. The Roman State was becoming larger, more complex and more prosperous; the opportunities for trade were far greater than they had been; there was more to life than long marches and the blood and dust of conflict. It was partly this mood, as well as the need for an outlet for the increasing frustrations of the poorer citizens, that led the consul Marius to make some radical reforms at the end of the second century BC.

Marius opened up the army to volunteers from the non-propertied class and paid them a salary. They were keen to join and saw the army as a good career that offered a reasonable living with the occasional perks of booty. By paying the soldiers, Marius was able to arm them all in the same way, so that the distinction between 'hastati', 'principes' and 'triarii' disappeared, although the names remained as a distinction of rank. The lightly-armed 'velites' also disappeared. The tactical formation of the maniple gave way to the cohort: each legion had ten cohorts and each cohort had six centuries. The tribunes, who commanded the legions, became young men doing their military service before taking up their first public job as quaestors. The cohorts were therefore placed under the command of more experienced legates.

Whereas the propertied citizen-army had looked to the State as the object of its loyalty, the proletarian army that Marius created looked to its generals, for they provided the victories, the booty and, often, the grants of land in the newly conquered areas. The later years of the Republic were a time of brilliant generals who won magnificent victories more for their own glory than for the glory of Rome. It was the loyalty of the legions to these generals – to Caesar and Pompey, for example – that was partly responsible for the Civil War that led to the end of the Republic.

Caesar himself was certainly one of Rome's greatest generals. He believed that it was essential to subdue the German tribes across the Rhine and realised that the only way to check them from advancing on Rome was to conquer Gaul, as well. He set himself this task and achieved his aim in Gaul. In the process he made two trips across the channel to Britain, mainly as a show of strength to discourage the British tribes from getting any ideas into their heads about encouraging the Gauls to resist. But Caesar did not have it all his own way. He met some stiff opposition on his first expedition to Britain, which he described with admirable honesty in his *Conquest of Gaul*. As an example of Romans encountering an unusual set of conditions, it makes good reading.

Caesar prepared eighty transports for his first crossing of the channel, to carry two legions. He embarked with a favourable wind at about midnight and reached the British coast at about nine o'clock the next morning but had to ride at anchor till the afternoon waiting for the rest of his fleet to catch up.

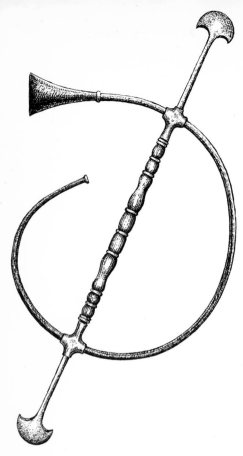

A Roman cornu. This instrument was a development of the trumpet and was in the form of a letter G. The wooden cross bar was held in the player's left hand and rested on his left shoulder. The trumpet part curved above his head. In tone the cornu sounded rather like a French horn. One found at Pompeii could produce a range of seventeen notes and was tuned in the key of G. Trajan's Column shows soldiers escorting the standards playing the cornu.

The Romans did not value music as much as the Greeks but they had a considerable variety of instruments and music played a great part in their lives. Most of the influences on their music were Greek or Etruscan.

Steep cliffs topped by a mass of enthusiastic British javelin-throwers made him decide to sail about seven miles up the coast, where he ran his ships ashore on an evenly sloping beach. But the British chariots had followed the fleet along the coast and were waiting to confront the landing party. Caesar takes up the story:

'The Romans were faced with very grave difficulties. The size of the ships made it impossible to run them aground except in fairly deep water; and the soldiers, unfamiliar with the ground, with their hands full, and weighed down by the heavy burden of their arms, had at the same time to jump down from the ships, get a footing in the waves, and fight the enemy, who, standing on dry land or advancing only a short way into the water, fought with all their limbs unencumbered and on perfectly familiar ground, boldly hurling javelins and galloping their horses, which were trained to this type of work. These perils frightened our soldiers, who were quite unaccustomed to battles of this kind, with the result that they did not show the same alacrity and enthusiasm as they usually did in battles on dry land . . . As the Romans still hesitated, chiefly on account of the depth of the water, the man who carried the eagle of the Tenth Legion, after praying to the gods that his action might bring good luck to the legion, cried in a loud voice: "Jump down, comrades, unless you want to surrender our eagle to the enemy; I, at any rate, mean to do my duty to my country and my general." With these words he leapt out of the ship and advanced towards the enemy with the eagle in his hands. At this the soldiers, exhorting each other not to submit to such a disgrace, jumped with one accord from the ship, and the men from the next ships, when they saw them, followed them and advanced against the enemy . . .'

However, there was some confusion, the soldiers were unable to form their ranks properly, they were harried by the javelin-throwers and, when they finally started to push the British back, it turned out that the cavalry had been blown off course and were not available to follow up the pursuit of the British. As Caesar put it:

'This was the one thing that prevented Caesar from achieving his usual success.'

Under Augustus, the army took up a new rôle, on garrison duty along the tender spots of the frontier. Augustus stalled immediate plans for expansion after the traumatic loss of three entire legions under Varus in the Teotoburger Forest in AD 9. He was so grief-stricken that he refused to re-create the lost legions and so reduced himself to twenty-five legions in all. Nero brought the number back to twenty-eight again: eight of these were based at the eastern end of the Mediterranean, thirteen were placed along the Rhine and the Danube, three were posted in Britain and one each in North Africa, Gaul, Spain and North Italy. By then only fifty percent of the legionaries were recruited in Italy; subsequently the percentage fell sharply and Hadrian actively encouraged the recruitment of provincials. Even so, legionaries still had to be Roman citizens; non-citizens could join the 'auxilia' and become auxiliaries.

The permanent establishment of legions in areas which remained their special responsibility and the traditions of long-term service gave the legionaries a great sense of loyalty to their own legion. Their fellow legionaries became their closest family and the legion's camp became their home. The legions acquired a very special sense of identity and usually had names associated with a particular campaign on which they had gained distinction.

Sometimes they shared a name and were distinguished by their number. Thus there were the Fourth and Fifth Macedonica legions. The Second and Third legions were privileged to hold the name of the emperor – the Second and Third Augusta.

In addition to the main legions, there was the Praetorian Guard. Their name came from the 'praetorium', the part of the camp where the general had his tent, and they were first established as personal bodyguards to consuls and generals in the field. Augustus had a personal bodyguard of nine cohorts of 500 men each. At first only three of these cohorts were kept in Rome; the rest were distributed round Italy. But Tiberius gathered them into one camp just outside Rome, where they were readily to hand in case of an emergency in the capital. The number of cohorts differed with various emperors but the Praetorian Guard continued to play an influential rôle in power politics. Those who wanted to seize the imperial throne tried first to win over the Guard – usually with promises of money.

The soldiers of the Guard were recruited from Italy and were considerably

*'All the Gauls are inclined to be contemptuous of our short stature, contrasting it with their own great height.'*

A detail from Trajan's Column shows Trajan's first campaign. Provisions are seen being loaded into ships, a religious, sacrificial scene is shown and the surrender of the barbarian chieftains to the Emperor.

Both sides of a Roman coin showing the head of Claudius and its reverse on which we can see the inscription 'de Britanni' on the arch-like structure with the mounted figure on top.

better paid than the average legionary. The more important they became politically, the more they could demand and they frequently received bonuses from the emperor or from rivals to obtain their loyalty. At one time, they openly auctioned the empire to the highest bidder. They wore traditional Republican uniform.

There were also three Urban Cohorts within Rome, which acted as the city police, with 1000 men in each cohort. And there were seven cohorts of fire-fighters, or 'vigiles'. The Praetorian Guard, as well as each of these forces, had a praefect in charge of them.

The organisation of the army under Augustus and subsequent emperors was not very different from that under the late Republic. The smallest unit remained the century, which generally had eighty men. On campaign, these were divided into ten 'contubernia' of eight men each who shared a single tent and ate together. Six of these centuries made up one cohort, of 480 men. Ten cohorts made up a legion but the first cohort was strengthened by having five double centuries instead of six single centuries – a hang-over from the days of the maniple: the first cohort therefore had 800 men. With an extra 120 cavalry attached to each legion as scouts and out-riders, and with officers and headquarter's staff, the total strength of an imperial legion was about 5500.

The 'legatus' now commanded the legion. He might well be a senator, who had already served as a praetor. He held his command for three or four years and was usually appointed by the emperor. His job was regarded as a stepping stone to becoming a consul and then a provincial governor. His second-in-command was the senior tribune. There were five other tribunes, all young men of about twenty-five, who were little more than staff-officers and were probably regarded with some scepticism by the older men in the army.

One of the most important officers was the 'Praefectus Castorum' – the Prefect of the Camp – a man of about fifty or sixty, who had probably risen from the ranks and achieved his present position after holding the job of senior centurion, or 'primus pilus'. This was the peak of the centurion's career: he was responsible for equipment, munitions, engineering and artillery.

The 'primus pilus' (literally, the 'first javelin') commanded the first century of the first cohort. The five centurions of the first cohort outranked all other centurions, who stood roughly in order of their length of service in the

A coin showing a Roman leader exhorting a group of soldiers.

A relief showing that 'moment of truth' for the gladiator. A lion and lioness leap in for the kill. To the crowds in the vast amphitheatre this was the supreme moment. For the gladiator it was the final test of courage, skill – and quick thinking.

*'You can guess at a young dog's strength by his weight and you can gauge his running by the size of his bones. But set fires in a circle and place the litter and yourself inside the fires. The bitch herself will choose without hesitation which of the litter should survive. She will select the most valuable dog first.'*

ranks. In principle all centurions were chosen from the ranks of their own legion but various factors cut across this: for example, a centurion might be commissioned directly from the Praetorian Guard. Subsequently, centurions might be posted from one legion to another. Petronius Fortunatus served as a centurion in thirteen legions during forty-six years active service. The centurion had a deputy, or 'optio', and a junior responsible for the appointment of sentries. Each cohort did not necessarily have a separate commander. Generally it was controlled by the senior centurion within the cohort; sometimes a young tribune was temporarily attached to the cohort from headquarters.

Centurions were distinguished by a fine corslet of chain mail. They also wore greaves and a transverse crest on their helmets instead of the front-to-back crest of the ordinary legionary. Both greaves and helmet might be finely decorated. He carried a twisted vine stick as an emblem of office and used it to beat the bare backs of his men for punishment. One centurion was known as 'Fetch-me-another' because he broke so many sticks on the backs of his men. The legates were very distinctive, with cloaks and armour made to their personal taste. Decorations or awards for valour – in the form of silver or metal torcs – were worn on a corslet over the chest. Awards were given out for a notable victory, for the first man over the wall in a siege, and for saving the life of another soldier.

Headquarters had a large staff of clerks, responsible for a wide variety of business including the troops compulsory savings bank. There were also engineers, surveyors, munitions workers and priests ('haruspices') to officiate at ceremonies and to interpret the auspices before battle. They were not concerned with helping legionaries with their personal problems as today's padré would be. The standard-bearer ('aquilifer') carried the precious eagle of the legion and the 'signifer' carried the particular standard of each century. There were trumpeters, torturers, doctors and vets.

Communication on the battlefield usually relied on horsemen carrying messages but methods of signalling were developed. Polybius described a system in which the alphabet was divided into groups of five letters. Torches were used to indicate the group first and then the letter within the group. Another writer, Vegetius, described a later method in which a beam of wood

*'The Roman soldiers are as quick to act as they are slow to give way, and never was there an engagement in which they were worsted by numbers; tactical skill or unfavourable ground – or even by fortune, which is less within their grasp than is victory.'*

was raised or lowered on a tower. Chains of such signal towers were set up for rapid communication over long distances but they were lightly constructed and none have survived.

The average legionary would be clothed in an under-garment, possibly of linen, over which he would wear a short-sleeved woollen tunic down to the knees. Trousers were originally considered effeminate or barbarian but were permitted in cold climates; they would usually be made of skin-tight leather and reached just below the knee. The cavalry wore trousers. Sandals were heavy and hob-nailed. The thongs came half way up the shin and both sandals and thongs could be stuffed with cloth or skins in cold weather.

Body armour changed considerably in the course of time. Officers continued to wear the Greek muscle-shaped cuirass well into the days of the empire and centurions retained the mail shirt but this was replaced by plate armour for the ordinary legionary. Horizontal plates of armour were hinged together either by hooks or straps or a combination of both. These covered the chest and upper part of the back and shoulders. The plates overlapped to give maximum protection with the greatest possible articulation. The legionary also wore a wide belt studded with metal plates, which carried his sword on the right and his dagger on the left (the centurion wore these the other way

A detail from the great Arch of Constantine showing Roman soldiers with a prisoner whose arms are secured behind his back.

round). An apron of thongs with metal rivets and weights was attached to the front of the belt to protect the private parts. To make long marches more easy, the greaves worn previously by heavy infantry were abandoned.

The helmet was made of bronze or iron; there were many different types. All were designed to protect the neck and shoulders with a projecting rear-piece. There was also a small projection at the front to protect the eyes and there were hinged cheek-pieces. The plume-holder on top was fixed for parade and occasionally for battle.

The large rectangular shield was carried by a strap on the left shoulder. It was made of thin sheets of wood glued together so that the grain of one sheet was at right angles to the grain of the other; this prevented the wood from splitting along the grain when the shield was struck. The shield was encased in leather and bound at the edges with metal. The centre was hollowed out for a hand-grip and protected by a metal boss. All shields were decorated in different colours for each cohort. We miss this mass of colour on the surviving reliefs of Roman soldiers. The orderly groups of red, blue, green, orange, yellow and so on must have added to the awesome impression of Roman power as seen by barbarian troops.

Each man carried two 'pila', more than two metres long: the first 70–90 centimetres were made of iron and the shaft of wood. The double-edged sword was about 70 centimetres long and was carried in a scabbard of wood and leather. The Romans retained this short-sword for nearly a thousand years. The dagger, which was probably used less and less, was about 20–25 centimetres long and usually held in an iron or bronze scabbard.

Throughout the ancient world, the heavy infantry was the dominant force, fighting shoulder to shoulder. The weight and strength of mature men was more important than the speed and agility of the young. Elite troops were therefore formed from men who, in more recent times, would have been relegated to the Home Guard. The middle-aged man remained a great deal fitter than he would today: he had to build camps, dig ditches, construct bridges and roads, and carry his own load. Soldiers with battle experience as far afield as North Africa, the Middle East, Spain, the forests of Germany and the fogs of Britain were greatly esteemed for their steadfast nature. Terrifying as the appearance of barbarians could be – with wailing priests and woad-coloured features – the legionaries were unlikely to be bothered by such novelties once the close fighting began. Polybius explained that they were:

'not so much bold and adventurous as men with a faculty for command, steady, and rather of a deep-rooted spirit, not prone prematurely to attack or start battle, but men who, in the face of superior numbers or overwhelming pressure, would endure and die in the defence of their post.'

The strength of the heavy infantry lay as a unit. They were not good at pursuing a defeated enemy nor at forcing lighter troops to give battle. When lightly-armed barbarians could not be brought to battle, the Romans could only press on to destroy their means of subsistence. But when the foe were nomadic pasturalists or when the terrain was only suitable for guerrilla tactics, the Romans could take little action. Thus the empire was bounded by nomadic tribes and guerrilla groups operating in rough or densely covered country. All that the Romans could do, when they did achieve any direct confrontation, was to demoralise others by making a ruthless example of their fellows and directing a massacre. Acts of such cruelty – sometimes against civilian populations as well – were not often gratuitous violence; they were the result of deliberate policy forced on the Romans by their own limitations.

*'In the midst of peace the soldier carries out manoeuvres, throws up earthworks against a non-existent enemy and tires himself out with unnecessary toil in order to be equal to it when it is necessary. If you want a man to keep his head when the crisis comes you must give him some training before it comes.'*

*'We Germans are not taking aggressive action against the Roman people, but we are ready to fight if provoked. For it is our traditional custom to resist any attacker and to ask no quarter.'*

For lighter and faster fighting, the army relied on auxiliaries and allies. Units of barbarians were adopted into the army for their specialist abilities and initially retained their traditional organisation under their own chiefs. Thereafter the leadership was Romanised and recruits to those units were often taken from other tribes as well. Auxiliary cavalry were particularly important because the Romans, despite their love of chariot-racing in the circus, were never great horsemen. When it became obvious that the 'knights' were no longer suitable as ordinary cavalry troopers, auxiliaries were adopted from nomadic and semi-nomadic tribes. They were organised into 'alae', 500 or 1000 strong, which were subdivided into 'turmae': there were about sixteen 'turmae' to an 'alae' of 500 horsemen and about twenty-four 'turmae' to an 'alae' of 1000. The 'alae' were often commanded by young tribunes promoted from the legion; the 'turmae' were commanded by 'decuriones' promoted from the lower ranks or transferred from the legion prior to becoming a centurion.

Cavalry were equipped with a double-ended spear: if one end broke off they

**The Roman Army,** left to right: an hastatus or front line soldier of the early army carried a sword and two javelins, one heavy and one light. The veles was lightly armed and carried a small round shield and light javelins. The later legionary had bronze helmet, mail shirt, carried shield, sword and light and heavy pila or spears. The tribune was usually a young

HASTATUS

VELES

LEGIONARY

TRIBUNE

could use the other end. Their sword was longer than the legionary's. Earlier shields were round but later they became oval. Horseshoes and hipposandals were fitted to the horses. The hipposandal was an alternative to the horseshoe; it slipped over the hoof and was easily detachable. Saddles, spurs and bits were all used but there were no stirrups. The subsequent introduction of the stirrup to Europe was a major innovation that paved the way for the heavily armoured knight of the Middle Ages. The North African horsemen rode without armour or bridle. They rode swiftly to the attack, threw their javelins and retreated before the enemy could respond.

Auxiliary infantry were also organised into cohorts of 500 or 1000 men, divided into six or ten centuries and commanded by a praefect, who ranked below the commander of the cavalry 'alae'. Equipment varied enormously but chain mail and scale armour were common and the short spear and legionary's sword were used for fighting. Bowmen used the short, composite bow made of wood and strengthened by sinew and bone.

After completing twenty years' service, auxiliaries were awarded Roman

aristocrat and his commission formed part of his political career. A Praetorian Guard in battle and dress uniform. He secured more than three times as much pay as a legionary. The signifer was also the 'banker' for his century. A Centurion in the ancient Roman army commanded the sixtieth part of a legion. Finally, a Roman cavalryman.

PRAETORIAN GUARD

Battle          Dress

SIGNIFER

CENTURION

CAVALRYMAN

citizenship, to which their children were then automatically entitled. Their children could therefore join one of the main Roman legions. The auxiliary was issued with a special bronze diploma from the emperor, acknowledging his service and granting citizenship. He would usually receive a grant of land in a colony and a sum of money; he might also have some of his own savings. He would then settle down and marry. Soldiers were not allowed to be married in the army. This did not apply to officers.

In Caesar's time, the ordinary soldier received about 900 sesterces per year, or from five to ten 'as' per day. From this he had to pay for his clothes, his weapons, his tent and, according to one soldier, 'bribes to the centurion to be let off fatigues'. There was constant lobbying for increases in pay and sometimes threats of open revolt. A centurion probably received about five times as much as a legionary and the senior centurion, the 'primus pilus', received a gratuity on retirement of 400,000 sesterces – enough to give him the property qualification for becoming a knight.

The soldiers lived primarily on wheat, cooked up in a stew or baked into transportable rations. Barley was despised and issued to troops as punishment; it was also used for fodder. Meat was available only on feast days, although units that were stationed in one camp permanently had their own meadows in which they grazed cattle. Wine and vinegar were an essential part of the soldier's diet.

Military hospitals had a high reputation and laid much emphasis on hygiene. There were doctors and medical orderlies in the field, who carried bandages, dressed wounds on the spot or brought the injured back to base. Stitches were used and amputations were carried out cleanly and efficiently – if painfully! Every permanent fortress had a legionary hospital, a bath house, drains and latrines. Where no river was immediately available into which the drains could flow, soak-aways were dug to act like modern septic tanks or latrines were cut too deep for flies and emptied regularly.

New recruits to the army were strictly trained in drill, discipline and the use of their weapons. Sword practice was carried out against a wooden stake. Pliny summed up the advantages of a military education for the young man who was going into public affairs:

'In ancient times it was the recognised custom for us to learn from our elders by watching their behaviour as well as listening to their advice, thus acquiring the principles on which to act subsequently, ourselves, and to hand on in our turn to our juniors. Hence young men began their early training with military service, so that they might grow accustomed to command by obeying, and learn how to lead by following others.'

Punishments were liberally handed out. Fatigues and a beating from the centurion's vine-staff were the most common form. Sometimes a soldier would be stripped and beaten insensible by several soldiers with staffs. Death was the penalty for any serious offence. The notorious penalty of 'decimation' was reserved for occasions on which the entire legion had disgraced itself, either by cowardice or by treasonable revolt: one in ten of all the legionaries were executed. There were, of course, the usual misunderstandings between soldiers and civilians, as Juvenal explained:

'Let us consider first, then, the benefits common to all military men. Not least is the fact that no civilian would dare to give you a thrashing – and if beaten up himself he'll keep quiet about it . . . and if he seeks legal redress, the case will come up before some hobnailed centurion and a benchful of brawny jurors, according to ancient military law: no soldier, it's stated, may sue or be tried except in camp, by court-martial.'

*Agricola, Roman Governor of Britain: 'His spirit was possessed by a passion for military glory – a thankless passion in an age in which a sinister construction was put upon distinction and a great reputation was as dangerous as a bad one.'*

*'The Germans either terrify their foes or themselves become frightened, according to the character of the noise they make upon the battlefield. . . . What they particularly aim at is a harsh, intermittent roar.'*

164

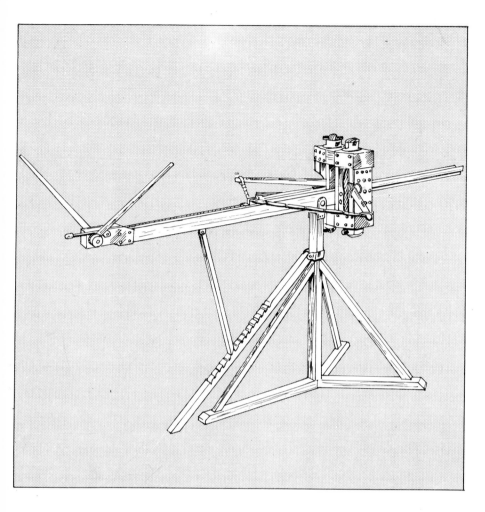

The Greeks, not the Romans, were the originators of the catapult, which could be a formidable weapon. Some of them were enormous contrivances which could hurl stones weighing around forty kilos. Catapults were also used to fire arrows, like the one we show here. The power came from twisted strings of sinews. There were also catapults for firing small stones of about the size of an apple.

Soldiers on police duties commonly extorted money and hospitality from local civilians and had plenty of opportunity for harassment. Jesus himself had something to say about this. According to the Gospel of St Luke, a group of soldiers, anxious to know how they should behave if they became Christians, came up to Jesus and asked him bluntly:

'And what shall we do?'
He replied:
'Never extort money or even lay a false charge, but be content with your pay.'

Much of the soldier's life was spent in camp. Temporary camps were always protected with a ditch and rampart, dug by the men in the form of a square, approximately 800 metres along each side. Tents were then laid out in an orderly fashion within the square. More permanent camps were fortified with wooden palisades and watch-towers or with stone walls. Many such camps were established along the frontier from the time of Augustus onward. Hadrian consolidated his frontiers by building a palisade joining the Rhine to the Danube. He also ordered the construction of Hadrian's Wall, from the mouth of the Tyne in northern Britain to the Solway Firth. The wall was 120 kilometres long, five metres high and two-and-a-half metres thick, with a series of little castles and turrets at regular intervals. A great deal of this remarkable demarcation line still stands, a substantial outpost of a vast empire that owed its success both to organisation and determination.

*'Think it no shame to be helped. Your business is to do your appointed duty, like a soldier in the breach. How, then, if you are lame, and unable to scale the battlements yourself, but could do it if you had the aid of a comrade?'*

The Jewish historian Josephus wrote a book about the Roman war against Jerusalem, waged by Vespasian and Titus in the first century AD. Josephus gave *his* opinion as to why the Roman armies were successful:

'Anyone who will take a look at the organisation of their army in general will recognise that they hold their wide-flung empire as the prize of valour, not the gift of fortune. They do not wait for war to begin before handling their arms, nor do they sit idle in peacetime and take action only when the emergency comes – but as if born ready armed they never have a truce from training or wait for war to be declared. Their battle drills are not different from the real thing; every man works as hard at his daily training as if he was on active service. That is why they stand up so easily to the strain of battle: no indiscipline dislodges them from their regular formation, no panic incapacitates them, no toil wears them out; so that victory over men not so trained follows as a matter of course. It would not be far from the truth to call their drills bloodless battles and their battles bloody drills.'

Josephus then described how the Roman camp was set up and fortified, with a wall, towers, artillery and gates to enable sorties against hostile troops:

'It all seems like a mushroom town, with market place, workmen's quarters, and orderly rooms where junior and senior officers can settle disputes as they arise. The erection of the outer wall and the buildings inside is accomplished faster than thought, thanks to the number and skill of the workers.'

Everything was done precisely to order. Eating, sleeping, guard-duty and reveille were all announced by trumpet call. When the time came to strike camp, it is almost impossible for the modern reader not to sense the parallel with the military precision and fervour of Nazi Germany:

'The trumpet sounds and every man springs to his duty. Following the signal huts are instantly dismantled and all preparations made for departure. The trumpet then sounds "Stand by to march!" At once they load the mules and wagons with the baggage and take their places like runners lined up and hardly able to wait for the starter's signal. Then they fire the camp, which they can easily reconstruct if required, and which might some day be useful to the enemy. For the third time the trumpets give the same signal for departure, to urge on those who for any reason have been loitering, so that not a man may be missing from his place. Then the announcer, standing on the right of the supreme commander, asks three times in their native language whether they are ready for war. They three times shout loudly and with enthusiasm "Ready", hardly waiting for the question, and filled with a kind of martial fervour raise their right arms as they shout. Then they step off, all marching silently and in good order, as on active service every man keeping his place in the column.'

Finally Josephus described the planning with which the Romans prepared carefully for battle, their training, discipline, obedience and order of march. He admitted a certain bias at the end:

'The purpose of the foregoing account has been less to eulogize the Romans than to console their defeated enemies and to deter any who may be thinking of revolt.'

On the march, great importance was given to scouts to prevent ambush and the best infantry cohorts were usually at the rear for the same reason. The Roman soldiers constructed their own roads where necessary and were acknowledged as masterly engineers. Bridges and siege structures were built

A military belt with dagger. This belt is designed to give protection to the lower abdomen.

Right: The Porta Palatina in Turin. Originally, Turin was a Roman military camp. It was rebuilt by Augustus in the form of a rectangle divided into 72 blocks or insulae. The city was encircled by walls and there were four gates. The Porta Palatina is the surviving example.

To the Roman army as to later armies, battle standards had great significance. Their loss meant defeat – and disgrace. This relief shows Roman soldiers carrying their standards.

on the spot from available material and only the lightest pieces of artillery would be carried with the army.

Rivers were crossed by fords wherever possible. Lines of cavalry would be placed above and below the ford: above, to break the force of the water; below, to pick up men and baggage that were swept downstream. If the water was only slightly too deep to ford, the level might be lowered by cutting trenches to let it flow away into the plain on either side. For a light bridge, empty casks were used, covered with boards. A stronger, pontoon bridge was made of light boats made from hollowed-out logs, with planks placed across them – they would be moored fore and aft. As enemy attacks were extremely likely at crossings where the troops were divided and preoccupied, defensive positions were built at the bridgeheads.

Bridges were important to the Romans, in preference to shipping an army across a river. They symbolised domination over the water. When Caesar crossed the Rhine, he described the bridge he built in great detail and added:

> 'A crossing by means of boats seemed to him both too risky and beneath his dignity as a Roman commander.'

Caesar's bridge was a model of its kind. Great wooden supports were hammered into the river bed at angles to give the greatest strength and tree-trunks were lashed across to hold them together. Smaller poles and bundles of sticks provided the surface of the bridge and wooden posts were set into the river bed upstream of the bridge to protect it from flotsam deliberately sent down by the enemy. The work was done with amazing speed, as Caesar proudly recorded:

> 'Ten days after the collection of the timber had begun, the work was completed and the army crossed over.'

Roman artillery was based on Greek developments and relied on two main principles: the bow and torsion. The artillery bow used a composite material similar to the hand-bow. A layer of wood in the centre formed a base; a layer of sinew on the outside expanded when the bow was bent back and contracted when the bow was released; a layer of horn on the inside did the opposite: it contracted when the bow was bent and sprung back to its original shape when the bow was released. The bow was fixed to a wooden frame and winched back. It could either fire bolts (long, heavy arrows) or be adapted to fire stones.

The torsion principle was based on a rope made of some elastic material – animal sinew or hair from horses' tails or women's heads. In the final defence of Carthage against the Roman attack, it was reported that the women cut off their hair to provide material for more catapults for the beleaguered Carthaginians. The material was wound repeatedly round a frame, an arm was inserted through the centre of the material and the material was then twisted by locks at top and bottom. When the arm was winched back against the twist, sufficient torsion was created for a projectile to be flung forward with considerable force when the arm was released. There were various types of light and heavy catapults but all worked on the same principle. Josephus recorded that stone balls weighing more than twenty kilos were thrown more than 400 metres at the siege of Jerusalem. Twentieth-century reconstructions of these catapults have succeeded in throwing bolts and stones up to 300 metres. 'Catapultae' used arrows for ammunition; smaller versions were known as 'scorpions'; 'ballista' threw stones.

Artillery was chiefly used at sieges, where it could rain a covering fire on the defenders, beyond the range of hand-bows and slings, while the attackers filled in ditches, built covered approach tunnels out of wood and hide,

*'The god within you should preside over a being who is virile and mature, a statesman, a Roman, and a ruler; one who has held his ground, like a soldier waiting for the signal to retire from life's battlefield and ready to welcome his relief. . . . We have to stand upright ourselves, not be set up.'*

*'Nothing can happen to any man that nature has not fitted him to endure.'*

constructed assault towers and brought forward the great rams within their sheltered housing. The ram itself was made of a single massive timber, bound with ropes and capped by an iron tip in the shape of a ram's head; the housing was made of wood and animal hides between which were layers of wickerwork, to break the force of stones thrown down by the defenders. There were also layers of damp seaweed to inhibit the action of fire-arrows. Soldiers also approached the walls in 'tortoise' formation: they advanced in a tight block with their shields completely covering them on all four sides and above their heads. Tunnels were dug beneath the defenders' walls to undermine their foundations and the defenders, not to be outdone, dug tunnels beneath the Roman assault towers to reciprocate.

One of the most determined and successful sieges was undertaken by Caesar, when he surrounded the Gallic leader Vercingetorix in the almost impregnable hill-village of Alesia, in 52 BC. Caesar made some remarkably thorough fortifications to encircle the town. The first circle of palisades, towers and ditches was sixteen kilometres round. It included ramparts, breastworks, trenches with sharpened stakes, spiked logs embedded in the ground and hidden by brushwood, and short bits of wood with iron hooks protruding upward. Vercingetorix failed to disrupt work on this construction with his cavalry, so he sent out horsemen to raise a relieving force from among the neighbouring tribes. Caesar responded to this new threat by constructing a second circle of fortifications, similar to the first but facing outward. This circle was more than twenty-two kilometres round. It had to be made particularly strong because Caesar did not have enough soldiers to man both lines at once: many legionaries were busy collecting wood and corn.

The relief force arrived and there was an initial engagement with the Roman cavalry outside the outer fortifications. The tribesmen were driven off temporarily but decided to make a night-time attack, which proved the effectiveness of Caesar's preparations:

'After an interval of only one day, however, during which they prepared a great quantity of fascines, ladders, and grappling hooks, the relieving army moved silently out of camp at midnight and advanced towards the entrenchment in the plain. Suddenly raising a shout to inform the besieged of their approach, they began to throw fascines into the trenches, drove the Romans from the ramparts with arrows and stones, discharged from slings or by hand, and employed every other method of assault. Meanwhile, hearing the distant shouting, Vercingetorix sounded the trumpet and led his men out of town. The Roman troops moved up to the posts previously allotted to them at the entrenchments, and kept the Gauls at a distance with slingstones, bullets, large stones, and stakes which were placed ready at intervals along the rampart, while the artillery pelted them with missiles. It was too dark to see, and casualties were heavy on both sides. The generals Mark Antony and Gaius Trebonius, who had been detailed for the defence of this particular sector, reinforced the points where they knew the troops were hard pressed with men brought up from redoubts well behind the fighting line. As long as the Gauls were at a distance from the entrenchments, the rain of javelins which they discharged gained them some advantage. But when they came nearer they suddenly found themselves pierced by the 'goads' or tumbled into the pits and impaled themselves, while others were killed by heavy siege-spears discharged from the rampart and towers. Their losses were everywhere heavy, and when dawn came they had failed to penetrate the defences at any point.'

*Spain and Gaul:*
*'They have changed their ways and altogether gone over to the Roman fashion. They wear togas and even speak Latin and have changed the pattern of their laws.'*

The Romans had various types of foot coverings. Their leather 'shoes' were made from small pieces of very supple leather and were shaped to the foot. They were frequently decorated, like the example below, and were tied with threaded thongs.

The plain sandal consisted of a simple leather sole held on to the foot by a thong which passed between the big toe and the second toe.

When a Roman wore his toga in town a *calceus* – a sort of high bootee – was the correct accompanying footwear.

Further attempts to co-ordinate the relief force and the besieged also failed and in a final engagement the relief force were driven off and Vercingetorix capitulated. A thanksgiving of twenty days was celebrated in Rome when the city received Caesar's reports of his victories during the course of that year.

The six-month siege of Jerusalem in AD 70 was far more terrible for the besieged than events at Alesia. Like Caesar, Titus built an encircling earthwork to confine the inhabitants. But his repeated assaults were constantly repulsed. Towards the end, famine within the city caused violence among the defenders themselves and Titus was able to over-run the entire place and destroy the Temple. He left three of the great towers as a reminder to others of the great city he had defeated. He then returned to Rome for a triumph. Prisoners and treasure from the Temple were paraded through the streets of Rome before the emperor Vespasian and a triumphal arch was erected in memory of the victory. Triumphs – voted by the Senate – had been common for victorious generals in Republican days but Augustus limited them to the emperor himself or members of his immediate family. Other successful generals were given certain honours.

*'The art of living is more like wrestling than dancing, in as much as it, too, demands a firm and watchful stance against any unexpected onset.'*

Although the majority of Rome's victories were on land, the one great victory to which Augustus owed his own position of supreme power was the result of a naval battle – the battle of Actium, in which he defeated Mark Antony and Cleopatra. The Romans were not a great seafaring people but they established naval supremacy in the Mediterranean and relied heavily on the use of their galleys for the transportation of troops and supplies. The largest warships, probably having three banks of oars, were about forty metres long and about five metres wide. They had a mast with a square sail and used a sprit-sail when convenient. They were equipped with a battering ram at the bow and a 'corvus' or raven – a boarding plank with a long spike sticking downwards from the end which locked on to the enemy ship. Each vessel had about 300 seamen and 120 marines, who were equipped in the same way as ordinary legionaries.

Ships were used for transportation around the coastline and up the main river routes. They could also be used for laying siege to forts along the coast; siege towers and artillery were set up on the ships and brought up against the walls of the fort. Augustus and later emperors had several fleets positioned at strategic points for policing sea lanes and for support duties. There were fleets, for example, at Naples, at ports in Egypt and Syria, in the Black Sea and on the Rhine and the Danube. Boulogne was used as one of the main ports for crossing to Britain.

*'Tuscany and the Aurelian highway have already fallen to the Goths. It is best to trust the sea because the rivers are not bridged and the land has become wild again.'*

But sea-power was no good against barbarians, nor in the end were the ingenuity of generals, the experience of mature legionaries, or the resolute determination and awesome reputation of the Roman army. The line was too thinly stretched along the frontier; the pressure was too persistent; and the barbarian Goths were themselves being pushed south-westwards by the Huns. These wild horsemen from the east, beyond the Sea of Azov, were described as horribly ugly, beardless and hairy-legged; they stayed constantly on horseback, yelled and screamed in battle, avoided any big engagement and used lassoos to bring down their enemy. They were always on the move. They were never reliable, never kept a truce, knew no sense of right or wrong, had no religion and no superstitions. The Roman army, through its permanent camps and by its incorporation of soldiers from every country under its control, was a vital leavening factor in the spread of Roman civilisation – but Romans had nothing in common with these 'senseless animals' who rode against their boundaries.

# The legacy of Rome

At the beginning of this book we looked at Roman deeds up to the time of the emperor Marcus Aurelius. He died in AD 180 and most of the Romans we have been listening to lived during the previous 250 years, a period that saw many changes in Roman attitudes and styles of living. If we were to go back 250 years in our own history, America would still be a British colony, Australia would still be undiscovered by Europeans and the industrial revolution would be unthought of.

We tend to think of Roman history after the death of Marcus Aurelius as a period of steady decline but Rome was not first sacked by the Visigoths for another 230 years and Julius Nepos, the last emperor in the west, was not murdered until AD 480. In that time many generations of Roman citizens continued to regard themselves as part of the unchanging, although at times

The aqueduct at Segovia in Spain is one of the best preserved of all the Roman aqueducts. It has a double-tier of arches and is still in use. The aqueduct is just over thirty metres high at its highest point and represents a triumph of Roman civil engineering. It was built from granite block without the use of mortar.

Arc de Triomphe, Paris.

Most of the great cities of Europe provide direct evidence of the enormous influence Roman architecture and design has had on European taste and style. The list of buildings, statues and memorials is legion. Here are a few prime examples – St Paul's Cathedral, London, the Tate Gallery, London, the Arc de Triomphe and the Louvre in Paris. Europe's debt to Rome is manifest and abundant.

The Louvre, Paris.

precarious, order of things. Rome remained a mighty empire in reputation at least, even if its problems steadily increased.

Of course, those Roman citizens did experience more and more changes. Many were caused by the confusions and tyrannies of short-lived emperors struggling for power. Other, more radical changes were caused by the occasional strong emperor who was only able to restore relative stability to the State by tightening his control over the bureaucracy of administration. One effect of this was to deprive people of their freedom of movement about the empire.

Marcus Aurelius was succeeded by his son, Commodus – reasonably able but vain, cruel and more interested in chariot-racing than in controlling the empire. Like many emperors to follow, he was assassinated but not before he had created a situation so unstable that the army was able to step in and auction the throne to whoever promised it most money. Into this confusion marched Septimius Severus, an army commander himself, who understood the need for keeping soldiers content as a priority in maintaining order throughout the empire. He improved their pay and conditions and encouraged officers to enter civil administration. It was believed by opponents of Severus that the effect of the first was to lower discipline and the effect of the second was to turn the empire into a military State.

In his efforts to control the frontiers, Severus also increased the number of legions but then had to raise taxes to pay for them. Upper class Romans rapidly became bankrupt and many forfeited their rank to avoid paying still more taxes. The numbers of the poor increased and Severus was forced to distribute more free social aid which in turn meant raising more money. The cycle was inescapable but Severus did succeed in remaining emperor for eighteen years and his own family line lasted another twenty-four years after his death. This included his immediate successor, Caracalla, renowned for the magnificent baths named after him in Rome and for granting Roman citizenship to all free men throughout the empire. The last of the Severan line was killed by his own legionaries and for the next fifty years a succession of more than twenty emperors and would-be emperors claimed sovereignty over all or part of the empire, backed by greedy soldiers.

The next emperor to take a firm hold on the State for any length of time was Diocletian, who ruled from AD 284–305. He faced pressure on his borders from north, south and east; inflation was running out of control and every taxable source of revenue had already been milked dry. He established an intricate bureaucratic administration whose prime purpose was to reorganise the provinces into units that could be more easily governed. These units included 'diocese' controlled by 'vicars' – terms which the Church took over when the civil administration withdrew to the east. He also began regular and frequent census-taking, which helped him to assess more precisely what taxes could and should be paid. The regular census and the increasing habit of paying taxes in kind rather than in cash were two of the main causes for fixing the inhabitants of the empire to their land: this paved the way for the feudal system of the Middle Ages.

Diocletian maintained overall control himself but divided the empire into two halves. He took the eastern half and Maximian took the western half. In addition, each had a subordinate or successor-designate, so that the shared system would continue. When Diocletian abdicated – the first emperor ever to do so – his concept of the succession failed dismally and there was further strife. Another of Diocletian's failures was his attempt to check inflation. His famous edict for fixing prices had to be dropped because it throttled commerce. Inflation kept on rising, sweeping aside all remedies.

It was Constantine who emerged from the ensuing struggle, as joint emperor in AD 306 and as sole emperor in 324. He defeated his partner and rival after a vision in which he was promised victory if he used the sign of Christ's name as his standard. It was the fulfilment of his vision that prompted Constantine to adopt Christianity. His second great achievement was the founding of Constantinople, on the site of old Byzantium, as the new capital of the empire. Western emperors continued to rule in Rome on and off for another hundred years or so but, by moving the focal centre eastwards, Constantine preserved one half at least of the empire for another 1100 years – until the Turks stormed Constantinople in 1453. He continued the administrative policies of Diocletian and increasingly gave Church officials more legal powers.

St Paul's, London.

While the eastern empire flourished and became responsible, first under Theodosius II and then under Justinian (in AD 533), for codifying the great traditions of Roman law, the western half did at last succumb to the pressures upon it. Rome was sacked by the Visigoths in AD 410 and by the Vandals in AD 455. Disease, Christianity and apathy have all been blamed for the collapse. Many reasons can be dismissed as highly improbable; apathy is the most likely. There was less and less incentive for Romans to support the central system that sucked them dry and barbarian invaders found increasingly little resistance.

When Italy was over-run, the Romans, of course, remained. At first things were extremely unpleasant for them. The invaders tried to destroy much of the physical evidence of the empire and they became the ruling caste. But they could not destroy everything. Barbarian vandalism was easily repaired. It was not until the Arabs in the eighth century that really intensive and intentional damage was done. Much of what the Vandals saw and experienced gradually impressed them as more desirable than conditions they had known back home. In time they adapted to what remained and the Lombard kings, who established a wide field of influence, took over many of the ancient Roman traditions.

It would have surprised the Romans to see themselves as an 'underground' movement or influence but that is what in effect Roman civilisation became. It was helped by the Church in the west, which carried on many of the administrative traditions of the empire and, above all, the concept of a single universal society. Depending on your point of view, we have been labouring under that concept or striving to realise it ever since. When Charlemagne went to Rome and was crowned emperor of the Franks on Christmas Day 800, he claimed direct succession from the Roman emperors of the past. Subsequently, the Holy Roman Empire played a central rôle in European affairs for a thousand years. When the Hapsburg empire disintegrated, Napoleon Bonaparte claimed the imperial title. Later still, Imperial Germany bore the Roman eagle through the First World War. Finally, the military machine created by Adolf Hitler bore a marked resemblance in style and in purpose to its Roman counterpart nearly 2000 years before, and Mussolini consciously recreated interest in the empire with such symbols as 'Fasces', 'Dux' and the 'Via degli Imperatori'. Meanwhile, in the east, Roman traditions were kept alive and passed on through Constantinople to Tsarist Russia.

Tate Gallery, London.

It was largely through the eastern centres of learning – at Constantinople and Alexandria – and through the Church in the west that Roman literature survived. In the east, Latin works were translated into Greek and then back into Latin during the Italian Renaissance in the fifteenth century. Greek texts were also translated back from Arabic which had been vital in the transmission of, for example, Aristotle. But by then scholars had already discovered the Latin texts that had been faithfully and repeatedly copied out and preserved in the monasteries of Europe. The self-conscious attempts of the Renaissance to recreate Latin culture were, in many ways, very artificial; there was already a natural tradition of learning that had come down almost unconsciously through the Churchmen of the Middle Ages.

Early Italian poets such as Boccaccio and Petrarch seized on Roman models such as Virgil and Horace. Dante gave Virgil an important place in his own epic poem. Milton's *Paradise Lost* is steeped in Latin construction. Romantic poets have constantly gone back to Roman models. The speeches of Cicero have been upheld by politicians of the past as the noblest examples of style. Catullus, Martial and Juvenal have not often been found in the schoolroom but Caesar, Livy and Tacitus have been thumbed through dutifully by innumerable generations of scholars.

The Roman language gave birth to French, Italian, Spanish, Portuguese and other 'Romance' languages. Latin roots lie at the basis of many English words, also. That dreaded 'urban' society in which we are supposed to live is a direct lift from the Roman word for a city – 'urbs'. Latin phrases are often used without any attempt at translation: 'ad infinitum', 'ad hoc', 'post mortem' and 'etcetera'. Until recently it was essential to know some Latin to get into a university; a knowledge of Latin is still helpful to the lawyer. The Bible was not translated from Greek or Latin into national languages until the sixteenth century. Even now, Latin is still used in many churches.

Roman currency and Roman weights and measures have had a lasting influence that, in some countries, has only recently been challenged. For example, the foot and mile were common Roman measurements and remain in use in the United States. Britain has only just begun to wean itself from them and has a long struggle ahead before they are finally forgotten. The British sign for a pound sterling, even after decimalisation, is still '£' for 'Libra' (a Roman pound weight). The original '£.s.d.' stood for 'Libra', 'solidi' (a Roman gold coin which was introduced in about AD 317) and 'denarius' (also a silver coin).

Roman law has probably been the most universal influence and one of the deepest. The very word 'justice' comes from the Roman word for law – 'jus'. Roman ideas of impartiality in judgement and of the right of the accused to face his accusers have become fundamental to all free societies. Roman law lay at the heart of the French Napoleonic Code and was used in many parts of Germany until 1900, when a national code was established. Democratic government, too, reflects many aspects of Roman Republican rule. In the United States the Senators themselves bear the name of their Roman model.

The barbarian invaders of Italy could do nothing to stop the underlying influence of these Roman traditions, even if they did drive some of them underground for a while. Nor did they pull down or destroy even an appreciable part of the material remains of Rome's empire. There was too much and it was too solid. From the amount that still survives we can only guess how much more fell steadily into decay during the centuries of barbarian occupation through lack of maintenance and repair work.

Among the constructions that have survived either in part or whole are temples, basilicas and churches, amphitheatres, theatres and circuses, aqueducts and baths, bridges, roads and arches, harbours, forums and villas. Some of them have enjoyed very chequered histories since Roman days. The

Right: The great oval colonnade at Jerash, Jordan, which surrounded a 'place' and was more than one hundred metres long.

Roman rule made Jordan a very prosperous province. The Romans established many new towns.

Bottom right: The modern city of Rome dwarfed by the splendid remains of the Basilica di Massenzio.

*'Go now, foolish man, and lay out acres of marble; build floors good enough to rest under the fine mosaics of your walls while I scorn the fruits of wealth and marvel at the work of nature rather than join that waste which only leads to poverty.'*

'Assyria attempted, but failed, to unite the world. Persia conquered only her neighbours. The empire of Alexander was torn apart by endless wars and rivalries. Rome was not larger at her birth, rather she had wisdom and judgement.'

amphitheatre at Nîmes, for example, was used by the Goths as a fortified castle against the Franks in AD 508. It became a fortress for the Saracens in the early eighth century, until they were driven out by Charles Martel. Then it was taken over by one of the orders of mediaeval knights. For a long time it was the communal home of nearly 2000 peasants who spoke a dialect entirely of their own. They were thrown out at the end of the eighteenth century and the amphitheatre reverted to what was, in effect, its original use: equestrian sports and bullfights.

The material remains of Rome are widely spread and so numerous that it is only possible to give scattered examples. Among many other buildings, Rome itself boasts the Pantheon, the baths of Domitian and Caracalla, arches, temples, parts of the Appian Way, and the Colosseum, or Flavian Amphitheatre, which remained intact until the Middle Ages, when it was partly destroyed by an earthquake. Warehouses have been reconstructed at Ostia; the remains of Hadrian's villa, with its swimming pool, its beautiful little

The great man presides in the seat of authority. He is raised above those who seek his patronage or his guidance. Rome had a vast system of patronage which stemmed from the Emperor and his court and permeated down through all the ranks of a most complex hierarchical system. Bureaucracy increased under the later emperors.

temple and its graceful columns, can still be seen at Tivoli; further south, villas and shops have been resurrected from the lava of Pompeii.

In Spain, the double-arched aqueduct at Segovia is still in use and the high bridge at Alacantra stands firmly, with its commemorative arch and its thirty-metre central span. The triple arch that forms part of the great aqueduct of the Pont du Gard at Nîmes, in France, is one of the most impressive monuments to Rome. France also has baths in Paris and a theatre in Lyons. There are Roman buildings at Cologne and Mainz, in Germany, and a fortified gateway at Trier on the Moselle. Belgium and Switzerland both have material evidence of Roman occupation. In Britain, the magnificent Roman baths at Bath still exist. Towns such as York and Silchester have revealed many details of the Roman way of life. A palace at Fishbourne, a villa at Chedworth and town houses at Verulamium, near St Albans, among many others, have given us glimpses of varying types of Roman buildings. The remains of Hadrian's Wall and the Antonine Wall continue to mark out

*'Anything in any way beautiful derives its beauty from itself and asks nothing beyond itself. Praise is no part of it, for nothing is made worse or better by praise.'*

*'The Roman world was struck in its heart by an enemy and then my father died, just at the time the empire fell. The invader ravaged my home but the ruin meant little when compared with the loss of my father.'*

the edge of the empire, though now they defy only the force of the weather.

North Africa and the eastern Mediterranean contain many of the best-preserved Roman constructions. Baalbeck, Palmyra, Petra, Timgad, Lepcis Magna, Sabratha, Cyrene, Volubilis, Carthage, Dougga and many other sites make Syria, Libya, Tunisia, Algeria and Morocco rich hunting grounds for Roman theatres, forums, arches, baths and harbours. Many of the North African towns were 'coloniae' of ex-soldiers settled in new areas to establish Roman civilisation. In many cases, the sand has recaptured the land they claimed. But in Europe many of the early Roman camps and settlements grew into thriving towns which have survived and prospered. Some European towns still show signs of their original Roman layout.

Many other material remains are steadily being unearthed by archaeologists. These include pottery, glass, coins, jewels, brooches, statuettes and busts, tools, weapons and domestic articles of every kind. One of the best hoards of Roman silver dishes and cups was discovered by a Suffolk farmer at Mildenhall, while he was ploughing, during the Second World War. Examples of Roman art have come to light in beautiful mosaics and frescoes, which have given us some idea of the Roman love of colour. The villas of Pompeii and North Africa are particularly rich in mosaics but villas in Britain and elsewhere have also revealed many.

More material remains will certainly be found. There are many archaeological digs now in progress that are turning up new and exciting evidence of Roman life. Aerial photography has helped enormously in the discovery of new sites. Mechanical excavation for roadworks and building sites has increased the chances of accidental finds. The buildings, artefacts and mosaics that the archaeologists reveal provide the background that has helped us build up a picture of the Roman way of life. Roman literature, language, traditions and law have all filled out that background.

The Romans were keen to be remembered for their material achievements but they knew very well that they had more to offer than conquest and concrete. Apart from a strong sense of destiny, they also possessed a clear concept of civilisation for which, on the whole, we are greatly in their debt. The scholars of the Renaissance who called themselves 'humanists' hit upon the one word that summed up the central idea of Roman civilisation. In Latin the word was 'humanitas'. Our nearest modern equivalent is 'humanity', which has various shades of meaning but carries at heart the Roman idea of human dignity and tolerance which were the mark of all that was best in the Roman empire.

It is very easy to praise general concepts in splendid phrases and to lose touch with the people themselves. In the end, civilisation consists of the assorted ideals of many individuals trying to live together in relative harmony. Each individual has his own ambitions and is thoroughly biased. None would wholly agree as to what they all want. So let Martial have the final word. If he sounds indolent, at least he is honest and much of what he wants has satisfied most people for a very long time:

> 'The things that make life happier, most genial Martial, are these: means not acquired by labour, but bequeathed; fields not unkindly, an ever-blazing hearth; no lawsuit, the toga seldom worn, a quiet mind; a free man's strength, a healthy body; frankness with tact, congenial friends, good-natured guests, a board plainly spread; nights not spent in wine, but freed from cares; a wife not prudish and yet pure; sleep such as makes the darkness brief; be content with what you are and wish no change; nor dread your last day, nor long for it.'

There were considerable regional differences in the mosaics of the Roman Empire. The most active period in mosaic work occurred towards the end of the second century AD. The emphasis in Rome was on black and white designs. At Antioch, where this mosaic was uncovered, the emphasis was on polychrome or multi-coloured mosaics. In the suburban villas of that area most main rooms had at least one beautifully worked, coloured mosaic. The subjects were mainly mythological.

# A Roman Time Chart

| BC | Events | Writers | The world |
|---|---|---|---|
| 753 | Traditional date of founding of Rome | | |
| 600 | | | Nebuchadnezzar in Babylon |
| 580 | Cloaca Maxima constructed | | |
| 550 | | Aesop's Fables | |
| 530 | | | Buddha preaches |
| 510–509 | Traditional date for expulsion of the kings and start of the Republic | Pythagoras dies | |
| 497 | | | |
| 494 | Rome joins Latin League of local tribes | | |
| 493 | Tribunes first introduced for plebeians | | |
| 490 | | | Persians defeated by Greeks at Marathon |
| 480 | | | Persian navy defeated by Greeks at Salamis |
| 478 | | | Confucius dies |
| 460 | | | Pericles in Athens |
| 456 | | Aeschylus dies | |
| 450 | Laws of the Twelve Tables | | |
| 406 | | Euripides dies | |
| 404 | | | Alcibiades assassinated |
| 399 | | Socrates dies | |
| 390–387 | Gauls sack Rome but fail to capture the Capitol building | | |
| 343–290 | War against the Samnites | | |
| 338 | Latin League disbanded by Rome | | |
| 333 | | | Alexander the Great defeats Darius of Persia at Issus |
| 321 | | | Alexander dies |
| 312 | Appian Way under construction | | |
| 300 | | Zeno of Crete (Stoic philosopher) | |
| 280 | | | Pharos at Alexandria built — Colossus of Rhodes built |
| 275 | King Pyrrhus of Epirus defeated by Romans at Beneventum | | |
| 270 | | Epicurus dies (philosopher) | |
| 264 | First public gladiator fights | | |
| 264–241 | First Punic War (with Carthage) | | |
| 218–201 | Second Punic War | | |
| 216 | Romans defeated by Hannibal at Cannae | | |
| 215c. | | | Great Wall of China |
| 212 | | Archimedes dies | |

| BC | Events | | Writers | The world |
|---|---|---|---|---|
| 202 | Hannibal defeated by Romans at Zama | | | Han dynasty in China |
| 199 | | | Naevius dies (comedy playright) | |
| 197 | Philip V of Macedon defeated by Romans at Cynoscephalae | | | |
| 190 | | Antiochus III of Syria defeated by Romans at Magnesia | | |
| 184 | | | Plautus dies (comedy playright) | |
| 170 | | | Ennius dies (poet) | |
| 168 | King Perseus of Macedon defeated by Romans at Pydna | | | |
| 159 | | | Terence dies (comedy playright) | |
| 149 | | | Cato dies (agriculturist) | |
| 149–146 | Third Punic War; Carthage destroyed | | | |
| 133 | | Tiberius Gracchus, tribune and reformer, assassinated | | |
| 123–122 | Gaius Gracchus, tribune and reformer | | | |
| 112–105 | | War against Jugurtha of Numidia | | |
| 105 | Gauls kill 80,000 Romans at Arausio | | | |
| 102–101 | | | Marius defeats Teutones and Cimbri; reorganisation of Roman army | |
| 91 | Livius Drusus, reformer, assassinated | | | |
| 91–87 | | Italian Social War: Rome v. Allies | | |
| 90 | | | Vitruvius *On Architecture* | |
| 88–66 | | Intermittent wars against Mithridates in Asia Minor | | |
| 82–79 | Sulla dictator | | | |
| 73–71 | Spartacus slave revolt | | | |
| 67 | | Pompey defeats Mediterranean pirates | | |
| 63 | Catiline conspiracy | | | |
| 60 | First Triumvirate: Pompey, Caesar and Crassus | Caesar founds news-sheet – Acta Diurna | | |
| 58–49 | | Caesar's campaigns in Gaul | | |
| 55 | Pompey builds first permanent theatre in Rome | | Lucretius dies (poet/philosopher) | |
| 55–54 | | Caesar's raids on Britain | | |
| 54 | | | Catullus dies (poet) | |
| 48 | | Caesar defeats Pompey at Pharsalia | | Library of Alexandria destroyed by fire |
| 48–44 | Caesar in sole power | | | |
| 46 | | Julian Calendar instituted | | |
| 44 | Caesar assassinated | | | |
| 43 | | Second Triumvirate: Antony, Octavian and Lepidus | Cicero dies (orator) | Cleopatra, Queen of Egypt |
| 42 | Brutus and conspirators defeated at Philippi | | | |

| BC | Emperors | Events | Writers | The world |
|---|---|---|---|---|
| 35 | | | Sallust dies (historian) | |
| 31 | | Antony and Cleopatra defeated at Actium | | |
| 27 | Augustus (27 BC–AD 14) | Octavian becomes Augustus Caesar | Varro dies (agriculturist) | |
| 20 | | Golden Milestone set up in Rome | | |
| 4 | | Probable date of birth of Christ | | |
| **AD** | | | | |
| 7 | | | Horace dies (poet) | |
| 9 | | Roman army under Varus defeated at Teutoburg Forest: 3 legions lost | | |
| 14 | Tiberius (14–37) | | | |
| 16 | | | Propertius dies (poet) | |
| 17 | | | Livy dies (historian) | |
| 18 | | | Ovid dies (poet) | |
| 19 | | | Virgil dies (poet) Tibullus dies (poet) | |
| 29 | | Probable date of the Crucifixion of Christ | | |
| 37 | Caligula (37–41) | | | |
| 41 | Claudius (41–54) | | | |
| 43 | | Roman invasion of Britain | | |
| 54 | Nero (54–68) | | | |
| 60 | | Boadicea's revolt in Britain | | |
| 64 | | Great Fire of Rome | | |
| 65 | | | Lucan dies (poet) Seneca dies (Stoic philosopher) Petronius dies (novelist) | |
| 68 | Galba (68–69) | | | |
| 69 | Otho (69) Vitellius (69) Vespasian (69–79) | | | |
| 78–84 | | Agricola governor of Britain | | |
| 79 | Titus (79–81) | Colosseum completed — Eruption of Vesuvius | Elder Pliny dies (scientist) | |
| 81 | Domitian (81–96) | | | |
| 84 | | Baths at Bath begun | | |
| 96 | Nerva (96–98) | | | |
| 98 | Trajan (98–117) | Empire at greatest extent | | |
| 100 | | | Quintilian dies (educationist) | Paper in China |
| 101–105 | | Dacian wars (shown in Trajan's Column) | | |
| 104 | | | Martial dies (poet) | |

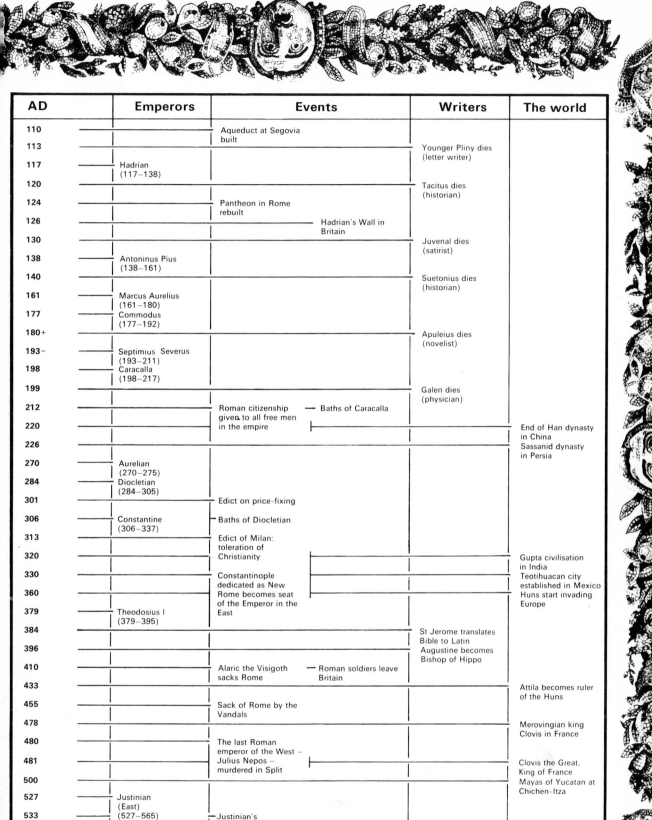

| AD | Emperors | Events | Writers | The world |
|---|---|---|---|---|
| 110 | | Aqueduct at Segovia built | | |
| 113 | | | Younger Pliny dies (letter writer) | |
| 117 | Hadrian (117–138) | | | |
| 120 | | | Tacitus dies (historian) | |
| 124 | | Pantheon in Rome rebuilt | | |
| 126 | | Hadrian's Wall in Britain | | |
| 130 | | | Juvenal dies (satirist) | |
| 138 | Antoninus Pius (138–161) | | | |
| 140 | | | Suetonius dies (historian) | |
| 161 | Marcus Aurelius (161–180) | | | |
| 177 | Commodus (177–192) | | | |
| 180+ | | | Apuleius dies (novelist) | |
| 193– | Septimius Severus (193–211) | | | |
| 198 | Caracalla (198–217) | | | |
| 199 | | | Galen dies (physician) | |
| 212 | | Roman citizenship given to all free men in the empire — Baths of Caracalla | | |
| 220 | | | | End of Han dynasty in China |
| 226 | | | | Sassanid dynasty in Persia |
| 270 | Aurelian (270–275) | | | |
| 284 | Diocletian (284–305) | | | |
| 301 | | Edict on price-fixing | | |
| 306 | Constantine (306–337) | Baths of Diocletian | | |
| 313 | | Edict of Milan: toleration of Christianity | | |
| 320 | | | | Gupta civilisation in India |
| 330 | | Constantinople dedicated as New Rome becomes seat of the Emperor in the East | | Teotihuacan city established in Mexico |
| 360 | | | | Huns start invading Europe |
| 379 | Theodosius I (379–395) | | | |
| 384 | | | St Jerome translates Bible to Latin | |
| 396 | | | Augustine becomes Bishop of Hippo | |
| 410 | | Alaric the Visigoth sacks Rome — Roman soldiers leave Britain | | |
| 433 | | | | Attila becomes ruler of the Huns |
| 455 | | Sack of Rome by the Vandals | | |
| 478 | | | | Merovingian king Clovis in France |
| 480 | | The last Roman emperor of the West – Julius Nepos – murdered in Split | | |
| 481 | | | | Clovis the Great, King of France |
| 500 | | | | Mayas of Yucatan at Chichen-Itza |
| 527 | Justinian (East) (527–565) | | | |
| 533 | | Justinian's Codification of Roman Law | | |

# Roman Authors

These are only some of the main writers from the central period of Roman history which this book covers:

**Apicius, Quintus Gavius** *1st centuries BC/AD*
Gourmet and cookery writer who lived during the reign of Augustus. The cookery book which bears his name was probably written much later.

**Apuleius, Lucius** *c. AD 120 – post 180*
Born in Morocco, went to Rome and travelled widely in Asia Minor. Wrote a book on magic and the renowned *Golden Ass*, a bawdy and adventurous novel about a young man who is turned into an ass.

**Caesar, Gaius Julius** *102 – 44 BC*
Patrician, statesman, general, dictator and author. His *Conquest of Gaul* describes his victorious campaigns which covered modern France, Belgium, Switzerland, parts of Holland and Germany, and two visits to Britain.

**Cato, Marcus Porcius** *234 – 149 BC*
Republican statesman, known as Cato 'the Censor' because of his reputation in that office. Persistently warned that 'Carthage must be destroyed'. Wrote a book on agriculture, which is the oldest surviving Latin prose work.

**Catullus, Gaius Valerius** *84 – 54 BC*
Lyric poet, famous also for his satire and epigrams. His love for the lady he calls Lesbia inspired many of his most passionate poems.

**Celsus, Aulus Cornelius** *1st century AD*
An encyclopaedist of the reign of Tiberius. Famous for his work *On Medicine*, in particular.

**Cicero, Marcus Tullius** *106 – 43 BC*
Statesman, orator and author. Published many of his great speeches and his letters and essays. The *Second Philippic against Antony* is probably his most famous speech. His essays *On Duty* and *On Old Age* greatly influenced later writers. Called by Augustus, 'an eloquent man and a lover of his country'.

**Columella, Lucius Junius Moderatus** *1st century AD*
A Spaniard who wrote in Rome during Nero's reign. Famous for his twelve books on agriculture, which attacked absentee landlords and dealt with every aspect of farming in detail.

**Ennius, Quintus** *239 – 170 BC*
One of the earliest Roman poets and one of the most influential. Famous for his *Annals*, an epic poem relating the story of Rome from the time of Aeneas to the poet's own day.

**Frontinus, Sextus Julius** *AD 40 – 103*
Governor of Britain from AD 75–78 and subsequently chief water-commissioner for Rome. Wrote books on military stratagems and on Roman aqueducts, based on his own experiences.

**Galen (Claudius Galenus)** *AD 129 – 199*
Greek physician who practised in Rome. Wrote several hundred treatises, of which only a few survive, but which have been very influential. Became physician to the gladiators.

**Horace (Quintus Horatius Flaccus)** *65 – 7 BC*
Friend of Virgil and given Sabine farm by wealthy Maecenas. His *Satires* and *Odes* were probably his greatest poems and give a marvellous picture of Roman society.

**Josephus, Flavius** *AD 37 – 98*
Jewish historian who first fought against the Romans and was subsequently brought to Rome and made a Roman citizen. His major works were a history of the Jews and a *History of the Jewish War*, in which he described the campaigns of Vespasian and Titus and the sacking of Jerusalem in AD 70.

**Juvenal (Decimus Junius Juvenalis)** *AD 55 – 130c.*
Brilliant Roman satirist who displayed his general indignation at Roman society in sixteen major *Satires*. Used as model by many subsequent writers, including Dr Johnson.

**Livy (Titus Livius)** *59 BC – AD 17*
Historian who wrote a *History of Rome* in 142 books, of which less than a quarter survive, although summaries exist of most of the others. Uses legend and folklore as well as historical fact. Favoured the Republic although he wrote under Augustus.

**Lucan (Marcus Annaenus Lucanus)** *AD 39 – 65*
Poet who described the war between Caesar and Pompey in *Pharsalia*, in which he praised Pompey as champion of the Republic. Favoured by Nero at first but eventually ordered to commit suicide.

**Lucilius, Gaius** *c. 180 – 102 BC*
Earliest poetical satirist in Latin, but little of his work survives. Often savage in attack on what he disapproves. Admired by Quintilian and influenced satires of Horace, who was considerably more mild.

**Lucretius (Titus Lucretius Carus)** *c. 96 – 52 BC*
Philosopher and poet. Famous for *The Laws of Nature*, in which he elaborated on Epicurean philosophy and the atomic nature of all matter.

**Marcus Aurelius** *AD 121 – 180*
Roman emperor and author of the famous *Meditations*, which were originally written in Greek. They contain his thoughts, in the Stoic tradition of philosophy, during his campaigns against the barbarians on his frontiers.

**Martial (Marcus Valerius Martialis)** *AD 40 – 104*
Wrote more than 1500 epigrams in twelve books, containing witty and realistic comments on Roman life.

**Naevius** *270 – 199 BC*
One of Rome's early comic writers of drama. His works are full of social satire and coarse plots. Less sophisticated than Plautus or Terence.

**Ovid (Publius Ovidius Naso)** *43 BC – AD 18*
Fashionable and witty Roman poet who wrote *The Art of Love* and *Metamorphosis* – a retelling of many ancient stories. Banished by Augustus to Tomis on the Black Sea for the immorality of his writing.

**Persius (Aules Perseus Flaccus)** *AD 34 – 62*
Very stylish poetical satirist who criticised much of the taste of Nero's court. He was a Stoic at heart.

**Petronius (Titus Petronius Arbiter)** *died AD 66*
Consul and Governor of Bithynia; favourite of Nero as an 'arbiter of elegance' but forced to commit suicide because of Court rivalries. Author of the *Satyricon*, a bawdy romance packed with incident and highlighted by the magnificent feast of the ex-slave Trimalchio.

**Phaedrus** *1st century AD*
Thracian slave who wrote social and political satire in the form of animal fables in the reigns of Tiberius and Caligula. Acknowledged his own debt to Aesop.

**Plautus** *254 – 184 BC*
Actor and playwright, famous for his comedies, many of which were based on Greek originals but transformed by Plautus into highly original plays with excellently depicted characters.

**Pliny the Elder (Gaius Plinius Secundus)**
*AD 23 – 79*
Wrote a *Natural History* in thirty-seven books, containing a vast assortment of information. Conscientious and hard-working, he condemned luxury and waste of time.

**Pliny the Younger (Gaius Plinius Caecilius)**
*AD 61 – 114*
Nephew of Pliny the Elder and at one time Governor of Bithynia. Famous for his *Letters* which cover a range of subjects reflecting the concerns of his contemporaries. His correspondence with the emperor Trajan is one of his most fascinating records.

**Plutarch** *c. AD 46 – 120*
Greek historian who wrote comparisons of twenty-three pairs of Greek and Roman personalities, known as Plutarch's *Lives* and used as source material for many plays including Shakespeare's *Julius Caesar, Coriolanus* and *Antony and Cleopatra*.

**Polybius** *c. 203 – 120 BC*
Greek historian who came to Rome as hostage after defeat of Macedonians and wrote forty books of history which are valuable sources for information particularly on the Roman armies.

**Propertius, Sextus** *c. 50 – 15 BC*
Contemporary of Virgil and Horace who wrote passionate elegaic poetry, mostly about his unfaithful mistress.

**Quintilian, Marcus Fabius** *c. AD 35 – 100*
Famous teacher and author of a work on oratory and education. Sponsored by the emperor Vespasian. Tutor to the Younger Pliny.

**Sallust (Gaius Sallustius Crispus)** *c. 86 – 34 BC*
Historian who recorded the events of the *Catiline Conspiracy* of 63 BC, which attempted to overthrow Pompey, and the war with Jugurtha in 111–106 BC. Powerful style that possibly influenced Tacitus.

**Seneca, Lucius Annaeus** *4 BC – AD 65*
Stoic philosopher and writer. He was tutor to the young Nero and later became an adviser to him but was eventually ordered to commit suicide by Nero. Wrote tragedies and *Dialogues* and *Letters from a Stoic*.

**Statius, Publius Papinius** *c. AD 45 – 96*
Epic and lyrical poet, contemporary of Martial. Became court poet under Domitian. Best known for his *Silvae* and *Thebais*.

**Strabo** *63 BC – AD 21*
Greek geographer and historian. Widely travelled but used other books as his main references for his *Geography*. Encouraged scientific approach.

**Suetonius (Gaius Suetonius Tranquillus)**
*c. AD 70 – 140*
His *Lives of the Twelve Caesars* reveals the inside stories of Rome's first emperors with no scandal or private indiscretion omitted. It makes lively reading.

**Tacitus, Cornelius** *AD 55 – 115*
Historian renowned for his *Annals* of Rome's history from the death of Augustus to the death of Nero, and for his *Histories*, from the death of Nero to AD 96. Also wrote highly original study of barbarian people in *Germania* and a eulogy on his father-in-law *Agricola* for his governorship of Britain.

**Terence (Publius Terentius Afer)** *c. 185 – 159 BC*
Probably came as a slave to Rome and became the second greatest comic writer of plays after Plautus. His plays are set in Athens and concentrate on character.

**Tibullus** *c. 55 – 19 BC*
Elegaic poet with strong emphasis on pastoral subject contrasted with city life. Many of his poems were written about his mistress Delia.

**Varro, Marcus Terentius** *116 – 27 BC*
Many-talented scholar and author. Despite his encyclopaedic learning, he is best known for his work *On Agriculture*, which extolled the Italian rural traditions.

**Virgil (Publius Vergilius Maro)** *70 – 19 BC*
Famous in his own lifetime as the greatest of the Roman poets. Under the patronage of Augustus and Maecenas, he wrote the *Georgics*, in praise of a return to the land, and the *Aeneid*, an epic on the traditional ancestry of the Roman people.

**Vitruvius (Marcus Vitruvius Pollio)** *1st century BC*
Architect and engineer, author of a famous book *On Architecture* which became a model for the Renaissance in Italy. His own work was based on experience and on Greek models; he was less enthusiastic about contemporary Roman architecture.

# The marginal quotes

**The marginal quotes**
The quotes in the margin, alongside the main text, have been selected from the following contemporary Latin authors. They provide additional glimpses of Roman attitudes and life, sometimes philosophical, sometimes critical, sometimes teasing; often, in just a few words, a whole scene comes to life. They are not necessarily appropriate to the text beside which they fall; they are meant to be asides; they could be spoken almost anywhere, by almost anyone.

# INDEX

# ACKNOWLEDGEMENTS

**Photographs**

The publishers wish to acknowledge the following sources of photographs: English Tourist Board; French Embassy; Michael Holford Picture Library; Italian State Tourist Office; London Tourist Board; Dr. R. Reece, Institute of Archaeology, London University; Spectrum.


**Translations**

The publishers also wish to acknowledge the following sources of translations: Loeb: Polybius, History (trans. W. R. Paton 1922); Select Papyri (trans. A. S. Hunt & C. C. Edgar 1932); Statius, Silves (trans. J. H. Mozley 1928). Penguin Books: Apuleius, The Golden Ass (trans. Robert Graves 1950); Marcus Aurelius, Meditations (trans. Maxwell Staniforth 1964); Caesar, The Conquest of Gaul (trans. S. A. Handford 1951); Catullus, The Poems of Catullus (trans. Peter Wigham 1966); Cicero, Selected Works (trans. Michael Grant 1960); Horace, Satires of Horace and Persius (trans. Niall Rudd 1973); Josephus, The Jewish War (trans. G. A. Williamson 1959); Juvenal, The Sixteen Satires (trans. Peter Green 1967); Lucretius, On the Nature of the Universe (trans. Ronald Latham 1951); Petronius, the Satyricon (trans. J. P. Sullivan 1965); Plautus, The Rope and Other Plays (trans. E. F. Watling 1964); Pliny, The Letters of the Younger Pliny (trans. Betty Radice 1963); Seneca, Letters from a Stoic (trans. Robin Campbell 1969); Suetonius, The Twelve Caesars (trans. Robert Graves 1957); Tacitus, The Annals of Imperial Rome (trans. Michael Grant 1956), Agricola and Germania (trans. H. Mattingly/S. Handford 1948/1970); Tibullus, The Poems of Tibullus (trans. Philip Dunlop 1972); The Last Poets of Imperial Rome (trans. Harold Isbell 1971); R. M. Barrow, The Romans. Apicius, The Roman Cookery Book (trans. Flower & Rosenbaum, Harrap 1974); Ausonius, Epigrams (trans. Janet Maclean Todd); Cyril Bailey, Legacy of Rome (Oxford 1923); Catullus, Poems (trans. James Michie, Hart-Davies 1969); Celsius, De Medicina (trans. J. Wight Duff, Literary History of Rome, Ernest Benn 1909); O. A. W. Dilke, The Ancient Romans (David & Charles 1975); Horace, Odes (trans. Sir E. Marsh); Ovid, The Art of Love (trans. Rolfe Humphries, Indiana University Press 1957); Varro, De Re Rustica (trans. Nichols & McLeish).


Artists:  Terence Dalley ARCA; Terry Gabbey; Trevor Newton; David Parr;
　　　　　 Jenny Thorne

Designer:  Peter Davies

Research Assistants:  Gaynor Cauter; Rachel Stainsby